AMERICAN VALUES PROJECTED ABROAD

A SERIES FUNDED BY THE
EXXON EDUCATION FOUNDATION

Vol. I   Western Heritage And American Values:
Law, Theology And History
By
Alberto Coll

Vol. II   Political Traditions And Contemporary Problems
Edited by
Kenneth W. Thompson

Vol. III   Institutions for Projecting American Values Abroad
Edited by
Kenneth W. Thompson

UNIVERSITY
PRESS OF
AMERICA

LANHAM • NEW YORK • LONDON

Copyright © 1983 by

University Press of America,™ Inc.

4720 Boston Way
Lanham, MD 20706

3 Henrietta Street
London WC2E 8LU England

Printed in the United States of America

Library of Congress Cataloging in Publication Data

Thompson, Kenneth W., 1921 —
    Institutions for projecting American values abroad.

    (American values projected abroad; v. 3)
        1. United States — Relations — Foreign countries.
2. Associations, institutions, etc. — United States —
International cooperation. I. Title. II. Series.
JX1417.A74   1982 vol. 3 [E840.2] 303.4'8273s   83-6948
ISBN 0-8191-3195-4   [303.4'8273'006]
ISBN 0-8191-3196-2 (pbk.)

INSTITUTIONS FOR PROJECTING AMERICAN VALUES ABROAD

VOL. III

EDITED BY
KENNETH W. THOMPSON

To
the
memory of
Joe Payton

and

To
those
unkown and forgotten
Americans
who lived the best years of their lives
engaged in
sharing American values
with
mankind around the globe

TABLE OF CONTENTS

CONTRIBUTORS

Edward W. Barrett was formerly Assistant Secretary of State for Public Affairs, and Dean of the Columbia University School of Journalism and editor of its *Journalism Review.*

I. L. Claude is Edward Stettinius Professor in the Department of Government and Foreign Affairs at the University of Virginia. He is the author of major works on international relations and international organizations including *Swords Into Ploughshares.*

Mary E. Cunningham is Vice President for planning and development of Joseph E. Seagrams & Sons, Inc., with an undergraduate background in philosophy and logic from Wellesley College and a Master's Degree from the Harvard Business School.

Thomas R. Donahue is Secretary-Treasurer of the AFL-CIO and a Trustee of the Carnegie Corporation. His essay is excerpted from a presentation in May, 1982, at the University of Notre Dame.

Emmett B. Ford, Jr. is a retired foreign service officer who has held diplomatic posts in the Middle East and Europe. He is currently an administrative officer at the University of Virginia.

Joseph Grieco is a member of the Political Science Department at Duke University. He is a former fellow of the Institute for the Study of World Politics.

Julian N. Hartt is Professor Emeritus of the Department of Religious Studies at the University of Virginia who was formerly a distinguished professor and head of religious studies at Yale University.

Soedjatmoko is Rector of the United Nations University in Tokyo. He has served as Indonesian Ambassador to the United States and is Asia's foremost social philosopher.

Ms. Valerie Sutter is a Ph.D. candidate in Social Foundations of Education and Comparative Education at the University of Virginia. She has had extensive international experience and is writing a book on refugees.

Clifton Wharton is President of the State University of New York, Chairman of the Board of Trustees of the Rockefeller Foundation and formerly President of Michigan State University.

Harris Wofford was one of the organizers of the Peace Corps while Special Assistant to President Kennedy, then Special Peace Corps Representative to Africa (1962-64) and Associate Director of the Peace Corps (1964-65).

PREFACE

American values and practices are projected abroad through a variety of institutions which are the channels for their dissemination and dispersion. The present volume seeks to fill a gap in the literature on cultural relations and international affairs by throwing the spotlight on the institutions which are the conveyor belts for the transmission of American values. They contribute to the process of the cultural exchange of values. Institutions are the instruments by which American values are carried to other peoples.

At the same time, institutions give new substance and content to American values. They provide a medical, agricultural, political or religious content to such values. Thus the institutions which are examined in this volume have both functional and structural characteristics. They are the means for transmitting values but also determine the ends which are to be disseminated.

Therefore, the volume has a dual purpose: one, to describe and explain the institutions which have been selected for review; and two, to illustrate the particular values which they embody and which in turn provide the substance of values projected abroad.

INTRODUCTION

American values as projected into the world affect four broad areas: human survival, economic well-being, international cooperation and the well-being of mankind in the broadest sense. Discussions in this volume group themselves naturally under these four headings.

Human survival needs include health, agriculture and food, and education. Not surprisingly, the earliest outreach activities of Americans in the world were concerned with the struggle against disease. Health was seen as the primary human need; without it no other needs could be served. Americans were in the forefront of an important movement to bring improved health services to all peoples, especially through the creation of schools of public health. The earliest chapter for the United States in seeking to help others was in the work of various health and sanitary commissions organized to seek improved health for peoples at home and abroad.

Agriculture followed health, and practitioners joined in a worldwide crusade to conquer hunger. The approach and methods of agriculturalists were not basically different from those of doctors and microbe hunters who had preceded them. In both cases, the objective was the eradication of a human condition that made impossible or unlikely the realization of other values. The specific movement for the agriculturalists was the green revolution which, whatever its shortcomings, did transform food production in important countries in Asia and Latin America.

A British historian once described education as the major force in society that could counter human destruction, and it completes the list of first order subjects. Through education, doctors, plant pathologists and agronomists in newly independent countries have been trained to combat hunger and disease. Educational institutions provide a framework for society to prepare to deal in turn with each emerging human need. The Unites States has been in the forefront of countries that have developed new patterns of education such as land grant universities and community colleges. Educators have gone abroad to live and work in foreign cultures as professors, administrators and advisors. Americans have participated in building new institutions and strengthening older institutions of higher education in the developing countries. They have sought to assure human survival by preparing others to meet the problems of an ever-changing future including those of the global environment.

Another fundamental sector in which American values come into play is economic well-being. The authors writing under Section II examine the core values of corporations, multinational corporations and of labor unions. Multinationals illustrate the form which relations with other cultures have taken and the issues that arise. The question of the interconnections of national and international economic needs is discussed and evaluated. The flight of international refugees and their struggle to gain a new livelihood is discussed. The chapters in this section are intended to raise questions and illustrate problems as much as they are to resolve outstanding issues.

The third section finds leading authorities addressing themselves to the modes of international cooperation in which American values are tested in relationship to the values of other nation states. The Peace Corps has brought Americans in direct contact with grass roots societies in other lands. Multilateral organizations have gained importance in the postwar world; traditional diplomatic relations are the historic channels of international politics. In the struggle of ideologies, Americans choose between truth and propaganda in extending American values. In all four arenas, American values must be studied from the standpoint of their relevance, coherence and adaptability.

A final area of consideration is one in which broader philosophical and spiritual issues come into play. The foundation in the United States is a unique invention for charitable and philanthropic action. The church has for centuries been the spiritual home for mankind in the West. For both secular and religious organizations, one important concern is how they interact with society at large and how effectively they understand and define their role. American developmental aid is a secularized version of earlier missionary endeavors and is continually being reassessed. These are the central issues discussed in Section IV.

I. AMERICA
AND HUMAN SURVIVAL
VALUES

The earliest American programs abroad rooted in certain underlying core values were in health, agriculture and education.

It was clear and self-evident to early leaders that health, food and education were primeval human needs in the absence of whose amelioration other basic needs were unlikely to be met. When the first private initiatives were taken, the trustees of these efforts asked themselves what human needs were basic to all the rest. Not surprisingly, health was chosen as *primus inter pares*. The first efforts rested on the premise that only men and women who were healthy could realize other goods and values. Adequate food and nutrition came next with education not far behind. Taken together, health, food and education were a triad of original human needs that must be met if mankind is to survive and advance responding to successive challenges.

As with the discussion to follow of the manifold values underlying the work of other institutions abroad, the interrelation of institutions and values effecting health, food and education programs merits study. Some values are universal as with the worldwide resolve to conquer infectious diseases that cripple man's search for a better life. Other values may have their source in deep-seated attitudes within particular groups as with the goal of service represented by the land grant colleges. Institutions spring up to meet human needs but change in response to changing human needs. Thus the Rockefeller Foundation first sought to assist overall institutional development in Third World education only to find that higher education for development was the most urgent need. Institutions, values and basic human needs form the main focus of the discussions which follow.

It was the editor's privilege to participate in the later phases of programs in all three areas as Vice President of the Rockefeller Foundation. The first two essays which follow are based on that experience. They have been prepared as examples of human survival responses. They are considerably modified and revised versions of papers that have appeared in another form in two books previously published, *Foreign Assistance: A View from the Private Sector* published by the University of Notre Dame Press and *Ethics, Functionalism and Power* published by the Louisiana University Press to whom credit is hereby given. The education paper is based on a review of the Rockefeller Foundation University Development Program, part of which was included in a foundation report and in a paper issued by the International Council for Educational Development.

The fourth chapter in this volume contrasts with the first three. The world in the 1980s is confronted with novel and unprecedented problems of global human survival including nuclear destruction and environmental deterioration. While the United States has responsibilities inherent in its national self-interest to arrest and turn back the grave consequences of such threats, the problem exceeds that of a single nation state. However, as Ambassador Soedjatmoko has observed, the worldwide hazards require for solution national cooperation and initiative. He asserts, by implication, that whatever their values neither the United States nor other nations have demonstrated the will to cooperate on a global basis to meet the challenge.

CHAPTER ONE
HEALTH AS THE EARLIEST VALUE
Kenneth W. Thompson

Looking back on the earliest history of international cooperation in the private sector, an air of predetermination hung over the focus and thrust of the American effort. In vast areas of the United States and across the world, the problem of disease stood out in stark relief as "the supreme ill of human life" and as "the main source of almost all other ills—poverty, crime, ignorance, vice, inefficiency, hereditary taint, and many other evils."[1] It was an area in which it was possible, as was less true in social relations, to search out the root cause, to cure evils at their source. A body of knowledge existed on which to build and some experience in applying it in regions of greatest need. The Rockefeller Sanitary Commission had achieved dramatic success in greatly reducing hookworm in the southern United States, and the stated objective of the International Health Board, created by the Rockefeller Foundation in 1913, was "to extend to other countries and people the work of eradicating Hookworm Disease as opportunity offers. . . ."[2] This board and its successor organizations, culminating in the International Health Division (established in 1927), sought to promote the spread of scientific medicine and to support or establish agencies for the promotion of public sanitation. The scope of the effort coincided with a mandate to conquer disease wherever it occurred. Its programs exemplified the dividends of concentration and of pursuing a clear-cut goal with singleness of purpose. There was a recognized need and solutions could be envisaged from work already in progress at the more advanced centers and in health centers in the field. The end pursued was improved health, the means a war against disease.

Hookworm is an anemia-producing disease contracted by contact with infected soil (especially through bare feet), which in the early twentieth century handicapped, debilitated and killed millions of people in the hot, humid regions of the world. In rural areas of the

South, the percentage of infected children ran as high as 90 percent, with the incidence also high among adults. The objective of the first phase of the campaign was to demonstrate that hookworm was a reality, a source of debilitation and weakness, but nonetheless curable and preventable. The task of the Rockefeller Sanitary Commission was to educate and to curb the lethargy and indifference of people and the medical profession. If illness is the supreme ill, bad health, like the weather, all too often was accepted as inevitable.

Here then was the classic instance of a private health body playing a catalytic and educational role. The Sanitary Commission appointed directors of sanitation in each of the eleven states in which work was undertaken. Traveling dispensaries brought knowledge to the people. The schools were enlisted, as were state departments of education. Following medical examinations, lectures, and demonstrations, more than 250,000 rural homes were inspected by sanitary personnel, and such measures as the construction of sanitary privies were undertaken to prevent recurrence of the disease. Over 25,000 public meetings were held with attendance exceeding two million people in 653 of the 1,142 counties in the eleven southern states. Voluntary groups such as women's clubs and school improvement leagues were formed and a massive cooperative effort was carried out involving state and county governments and the Sanitary Commission. As a harbinger of future patterns of international cooperation, the professional staff everywhere functioned under state control. The commission leader, Dr. Wickliffe Rose, wrote: "The eradication of this disease . . . is a work which no outside agency working independently could do for a people if it would, and . . . no outside agency should do if it could."[3]

The leadership of the Sanitary Commission was imbued with an international outlook even before it merged in 1913 with the Rockefeller Foundation as the International Health Board. Its outreach was worldwide because medical science was universal and knew no boundaries. Government agencies in Washington and abroad established the fact that hookworm extended around the world from approximately the thirty-sixth parallel north to the thirtieth parallel south, involving a population of a billion people. The work of the International Health Board in its war against hookworm reached out to fifty-two countries on six continents and to twenty-nine islands, extending from Fiji and Samoa westward through the Antipodes and the Far East to Africa and the Mediterranean and on to the West Indies and the Americas. The board patterned itself after an operating model. Wherever it went it sought to apply the lessons of the Sanitary Commission: to work through established and responsible indigenous institutions, to ask that governments contribute, and to be "a partner, but not a patron." In. Dr. Rose's instructive phrase:

Demonstrations in which the . . . authorities do not participate . . . from the inception . . . are not likely to be successful; . . . the state must be sufficiently interested to risk something, to follow the plan critically, to take over the cost of the work gradually but steadily, and within a reasonable period to assume the entire burden of direction and expense. [4]

For today's practitioners of international cooperation, this early principle for the extension of health suggests there is nothing new under the sun.

From the start, the International Health Board followed another precept that was to become the hallmark of private initiative. It sought to attract and hold the ablest young professionals as part of a cadre of career servants. Such men were to write history in the public health area and to live out their lives, or substantial parts thereof, in far-flung corners of the world: Dr. Victor G. Heiser in the Far East; Dr. S. M. Lambert in Fiji, Samoa, and Polynesia; Dr. Wilbur A. Sawyer in Australia; Dr. George K. Strode in Brazil; and others in various world regions, like Dr. Lewis W. Hackett and Dr. Charles N. Leach. The success of the board and of its successor, the International Health Division, would have been impossible without the work of these legendary figures and younger scientists emerging under their tutelage.

The International Health Division ranged around the globe for thirty-eight years. Its staff, which numbered annually seventy to eighty professionals—about the size of the Foundation's agricultural staff three decades later—worked with seventy-five cooperating governments. It broadened its approach to include twenty-one specific diseases or health problems, including tuberculosis, yaws, rabies, influenza, typhus, amebiasis, schistosomiasis, dysentery, typhoid fever, hepatitis, undulant fever, and nutritional deficiencies. But in keeping the concept of a central focus, the three major centers of effort were hookworm, malaria, and yellow fever.

The IHD learned from doing and through trial and error. For example, in hookworm, the staff, early in its Asian program, treated people en masse on the theory that in hookworm control the essential objective was less to cure each infected person than to remove the largest number of worms from the largest possible number of people, thus lowering the severity of infection. In the Dutch East Indies, India, Thailand, and other heavily infected tropical countries this mass approach supplanted the procedure of individual examinations which had been taken over from the Sanitary Commission. Later, mass treatments in turn were abandoned and emphasis was placed on improved sanitary arrangements and treatment only of those persons who were seriously infected. Laboratory tests had shown that some individuals carrying a small number of hookworms were not necessarily ill, that through the workings of antibodies many had relatively harmless infections and had acquired immunity to future infection even though constantly exposed to infecting larvae. A distinction came to be made between hookworm disease and harmless infection.

Eventually, a shift of emphasis in the hookworm campaign led to dropping the term "eradication." Eradication remains, as with most "total solutions" to most human needs, a goal that has never been reached. Advocacy in foreign assistance, as in politics, leads to overstatement, and private organizations are not immune. The battle cries are unqualified: the conquest of hunger, eradication of disease, etc. Results inescapably fall short of the goal, but there is probably some virtue in formulating human goals that exceed man's grasp. In the end, the prevalence of hookworm was sharply reduced so that today, like smallpox and typhoid, it is subject to control by modern public health methods.

The lore and legend, myths and miracles, triumphs and tragedies encountered in moving ahead with world health could fill volumes. Some stories are particularly well-known and often told. Dr. Wilfred E. Barnes in Siam encountered a Buddhist priest forbidden by his religion to take life and therefore he was resistant to anything that would "kill the germs." Finally, Barnes, having been rebuffed on every other ground, persuaded the priest to take hookworm medicine by displaying the washings from the stool which showed that the worms were still alive when expelled. Dr. Lambert, in his work in Polynesia and Micronesia, found the Papuans hesitant to give their names for labels on specimens, lest in speaking their names aloud the spirit of a dead relative would hear and come back to haunt them. The problem was solved by having the individual whisper his name to a bystander, who passed it on—also in a whisper. Scientists told of a thousand or more encounters with the folklore and the faith of other peoples.

Then there was the eternal debate over research. At first, Rose and his associates assumed that eradication would take place through the mere application of known scientific methods. Experience put question marks after this assumption. A debate broke out within the IHD, with men like Dr. Simon Flexner, director of the Rockefeller Institute for Medical Research, asserting that the IHD was not a research organization and others, like Dr. William H. Welch, the first dean of the Johns Hopkins Medical School, calling for a joint Johns Hopkins-Rockefeller Foundation twenty-year program of "wormology." In this debate, the researchers won out and studies at Johns Hopkins and in field and laboratory stations continued well into the 1940s. They included investigations of the interplay between man's relative immunity and his nutritional balance and the discovery of a hookworm egg-counting technique that enabled doctors to estimate the number of worms in a patient from the number of eggs in one gram of his feces. Men like Frederick F. Russell, a giant in the medical sciences, were impressed with the gap, not between scientific knowledge and its application, but between what science knew and what it needed to know.

The IHD remained primarily a field program and an operating agency but was flexible enough to support and draw upon other scientific institutions in doing needed research. Again and again, this was the case with operating programs abroad; those who disparage research in the name of action have been as wrong as those who call only for research. In all candor it should be added that for the most part the basic research left the plight of barefoot, hookworm-infested humanity largely where it found them. No one discovered a simple vaccine or a soil disinfectant, and the gains in hookworm control went on within rather severely defined and narrow limits.

It must have been tempting in those early days for the doctors, as with population specialists today, to feel discouraged, defeated, and depressed. Yet in the end, the results were impressive. A study of fifty-two counties in Mississippi showed that hookworm had been reduced by two-thirds between 1910 and 1933. A companion study in eight southern states disclosed a similar overall trend but with substantial residual pockets of resistance persisting along the sandy coastal plains from North Carolina to Mississippi. Outside these areas, if hookworm has not been eradicated, the disease is rarely seen. Although it still has not died out, no one today considers it much more than a minor problem. But what was the cause of this change, or the causes? Was it the education of local doctors, increased incomes for the purchase of shoes, the drift to the cities, improved diets, or the catalytic effect of the IHD? Undoubtedly the answer is that it was a combination of medical, economic, and social factors, but a further question worth asking is whether these energies would have been unleashed in the absence of an organizing driving force such as the IHD.

Worldwide, the picture is less clear in the absence of convincing statistics and the geographical sprawl across six continents. One estimate suggests that more than six hundred million people are still infected, but this must be balanced against the fact that a study of tropical health published in the 1960s ranked hookworm ninth in cases reported (in a survey population of 1.2 million) and twenty-third as a cause of death. Further progress depends as much on break-throughs in nutrition as on advances in the always difficult sanitation field because it appears increasingly self-evident today that the quality of food consumption is related to susceptibility to disease. To have discovered this, an organization had to be active and alert in a broad social and scientific front, not narrowly concentrated in its work on the cause and prevention of disease.

Once again, we can ask what might have been the outlines of the problem if a private agency with a modicum of national success had not extended its efforts to the world at large. The strength of the Rockefeller Foundation, as of its International Health Division, stemmed from the ability of its staff to move back and forth, now within the territorial limits of a scientifically advanced country, thereafter in some of the least developed countries of the world. It was stronger because it was a national institution with an international outreach than if either of these elements were lacking. Understanding the cultural context in which health problems exist can be as vital as understanding their epidemiology. It is difficult enough to understand one's own culture and the interplay of social, economic, and health factors within it. How much more difficult to penetrate the enormously complicated layers of culture in other lands. In the words of Dr. John B. Grant, who served in China, India, and Puerto Rico: "Technical solutions to health problems should be humanized by an understanding of the existing cultures and subcultures and the ways these are changing."[5] Only a group of men who combine love for medicine with love for foreign cultures would be capable of penetrating these subtle realms.

Yet something more was involved than the knowledge of foreign culture or a single disease. From the outset, the war against hookworm was seen as important in itself but even more as "an advance agent of preventive medicine." It was both an end in itself and a means to a larger end. It was a demonstration project in disease control; and if it could succeed, the doctors in the IHD had faith that the Asian peasant or South Seas islander would trust himself more generally to scientific medicine. It was widely believed that the same organizational patterns and sanitary practices could be applied to other diseases. In the south, malaria, which was responsible for a larger fraction of sicknesses and deaths than all other diseases combined, existed side by side with hookworm. It is another anemia-producing disease, and like hookworm, economically practical control measures were known to exist through simple anti-mosquito steps.

After five years of expanding effort in the south, the campaign was extended across the globe. The same pattern was followed with tuberculosis and then with yellow fever. The ultimate goal was not any one disease but a worldwide campaign for preventive medicine through official agenices, full-time professional staff, and modern facilities. It was the modern machinery for administering sanitary and medical care that would count, along with the awakening of public consciousness.

The task was to build up local and regional health agencies; in this, the United States had lagged behind Great Britain and Germany. Where agencies existed, they lacked funds for their work and functioned, if at all, only in times of epidemics. The technique used to strengthen county health organizations was pump priming—$2,500 a year from the external agency, with assurances that at the end of at most three years the county would take over. In Puerto Rico, Brazil and the Philippines, it was the *municipio,* in Austria the *bezirke,* and in France the *departement.* All told, the IHD appropriated more than $4 million for this purpose and today the organizational pattern for rural health services, while still needing improvement, is firmly established in many places. At the state and national levels, in more than forty countries in Europe, Asia and Latin America, a similar scheme was pursued: "Vital statistics in Colombia, public health laboratories in Costa Rica and the Philippines, a hygienic institute in Hungary, a statistical bureau in Bulgaria, a laboratory in Peking—these are random samples of the sweep and scope of the work."[6] The seeds of eventual international cooperation were planted in countries that hopefully might someday reach out to work together across ideological lines.

If ever there were a private venture in which scientific objectives were matched up with an institution's international outreach, it was the yellow fever program of the International Health Division. Stories are legion of personal bravery and human tragedy. Six scientists lost their lives in the search for a "solution;" on no disease up to then had a private agency placed greater emphasis or a larger proportion of time and financial resources. Slow progress had been made until Major Walter Reed of the United States Army Commission demonstrated in Cuba, at the time of the Spanish-American War, that yellow fever is transmitted by the mosquito *aedes aegypti,* and not by human carriers or contaminated objects. General W. C. Gorgas, the Chief Sanitary Officer of the U.S. Army in Cuba, seized on this discovery and "eradicated" yellow fever from Havana. Three years later he extended his success in Panama, making possible the building of the Panama Canal. This led Gorgas to prophesy that yellow fever could be "eradicated from the face of the earth within a reasonable time and at reasonable cost." His approach rested on two assumptions: (1) the *aegypti* mosquito is the sole carrier; breeds almost entirely in urban areas as distinct from the malaria mosquito which is found in swamps, rivers, and lakes; and carries infection through the man-mosquito-man cycle; and (2) key endemic centers such as Guayaquil in Ecuador are seedbeds of infection and the only source of epidemics. Both assumptions proved faulty and the epidemiology infinitely more complex.

A decade later, when the disease seemed under control, if not eradicated, it struck back with savage and unrelenting fury. It was discovered that yellow fever can occur in areas where there are no *aegypti* mosquitoes but where there are other carriers. It was also found, in opposition to the endemic center idea, that a form of yellow fever which existed in tropical forests in South America and Africa was the same as the disease carried by *aegypti* mosquitoes in urban centers. Thus it was not enough to destroy a few endemic urban seedbeds and assume this meant the end of yellow fever. Such knowledge could not have been obtained through anything less than an international inquiry. Peru and Brazil in South America; Honduras, El Salvador, and Nicaragua in Central America; Mexico; and West Africa each in turn were the scenes of fateful epidemics and became thereafter essential areas for research.

Science made possible the bringing together in the laboratories of the Rockefeller Institute for Medical Research in New York the yellow fever viruses of Africa and Latin America and the making of cross immunity tests in monkeys which led to the development of a vaccine. By the end of 1938, 1,040,000 people in Brazil and Colombia had been vaccinated and more than 90 percent developed immunity. British and American soldiers in World War II were protected in Africa and Latin America by this vaccine.

Practically all the vaccine produced since 1937 by private and public agencies derives from an original strain of virus taken in 1927 from a West African native, Asibi, who had yellow fever. The rhesus monkey from India which was inoculated with Asibi's blood specimen died, but Asibi lived and the virus taken from him has been carried down to the present day from one laboratory animal to another through repeated multiplications and tissue cultures, affording immunity to millions of people. The blood of a single West African has served the whole human race. Because the worldwide attack on yellow fever was sustained over three decades, the disease has been pushed back from the frontlines into a secondary position. It remains capable of erupting in violent epidemics, but present techniques appear capable of bringing it under control. The world is the laboratory in which the control was achieved and Asibi is the human symbol of the host of mankind who contributed.

It is significant that the sites of medical and scientific work conducted by the IHD on other diseases dramatize their worldwide distribution. Rumania was the principal site for field research on scarlet fever; Puerto Rico for anemia; Tennessee for amoebic dysentery; Peru for oroya fever; Johns Hopkins for syphilis; France for undulant fever; Polynesia and Micronesia for dengue fever; and Mexico, Canada, England, France, Spain, and the United States for nutritional studies. Disease, as science, knows no nationality or boundaries.

Malaria, which has been the major health problem of a large proportion of mankind, was the third major disease on which the IHD worked. Before a demonstration of malaria control could be undertaken intelligently, the insect vectors had to be identified and the biology of each species investigated. It became clear that methods and techniques applicable in one world region could not readily be transferred to another region, sometimes not even to a different region within the same country. More importantly, *anopheles gambiae,* a carrier of particularly severe type of malaria previously unknown in the Western Hemisphere, had in 1930 made its way from Africa to Brazil, thanks to modern means of transportation. If the argument for confining scientific activity to local diseases had merit before the era of fast destroyers and airplanes, it lost it with their birth. Intercontinental and international travel necessitates international science. In 1930 and 1931 an outbreak of malaria occurred near Natal, and by 1931 *gambiae* mosquitoes had traveled 115 miles up the coast, following prevailing winds and penetrating the flat alluvial shelf at a rate of about forty miles a year. One valley had fifty thousand cases. For some districts 90 percent of the population was affected with up to 10 percent mortality. Consternation spread, not alone in Brazil but throughout Latin and North America. The risks were described as more ominous than the penetration of yellow fever into the Far East.

In 1938 the Brazilian Health Service and Rockefeller Foundation staffs moved into North Brazil, the former with over two thousand doctors, technicians, and laborers, the latter with key organizing scientists who brought skill and resources. While this combined group, through field personnel, distributed quinine and atabrine, their main purpose was to draw a circle around the location of the *gambiae* and try to exterminate it there. The assumption was that if the *gambiae* broke through to the Parnaiba and Sao Francisco river valleys, its spread through the rest of South, Central, and perhaps North America could not be resisted. The *gambiae* had by then advanced halfway to the Parnaiba from Natal, spread over 300 miles, and were infesting an area of 12,000 square miles.

At first climate and geography were allies of the *gambiae*, which breeds in shallow pools of rainwater and thrives in rainy seasons. But a highly organized campaign with fumigation outposts for cars and trains entering or leaving the area, a maritime service which disinfected every boat or plane bound for clean ports and a "scorched earth policy" of spreading substances like Paris green over the ground ten miles beyond the mosquitoes' advance turned back the enemy and the spreading malaria epidemic. The campaign involved an immense effort, cost \$2 million but saved the Western Hemisphere.

The story of malaria dramatizes the problem of a tightly interdependent world and of the flight of carriers of disease and death from one continent to another, transported by modern aircraft and ships. Three years after the 1939-40 threat in Brazil, another invasion of Natal by *gambiae* from Accra and Dakar occurred, and Brazilian authorities again acted to turn back the threat. The lessons of these events made it plain that a spray-gun campaign at airports would never suffice—scientists must carry the war to the sources and sites of infestation in West Africa. In 1944, Egypt called for help as the *gambiae* moved north through the Nile Valley, killing 135,000 people. Once more, Foundation staff under Dr. Fred Soper and thousands of Egyptian Ministry of Health personnel met the challenge and stamped out the *gambiae*. With malaria, there can be no test of success short of exterminating the last pair of the disease-carrying mosquitoes within the area concerned.

The story is not complete unless some mention is made of the most serious bottleneck of all, namely the lack of trained manpower. It soon became evident that ordinary physicians were not necessarily qualified as public health officers. It was decided to create an autonomous school of public health with an institute of hygiene at its center and closely affiliated with a medical school—a "West Point of public health." To this end, the Rockefeller Foundation built and endowed the School of Hygiene and Public Health at Johns Hopkins and subsequently supported the London School of Tropical Medicine and the Pasteur Institute in Paris. Thereafter schools and institutes of public health were developed in Prague, Warsaw, London, Toronto, Copenhagen, Budapest, Oslo, Belgrade, Zagreb, Madrid, Cluj, Ankara, Sofia, Rome, Tokyo, Athens, Buchrest, Stockholm, Calcutta, Manila, Sao Paulo, and at the University of Michigan. More than $25 million went into this monumental effort with incalculable consequences for public health. The first large-scale Foundation fellowship program was launched in health, to be replicated in other fields. From nearly every country in the world, promising young students, scrupulously chosen and with assurance of scientific appointments on their return, matriculated at the new public health institutions. Other men, already trained as public health officers, were given refresher or postgraduate courses. The aim was to link the needs in the field with powerful advanced educational centers and foster an enriching interchange of knowledge and experience. The fellowship program—an investment in leadership—gave a model that was to be followed in almost every sphere of the Foundation's work. It would be difficult to match its importance with any other social or scientific invention in the private sector.

All told, from 1913 to 1950, the Foundation allocated $100 million to health activities, including the awarding of 2,566 fellowships. The operating cost of field staff and offices totaled $22 million, and $8 million was appropriated for state and local health services. A total of $22 million was spent on the control and investigation of specific diseases, including $8 million for yellow fever, $4.5 million for malaria, $3.8 million for hookworm and $3 million for tuberculosis. For a private organization in the first half of the twentieth century the figures are staggering; but in response to this pump priming, the cooperating governments spent far more. The total field personnel of the IHD through its history numbered more than four hundred public health physicians, nurses, engineers, bacteriologists and others— again a mere handful in comparison with the thousands with whom they worked. Few men have won the affection and respect of as many foreign peoples or been trusted more fully. It is a classic story of partnership.

The single most important lesson to be drawn from the work of the International Health Division on specific diseases is that the acquiring of experience and the developing of machinery for an attack on specific diseases has a cumulative and aggregating effect. Momentum is built up and professional competence established. The most natural question for the scientific body is: What disease problems should now receive our attention? For an international foundation, the worldwide character and epidemiological relationship of a disease provides one set of guidelines. The other is set by its overall priorities in programming and its estimate of urgent needs.

Still another consideration has importance and for private agencies can be determining. It is the presence or absence of massive competing resources that are being directed to particular needs. The original position of the IHD and its predecessor boards was an isolated and solitary one. It crossed paths with few organizations with a similarly broad and comprehensive mandate. To be sure, there was some degree of contact with the Health Organization of the League of Nations, but its field operations were limited. As time went on, private and public bodies entered the world arena with resources dwarfing those of private bodies. The Pan American Sanitary Bureau, covering twenty-one Latin American republics, had been organized in 1902 and reorganized in 1947. Its major activities included epidemic disease control, improved national health services, and public health education. By the 1950s, its annual budget was $1.9 million. The Institute of Inter-American Affairs created in 1942 devoted a part of its budget of $6 million to health and sanitation. The World Health Organization, with a basic budget of $6.15 million, provided technical experts, awarded fellowships and travel grants and undertook demonstrations and field studies. UNICEF had funds which varied from year to year depending on contributions, but in the period 1946-50, its total funds were $150 million, part of which went to WHO activities. U.S. foreign aid included funds for health and education, and the Colombo Plan funds exceeded $5 million. The United States Public Health Service represented the American government in international health relations and selected fellows and foreign service personnel. Finally, new funds entered the field from other U.S. agencies, which came to exceed those of all other bodies.

Faced with the introduction of these massive new resources and the addition of new areas of interest within the Rockefeller Foundation, such as medical education and public health, the IHD more and more turned to the clarification of basic principles rather than the application and demonstration of tried and tested technologies. It shared its knowledge with others and assigned personnel to newer bodies. The IHD lives on in a smaller and reorganized Foundation program and in new scientific adventures continuing to the present day, at one time the international program in virus research and more recently in contagious diseases.

The enduring contribution of the IHD was the structure it evolved, the professionals it attracted and the goals it pursued. For a brief but critical period in the long history of man, it played a solitary role, demonstrating what an international health activity under private auspices could accomplish. It left footprints that have guided others and a rich legacy that proved what can be done through people working together and through generating resources from the private sector. There can be little doubt that current priorities and activities in population control and health care draw working models from this respected and pioneering body.

Yet the new areas run the risk of being more politicized than professionalized or of reflecting the noble impulses and energies of a few powerful and fanatical reformers. These impulses, however worthy, are mixed with an immense amount of selfish pride and desire for personal advancement. Those who hold them are sometimes oblivious to the need for institutions such as the IHD. Or when the instruments exist, they are not always wisely and fully used. To the extent reformers leave to scientists the shaping of scientific decisions, the more likely they are to carve out a place in history comparable to that of the IHD. The quite modest advances that have been made thus far in fields like population and environmental studies underscore this warning. The same need for clarity of objectives and sharpness of instruments exists in these complex fields as it did six decades ago in health. It is instructive therefore to review and reexamine this earliest value in America's adventure with international cooperation.

CHAPTER TWO
AGRICULTURE AND THE CONQUEST OF HUNGER
Kenneth W. Thompson

A second broad area in which American values have come into play has been in agricultural assistance programs. International agriculture involves the work not of political figures but of scientific and technical professionals. It starts with a problem—world hunger—and moves forward in the social and economic realm. Its concerns are neither local nor regional. They are worldwide, for feeding mankind and averting famine is an international need. The problem of hunger is universal.

The approach to this urgent need is one in which agricultural scientists, wherever they may be, build on a tradition and established skills and techniques developed elsewhere in the world. For example, various rice-growing techniques developed in Louisiana and Japan have provided an important basis for experimentation at the International Rice Research Institute in the Philippines. Similarly, agronomists and plant pathologists who had worked on new varieties and production techniques for corn and wheat in the heart of America have put this knowledge to work at the International Corn and Wheat Center in Mexico. Since what has been learned in one area cannot be applied without modification in another, a significant amount of adaptation and modification has been required: research on plant-breeding, testing for disease resistance in different circumstances, and studying the characteristics of individual varieties in relation to local tastes and cultural preferences.

In all these efforts food production is aimed at meeting a primary, not a secondary need. Nothing less than the survival of humanity is involved. To this end, the activities of professionals working on improved food production must proceed with a degree of freedom from politics and governmental pressures. It is possible to see agriculture as primarily a technical and an applied scientific activity, less subject than other types of international cooperation to politics and hence to the dictates of national sovereignty. It can also be shown that cooperative programs in agriculture, much as with medicine and public health, can pave the way for international programs in other fields, such as education.

Agriculture as a Success Story

Notwithstanding its failure to change the patterns of political organization in the world, American agricultural efforts, both nationally and internationally, have been a success story. Agriculture is a field of technical assistance in which the donor agencies have something to give the poorer nations; agricultural accomplishments in the developed countries are relevant, at least in broad terms, to the needs of the world community. This is particularly true of American agriculture in its various manifestations.

In part the success of American agriculture can be attributed to the historic role of the land-grant colleges, the most significant educational innovation in the United States in the nineteenth century. A group of English academics described them off-handedly as "places where men are taught to throw manure about and act as wet nurses to steam engines." Nevertheless, the Morrill Act in 1862 created a novel system of higher education. Whereas the distinguished universities of the East had dominated the American educational scene seeking as the highest end of education the training of broadly educated men, the land-grant institutions put stress on the practical— the applied sciences and arts. Universities destined to become large-scale educational centers appeared out of nowhere. A vigorous and dynamic chicken farmer in Michigan brought a new institution, Michigan State, from being a rather small and provincial university to an institution of national and international standing. What John Hannah accomplished in East Lansing, Michigan, had earlier occurred at Cornell, Minnesota, and Wisconsin.

What are the principal characteristics of the land-grant university as it has developed throughout the United States? In the first place, it has been more vocationally oriented than have Ivy League universities and their counterparts. The links between study and work are closer than in other universities. Education is tied to the labor market within the region and the nation. Students of education point out that such emphasis means that enrollments remain stable or significantly increase when declines occur in more traditional liberal arts institutions because of the decrease in job opportunities for arts and sciences graduates.

Second, the curriculum and programs of land-grant institutions are geared to local needs and problems. Some of the great private universities located in large metropolitan areas take pride in being "in but not of their cities." It is said that Harvard University contributes little to the political and economic life of Cambridge. The same has been true in recent years of the University of Chicago, though men like Julian Levi, brother of former president Edward Levi, have played a decisive role in neighborhood redevelopment. The educational philosophy of land-grant institutions is the direct opposite. Faculty of these colleges and universities insist on taking a direct and continuing interest in the problems of their communities. If concern with problem-solving directed at the needs of immediate localities has somewhat diminished or been redirected to nationwide problems as land-grant universities have grown in size, their underlying philosophy remains intact.

Third, land-grant institutions have designed and carried out programs involving substantial adaptation and extension of the university's work and outreach. Examples include programs for the training of county agents and short courses and summer programs in agriculture. My father, who lived throughout his youth in rural Wisconsin and other members of his family devoted three or four weeks each summer to study at the University of Wisconsin learning new and improved approaches to agricultural production. Such universities as Wisconsin, Minnesota, and Cornell also developed radio and publication programs to aid the farmer, issuing leaflets and brochures written in simple, nonscientific language and applicable to local circumstances.

Fourth, land-grant institutions were in the forefront of educational centers that brought education to the people. Branches of major state universities were established in other parts of the state and, carrying the land-grant philosophy another step, these branches geared their offering to whatever needs were more pressing within each particular locality.

Fifth, it was recognized early on that educational institutions in the twentieth century must think in terms of lifelong learning. In this the land-grant institutions anticipated an educational viewpoint that came into prominence in the 1960s with a widely discussed report by UNESCO on the need for continuing education of adults as well as young people. It is obvious that the industrialized and non-industrialized countries respond to this need in the light of different problems and circumstances. In the industrial countries, the growing mechanization of work and life has driven many adults to seek human satisfaction and self-realization outside their day-to-day employment; they are turning in ever larger numbers to continuing education and community college programs. Liberated from long hours of drudgery by shorter work weeks, they are seeking renewal in the offerings of adult education. In the less developed countries, economic pressures and trained manpower shortages, rather than increased leisure, have brought adults into educational institutions. So-called mature student programs are now an established part of educational opportunities in most African universities. If one were to look for the sources of these educational innovations, many of them go back to concepts of the land-grant college movement.

Sixth, land-grant education begins with an urgent problem. The core precept rests on the belief that the main business of education is to prepare men and women to cope with the amelioration of difficult and pressing circumstances. Its process is problem-solving; its approach is inductive, not deductive. The starting point is not a general principle, but a problem to which education can make or discover a way to make a contribution.

Seventh, the leadership of land-grant institutions, it follows, is composed not so much of educational philosophers as of technical professionals. They constitute a network of experts rotating in and out of positions of power in the public and private sectors. One example can be drawn from the field of agriculture. An extraordinarily capable group of scientists are the agriculturalists who have served as leaders of the land-grant institutions, men like Clifford Hardin, Earl Butz, James Jensen, Louis Morrill, Clifton R. Wharton, Jr., and John Hannah, who later served as secretaries of agriculture or leaders of technical assistance programs. These men have constituted an educational and scientific elite, a group set apart from the foreign policy establishment. They have been trustees and advisors to foundations and government agencies who have provided agricultural assistance to the less-developed countries. They are known in these countries as trusted friends and consultants who have played an important role in the shaping of agricultural education and policy.

Eighth, the land-grant institutions in the United States have emerged as important clearinghouses and repositories of agricultural know-how and information. They are centers in which new varieties of basic food crops have been developed, and their leaders are always willing to share their findings and their expertise with international agricultural institutes and ministries of agriculture in other countries.

Ninth, the most distinctive characteristic of the land-grant institution is its emphasis on service. There is widespread agreement that the threefold task of those in higher education is to teach, to engage in research, and to render service. Different educational institutions have emphasized these functions in varying degrees. The great private institutions such as Harvard, MIT, and Stanford have gained fame and renown as research institutions. Although land-grant institutions have not neglected research, especially in applied scientific areas, their greatest contribution has been the service they have rendered to agencies of government and to private corporations. A unique tradition has grown up that enables at least some of these institutions to make their best scholars and scientists available to developing countries for extended periods of residence and for the training of indigenous leaders. It is increasingly common for them to grant academic leaves to their strongest faculty members for three or four years of service abroad, much as strong research universities grant similar research leaves to their most outstanding basic research scientists. For example, a well-known agricultural economist from the University of Minnesota has over a dozen years been a regular faculty member of Kasetsart University in Bangkok, Thailand, while retaining his professorship at Minnesota. Some land-grant universities have in effect two faculties in certain fields, one for teaching and research at home and the other for similar work abroad. Thus these institutions include in their budgets provision for a cadre of professors engaged in international service. Moreover, the land-grant colleges have taken the lead in initiating sister-university relations with institutions in the Third World. Their willingness to undertake such missions can only reflect a deep commitment to service.

The special problems of the less-developed countries and their most urgent needs and priorities have made the land-grant pattern congenial to the thinking of their leaders. But even for those whose educational formation and background falls within non-American-developed educational systems, the land-grant system is attractive. Sir Eric Ashby (now Lord Ashby) of Clare College, Oxford University, in England, was the author of a major review of higher education in Nigeria following that country's independence. Sir Eric urged Nigerians, and donor agencies that might assist them, to revise the inherited educational system that was patterned after the University of London and kept a continuing special relation with that institution. The Ashby Commission asked if the land-grant institution was not more relevant to local needs in Nigeria. Members of the commission proposed a series of new universities in Nigeria, providing clear educational alternatives to the Ox-bridge model; and shortly thereafter a new university based on these proposals was created in the eastern region at Nnsuka, with a special relation to Michigan State University.

Although it is still too early to measure the results of these changing educational patterns in Nigeria, it is significant that the other new universities there—especially at Ife near Ibadan and in Zaria in northern Nigeria (Ahmadu Bello University)—have patterned themselves more after the American land-grant university than after the British model. Slavish imitation of any outside model is risky, and the Nigerians and other African educators have struggled to avoid this mistake. It is also true that the existence of such alternative educational systems has influenced and led to change in a more traditional British institution such as Ibadan University. The African experience teaches that the existence of these alternatives and more serious attention to problems in the agricultural and non-agricultural faculties has had a constructive effect.

The Capacity of American Agriculture

The success story of American agriculture and the unique strengths of the land-grant college movement provide only a partial explanation of the capacity of American agriculture. Its resources are also a result of its heritage—the quality and vitality of its leaders, its curious intermingling of individualism and communalism, its blending of parochialism and universalism.

The herîtage of American agriculture stems from its noteworthy achievements in opening a vast continent to settlement and feeding an expanding population. Many of the nation's first immigrants arrived in the new land from western and northern Europe where they had farmed the land, raised livestock, and experimented agriculturally. As the early settlers moved westward they looked for a terrain of rivers and plains such as they knew in Europe. Ole Rolvaag and Herbert Krause, respectively, in *Giants in the Earth* and *Wind Without Rain,* have written of the suffering and adversity, the courage and inventiveness of the Scandinavian immigrants. Later waves of migration brought workers and technicians from southern and eastern Europe. Because those who made up the agricultural stratum were so resourceful, the specter of hunger and famine that has threatened other societies was not as forbidding to the new Americans. To credit the skills of the American farmer is not to minimize the advantages of the abundant productivity of the soil or of an equable climate and rainfall.

The triumphs of the American farmer in conquering the wilderness and his survival against great odds produced a new breed of fearless and outspoken leaders whose thinking and attitudes were rooted in local needs and circumstances. Social and political movements such as populism, the Farm Labor party, and the Progressive party drew on the drive, ambition, and discontent of these men. They were symbols of the sturdy individualism and stubborn persistence in the face of ever-changing conditions of winds and weather. At the same time, they spoke out against early injustices and exploitation by the railroads, utilities, and a government that was remote and indifferent to their needs and problems. Less polished and urbane than business and industrial leaders, the nation's agricultural leaders were blunt and plainspoken, wary of domination by the favored few of an eastern elite.

Yet individualism alone is not adequate to describe rural motivation. When disaster struck, it was the whole community that helped raise homes or barns that had been destroyed—and then celebrated with revelry and dance what people joining together had accomplished. Individualism and communalism coexisted in practice, however much they conflicted in theory and logic. Because men had learned to help themselves, they were better able to help others. Service had its birth in these early community beginnings; and it comes as no surprise, therefore, that individuals in the rural sector were responsive to the mid-twentieth century calls for help from abroad.

Finally, paradoxical as it may seem given its motivation to serve mankind, no group in American life has been, from a certain standpoint, more parochial. It is the American farmer who, until recent decades at least, has protested the acts of faraway government, resisted cries for help by the cities, and questioned internationalism whatever its creedal or political formulations. Rural areas have cradled isolationism, welcomed opposition groups such as America First, nurtured xenophobia, and doubted the value of any foreign involvements. Whatever the motivating force, whether it has been fear and resentment of the rich and powerful or the Jeffersonian belief that it was impossible to find human virtue outside of small cities and rural areas, agricultural America has affirmed loyalty to what was local and immediate and questioned cosmopolitanism and internationalism as leading to an effete way of life.

Yet rural peoples have also clung to a dream that was universal, a belief that the good life was rooted in religion, hard work, and the family. Men who lived close to the soil were assumed to have integrity and moral stamina, whether they happened to be in Iowa or Nigeria. Their religious heritage had bound them together in the Christian missionary movement, and it was not too farfetched for American agronomists or plant pathologists to see continuity between their missionary forefathers and themselves as they worked in a secular and scientific world. Religious precepts taught that all men were brothers. Mankind everywhere had both spiritual and material needs to which the privileged few were duty bound to contribute. It was not surprising, therefore, that despite a certain strain of parochialism, rural America rose to the challenge of helping feed the world. Such universalism was linked to the simple and rudimentary aspects of life even as farm people continued to look with distaste and suspicion on clever international diplomacy or high-flown language concerning world power and national interests.

Taken together, these four factors—the heritage of rural America, the energy and convictions of its leaders, its intermingling of individualism and communalism, and its blending of parochialism and universality—combined to give American agriculturalists a unique capacity. Here was an identifiable group with a mission of its own, willing and able to contribute to the world not as nations had traditionally assisted one another through arms and trade but through people working together for agricultural development. American agricultural scientists were carried along in their mission by the conviction that they could work not necessarily with Nigerians in general or with any other nationality but with Nigerian agriculturalists. Despite the parochialism that pervaded some of their thinking, they were internationalists in the sense that they had confidence that their capacity in agriculture was relevant to what they called the conquest of hunger everywhere. American agriculture had fed a growing population, and those primarily responsible were convinced they could help others to revolutionize agricultural productivity, to turn their systems around and feed their own people through strategies of self-help. This wider task required not the usual patterns of emergency food aid, but new forms of functional cooperation on which American specialists would stake their prestige.

Agricultural cooperation, as described here, begins from an American base. Its core is American agricultural know-how. However, as agriculturalists envisage the effort, its ultimate goal is to assist the "well-being of mankind." It is grounded in agriculturalists working with agriculturalists regardless of national origin. For this reason, and particularly because the initiative in the 1950s and 1960s came from private organizations, it is an experiment in functional cooperation, not one more instrument of American foreign policy.

The Internationalization of Agriculture

That the improvement of agriculture is viewed as a worldwide challenge is in part a result of the success and capacity of American agriculture, reflected in the land-grant college movement, and in part a result of the desperate straits of the poorer nations struggling to feed themselves. American efforts to help other peoples began with private and public efforts in emergency and rescue operations. When disaster struck, whether in catastrophes of nature or in unremitting famines, Americans were among the first to respond. Church groups and other humanitarian agencies rallied to deliver food and other forms of relief. The Food for Peace program of the government is only the most recent large-scale attempt to help the starving and the homeless. The practice of needy peoples turning to America testifies both to our recognized humanitarianism and to the successes of American agriculture. Negatively, it demonstrates a sense of dissatisfaction with the failures of other agricultural approaches, whether the Russian attempt to feed the peoples of the Soviet Union or the less-than-spectacular success of the French and the British in Africa and Asia.

The American approach to feeding the world represents the convergence of a missionary spirit of a people and of a felt need expressed particularly by the governmental leaders and educators of Africa and Asia. I learned this in numerous conversations from the late 1950s to early 1970s as the coordinator of international programs for the Rockefeller Foundation. By the 1960s, African leaders in particular were growing restive with existing assistance programs and, as already noted, the Ashby Commission called for another type of education in Africa. The late Sir Alexander Carr-Saunders, a renowned British demographer and social scientist, headed several survey teams that made similar recommendations to universities founded by the British in Africa. Asians expressed concern with the high price of the brain drain, as national educators trained abroad were attracted by institutions outside their own countries. Asian and African universities whose agriculture programs had enjoyed at best limited success under British, French, and German tutelage requested American technical assistance. Several institutions, including Makerere College in Uganda and Asian universities in India and Indonesia, went so far as appointing American agricultural educators with land-grant college backgrounds as deans of their agriculture faculties. Ralph W. Cummings, director of the Rockefeller Foundation's agriculture program in India who later headed the International Institute on Arid Lands Agriculture Research in Hydrabad (ICRISAT), promoted the development of seven agricultural universities in India, all modeled after the land-grant universities. Indonesia turned to the Rockefeller and Ford foundations for the strengthening of its agricultural institutes and universities. The University of the Philippines reorganized its system of agriculture education with help from Cornell University, the International Rice Research Institute (IRRI), and the Ford Foundation. Kasetsart University in Thailand drew heavily on the agriculture staff of the Rockefeller Foundation and several land-grant universities. Zaire, Tanzania, Ethiopia, and Kenya in Africa made similar calls on professional agriculturalists from the United States. Indeed, it is difficult to think of a major country in Africa and Asia that has not been touched by American agriculture, bringing to fruition the internationalization of this nation's effort to be helpful not only on these continents but in Latin America as well.

The Common Emphasis of the American Agricultural Effort Abroad

How can we account for the spread of American agricultural ideas and practices? What have been the working principles and the common emphases of the effort? What explains its widespread influence throughout the developing world? There are at least eight distinguishing characteristics of the approach that strengthen and reinforce one another.

First, American agricultural scientists at work in the Third World have given the highest priority to improved agricultural production, not to research for research's sake. Other traditions, and in particular the British, had laid greater stress on a form of agricultural education aimed at training broadly educated agriculturalists. As one traveled by airplane in the 1960s from London to universities in West or East Africa, it was commonplace to meet British-trained agriculturalists who could recite the history and culture of every major crop in Africa. At early morning refueling stops en route to their destination, these remarkably cultured men put Americans to shame with their encyclopedic knowledge of the origins and development of plants and animals across the continent, many introduced or cultivated by the colonial power. What was missing, however, was the passionate concern of American agronomists or plant pathologists for expanding and diversifying agricultural production in order to eliminate the hunger of the people of the country or region, a lack some Englishmen were frank to admit to their American friends in moments of candor. It was this passionate concern that inspired American agriculturalists to work long hours side by side with agriculturalists of other nations, without ever asking who would receive the credit for their functional endeavor. Anyone who looked in on the agricultural research institutes left with a sense that here were men laboring with a "grand obsession." They were men of action, not historians or philosophers.

Second, the Americans had one all-consuming objective, if not obsession, in their blueprint for agricultural universities. It was essential that experiment stations be established for practical work with these institutions. Many Asian and African universities lacked such a facility, putting more stress on the theory than the practice of agriculture. Americans insisted there must be a place where fledgling agriculturalists "could learn to grow a crop."

Third, Americans maintained that there must be links with ministries of agriculture. Universities must not exist in isolation from the principal actors in the agricultural scene. The British had separated governmental research stations from educational institutions. At least partially in response to American influence, these two parts of the agricultural system were joined when the newer universities came into being as with the new university in Northern Nigeria, Ahmadu Bello. When the Rockefeller Foundation agreed to help the agricultural faculty at Gadja Mada University in Jojakarta, Indonesia, it did so on condition that various plots of land spread over wide areas remote from the university be joined together in an experiment station with links to the ministry of agriculture.

Fourth, the American approach also laid stress on the building of substantial storage and retrieval systems. It was essential, the Americans argued, that a vast array of plant varieties be brought together in one place readily accessible to agricultural researchers. Corn and wheat banks were established at almost every center where work was undertaken. This was also done for potatoes, sorghum, and beans, as well as indigenous crops with which Americans had little initial familiarity.

Fifth, Americans insisted that trainees put on overalls and go out into the field. Book learning was not enough. The Rockefeller Foundation staff, when it went into Mexico in 1943, found that young Mexicans had imagined they were to be trained for desk jobs. Their resistance to soiling their hands was overcome, however, when they found their American colleagues spent most of their working hours teaching themselves and their students "how to plant a crop of wheat in Mexico." Nobel Prize winner Norman Borlaug set an example by working from sunup to sundown in the wheat fields of northern Mexico, and his example proved contagious.

Sixth, another point of doctrine emphasized the integration of training and research. Although the American team of the Rockefeller Foundation in Mexico began its work under the auspices of the so-called Office of Special Studies within the Ministry of Agriculture, it quickly turned its attention to the creation of a first-class Graduate School of Agriculture at Chapingo. There the emphasis, as in the land-grant colleges, was on training for agricultural production, not on agricultural theory.

Seventh, it was also taken as a given that what was learned in one place in agricultural sciences must be shared with others. Far-ranging exchange of information and materials and, wherever possible, of trained personnel, was encouraged. Nor were the learners to be exempt from such exchange, for it was assumed from the beginning that Mexicans, for example, had a responsibility to share information and know-how with agriculturalists in Central America.

Eighth, the overall activity of building agricultural capacity and its success was dependent upon the existence of highly qualified professionals who had something to contribute to colleagues in other countries. A career service was established by organizations such as the Rockefeller Foundation and by the land-grant institutions financed from private and public sources. The concept of a career service reached its culmination in the establishment in 1975 of an International Agricultural Development Service (IADS), composed of agricultural personnel who had had experience in one or more developing countries and were available for service elsewhere.

Reinforcing Programs

The approach of the land-grant institutions was strengthened and reinforced by what were called country programs brought into being by agencies such as the Rockefeller Foundation. In 1943 that organization, after long and careful study launched its first country program in agricultural research and training in Mexico and followed this by establishing additional programs in Colombia (1950), Chile (1953), the Philippines (1959), India (1960), and Nigeria (1962). Not only did these programs call on the resources of skilled professionals from land-grant institutions; they also helped such scientists and technicians to develop an identity and an *esprit de corps*. The leaders of the programs developed pride in their own approach and a mild skepticism with the fixed concepts of the land-grant approach. They constituted themselves into small, close-knit bodies of professionals who never doubted their ability to so alter the agricultural production system of the countries in which they worked as to move from a crop-deficit to a crop-surplus position. So single-minded was their commitment that they were reticent about exploring broader issues of agricultural economics, agricultural policy, and land reform. Through their efforts, Mexico was able to terminate the importation of corn and wheat, thereby protecting scarce foreign-exchange reserves.

Success in country programs led to larger regional efforts and to the creation of international agriculture institutes manned by experienced leaders from the country programs who followed the example set by the International Health Division of the Rockefeller Foundation, as well as other medical and public health agencies. Their aim was to keep intact the human capital developed by the country program and make it available on a wider geographical basis.

Finally, a coalition of some twenty-five or thirty donor agencies—private and public—joined in the 1960s to form a consortium of policy and fund-raising bodies constituting the Consultative Group of International Agricultural Research. The efforts of this group assured that the necessary support for the continuation of a wide range of cooperative activities in agricultural research and training in the developing countries would be forthcoming.

The World Food Conference and the World Food Council

The efforts made by these private bodies and others who have marshaled the skills and talents of the international community of agricultural scientists were a prelude to a far larger effort in the 1970s to meet the problem of world hunger. In 1972 the World Food Conference was convened in Rome, bringing together representatives from both the developed and less-developed countries. The conference was an expression of the desire for a North/South dialogue; it represented the same type of producers' and consumers' conference that had been held in the energy field. Such a meeting was also a further sign of the equality of nations exemplified in the work of the United Nations and evidenced by the fact that the existing international specialized agency in agriculture, the Food and Agriculture Organization (FAO), had left something to be desired. The World Food Conference, and the World Food Council it brought into being, represented the chance of carrying further the important effort begun in the 1940s to feed the world. It demonstrated the organic growth from the small beginnings of a handful of agricultural scientists laboring to end the crop-deficit position of Mexico to a broad-based worldwide consortium of donors and experts.

With the World Food Conference in Rome, the international agricultural effort moved across the threshold that separates a private endeavor from one involving politics and the high governmental policies of nation states. It engaged domestic political groups in every participating country. For example, the chief spokesmen for the United States on issues in contention were Secretaries Henry Kissinger, Earl Butz and President Ford for the Republican administration, and Senators George McGovern and Hubert Humphrey for the Democrats. In international politics, it involved the clash of interest between the developed and the developing countries. Politicians, not agricultural scientists, moved to the center of the stage. It was no longer possible to describe the international agricultural cooperation in primarily technical and economic terms. The issue that remains unresolved is whether the functional cooperation that prevailed from the 1940s to the end of the 1960s has been superseded by new groupings with political clash of interests or whether functionalism has worn away some of the extreme loyalties that have dominated other sectors of international relations.

CHAPTER THREE
EDUCATION PROJECTED ABROAD:
INSTITUTION-BUILDING IN THE THIRD WORLD
Kenneth W. Thompson

Americans have been rightfully proud of an educational heritage which has been as varied as it has been distinguished. American educators have taken initiatives around the world to assist educational development extending from work by distinguished research scientists to literacy training by Peace Corps volunteers. One program of educational assistance was the university development program of the Rockefeller Foundation which I was privileged to direct as vice president in the 1960s and early 1970s. It followed programs in health and agriculture which laid a foundation for a wider educational effort. The trustees of the foundation authorized the undertaking with assurances of a ten to fifteen-year commitment.

Beginning in the early 1960s, the foundation undertook to provide technical assistance for overall university development to a few selected institutions in developing countries. The program had a definable *rationale,* involved institutions selected in accordance with explicit *criteria,* proceeded according to a design or *plan* through various stages of development, and undertook to assist the building of institutional *capacity* for grappling with problems of national development. These four topics provide a focus for the description of the particular approach to university development which follows.

Rationale

Institution-building is at the heart of the foundation's tradition as well as of American education generally. Its beginnings go back to the birth of two score schools of public health in the 1920s and 1930s, to area-studies centers in the 1950s, and to international institutes of agriculture in the 1960s. The rationale of the University Development Program (UDP) was rooted in this tradition plus the belief that, for the Less Developed Countries (LDCs), the missing factor was educated people or trained leadership. Needed were not only the doctors, engineers, agronomists, and economists who would chart the nation's course but also those who could multiply themselves by training men to fill such posts. The single most important factor separating the successes of the Marshall Plan from the problems of Point Four was the human and organizational infrastructure. From Point Four to the present, assistance to the developing countries has oftentimes been held in suspense when local counterpart requirements could not be met, whether in trained manpower or effective institutions. The remedy lies not with outsiders; to meet these human deficits, indigenous institutions are needed to prepare the missing leaders.

A second part of the rationale underlying institution-building is that a concentrated attack on a single urgent problem, while necessary, is insufficient in and of itself. Often the only thing worse than failure may be success. It is imperative to identify pressing human needs, but no less imperative to grasp their interrelationships. The earlier triumphs of public health in reducing mortality have had some part in ushering in the population explosion. The "green revolution" of our time will ultimately prove successful only if its relationship with employment, internal migration, and political structures is recognized and dealt with.

Developing universities provide a framework within which problems of this order can be considered as part of an integrated effort. One of the dividends of a technical assistance staff working together on an across-the-board basis within an institutional framework is the possibility of interdisciplinary approach to local development problems for a well-defined and delineated geographical area. The one attempt which had been made was in the late 1940s, in Crete. It was at best a partial success but valuable lessons were learned. The foundation's professional staff had a long tradition of operating abroad but characteristically in the more or less isolated medical or agricultural sectors. University Development brought staff and resources together to join in the task of building educational institutions. A university can be a prime mover in the transition from traditional to modern ways of life but this requires many different kinds of trained people. It must build professional competence in key disciplines and furnish a scientific and scholarly base for relevant problem-solving. The provision of human and material capital, of people and things, is directed toward this purpose.

Criteria of Selection

Once the Rockefeller Foundation decided in the 1950s to shift program emphasis from Europe and the United States to the developing countries, it was faced with critical problems of choice.

It had to measure unlimited human need against severely limited resources. There was concern that, even with income being augmented through expenditure of capital, the comparatively small sums available could readily be frittered away, leaving hardly a trace over the vast reaches of Asia and Africa. At an earlier point, scatteration had prevailed: in a single year, grants or study awards were made to approximately 50 separate institutions in Latin America alone. What was the effect? Institutionally, it was minimal; for the individual returning from study, he was bereft of a post and driven into the general labor market.

This led the trustees and officers to evoke once again the principle of concentration. In the same way that an earlier decision had been made to work with one Ministry of Health or Ministry of Agriculture in a chosen country, it was decided to work with one university. The choice of the right university was a difficult one. The foundation was determined to work only with institutions that had the potential of serving national or regional needs. As the program unfolded, a set of criteria evolved for the selection of UDP centers. The first was the existence of a genuine request for help formally and informally communicated. Review teams comprised of representatives of all sectors of programs at the foundation visited each prospective center to determine whether help was desired and to what extent conditions for indigenous growth in a given discipline were present. They "put down the scientists' rod" to test the depth and potential of resources in fields in which the foundation could be helpful. They looked for determination to move ahead, for academic and administrative leadership committed to change, and for the prospect of increasing support from other sources.

In the same way that not every nation had made the hard decisions prerequisite to benefiting from foreign assistance, not every institution has prepared itself for genuine organic growth. Some had failed to come forward with a practical design for upgrading faculty, neglected research opportunities, overlooked salary problems, or forgotten about community support. Others lacked a nucleus of devoted and responsible leaders willing and able to foster institutional growth at the expense of their own professional advancement and prestige, if necessary. There are certain matters that institutions, no less than individuals or nations, cannot leave to chance. What is to be their role in a wider geographic region? How are they to weigh numerical growth against the pursuit of excellence? How much or how little should they undertake in a specific field? Is their mission to train the teachers, public servants, engineers, and doctors to serve the nation and other social and educational institutions? Or is their role conceived in the more parochial, if worthy, terms of building a civic culture for their immediate constituents? Finally, has the leadership made a fresh and self-critical review of strengths and weaknesses and laid down the broad guidelines for responding to institutional needs?

Recognizing that its resources are always more restricted than its needs, how far has it gone in establishing priorities for determining points of emphasis next year, three, or five years hence?

Partners in institution-building, who can at best assist only a few institutions, cannot escape the obligation to assess the many factors essential to growth. Perhaps what is needed is an institutional equivalent of the pilot's check list before clearing the aircraft for flight. But in the end, when the many factors essential to growth have been considered, partners must consider the institution as a whole. For whether the aim is developing a university or building a strong and vital research institute, the organization is somehow more than the sum of its parts. Those who assess in order to help must acquire the knack of measuring the potential and strength of institutions in the process of evolving. Universities in some parts of the world are little more than loose collections of faculties. If it is only an isolated faculty in the university that invites development, this fact may lead to exclusion, or may require a new approach to institution-building. If outside donor organizations concentrate their resources at a few developing institutions, the corollary of external assistance is single-minded concentration by indigenous leadership on the central problems of institution-building.

Perhaps the most crucial criterion of all is the estimate those who assist must make of the prospects of partnership. Full and frank exchange of ideas is the result, not the forerunner, of mutual commitment. Yet intimate, unguarded, and self-critical discussion is vital if assistance is to make a difference. To mold a partnership in institution-building is to build a framework within which consultation goes on and mutually acceptable, far-reaching decisions are made. By contrast, casual involvement in institutional development results in hit-or-miss direction of those actions that shape the future. Whether the subject is selection of a fellow or reworking the syllabus or planning a new curriculum, the partners are engaged in what is ultimately the institution's most serious business. Whether they succeed or fail depends on whether these topics are considered casually en route to the airport or through the solemn and deliberate processes of ongoing institutional life.

The Foundation's Plan

If the foundation could call on universities to have a plan, it was obligated to have one, too. The great issue was whether its staff could match up resources and capacities with urgent needs at selected institutions. Objectives had to be formulated in terms of definable tasks. It was vital that there be a timetable; the plan required a beginning, a middle, and an end. In operational language, the foundation had "to get in and get out." In 1961, the foundation's president, J. George Harrar, in presenting the program, spoke of a possible twelve to fifteen-year effort which might cost up to $100 million. The trustees accepted the proposal without blinking. In fact, expenditures over the first eight years totaled about $40 million.

Broadly speaking, the plan envisaged at least four distinct phases, varying as between the several UDP models described below. Phase I involved the giving of assistance in speeding the transition from a colonial to a national university. Toward this end, the foundation made available, on long-term assignments, a few members of its professional staff. The prior question involved identifying and defining discrete and manageable areas of assistance. This need is an outgrowth of the essential nature of technical assistance. Outside help, even public and international agency help, is inevitably marginal help. (At the peak of the Marshall Plan, the flow of aid never exceeded 4 percent of Europe's capital needs.) Private foundations particularly must come to a judicious determination of the focus of their aid. Policies follow questions that go to the heart of cooperative efforts. What are the recipient country's most urgent and pressing needs and what is it doing about them? What is it doing for itself and what does it seek from others? Viewed realistically, what capacity does the donor agency possess, or can it acquire, for assistance in those areas where it can make a genuine difference? Whether the choice is agriculture or virus research or improving an economics faculty, there are dividends in defining and identifying areas of need and matching them against available outside resources.

In Thailand, the Rockefeller Foundation concentrated its efforts in university development on the strengthening of three basic disciplines: medical and basic sciences, agriculture, and economics. Within its operating agricultural programs, the emphasis was on research and training programs directed toward strengthening various countries' ability to produce certain basic food crops, such as corn, wheat, sorghum, potatoes, and rice. Crops were chosen because they were crucial for specific economies—corn and wheat in Mexico, rice and sorghum in Asia. The goal was improved varieties and techniques, not across the entire agricultural spectrum, but in areas where need and capacity could be joined. Again, in the foundation's university development efforts, its focus was on disciplines ready and able to use assistance for which the sources of intellectual cooperation were in sight.

Career Service

Once the major thrust was determined, the selection of visitors and professionals skilled in the complexities of institution-building followed. Here a career service of men engaged in assistance to developing institutions was essential. The Gardner Report[1] proposed an Agency for International Development (AID) career service backstopped by a cadre of AID reservists. Experience that harked back to the International Health Division of the Rockefeller Foundation pointed the way to the maintenance of professional competence for international service. If Henry Wriston was right when he declared that first-class problems attract first-class minds, the rallying of qualified personnel was not impossible. The foundation in its University Development Program, was encouraged by the interest of first-rate scholars in serving abroad as visiting professors, heads of departments or research institutes, and even as deans. Some were recruited as regular foundation staff, others as temporary personnel, and others as scholars on leave from their own universities. A career service for university development must be flexible enough to provide for commitments ranging across a sliding scale of interest. Some will be engaged more or less permanently, others for a year or two. It is obvious that any plan for a career service that would attract the best minds must allow for both service and research—the continuation of a scholar's most deeply cherished interests. Essential will be the presence, in any organized effort at a university development center, of a least a few top-flight leaders devoting themselves full-time to academic administration and teaching. Their presence at the heart of the development enterprise leaves room for researchers who teach by carrying forward their own scientific inquiries.

In the end, the fate of American education abroad is dependent on responsible and well-qualified people engaged in tasks for which there is a recognized need. Sometimes this involves doing well what a scholar is required to do in any educational setting. At other times the adaptation must be more drastic. Perhaps the success of the American effort has been greatest when the approach is indirect and oblique. American agronomists, economists, or virologists probably contribute most when they labor as scientists and scholars drawing on the full range of knowledge which they can appropriate not because they are Americans, but because of professional competence. If this is the test of American education, it is more likely to be realized within the framework of an organized, concentrated career-oriented approach to institution-building abroad.

The corollary of the concept of a career service is the need to build supplementary structures and arrangements for strengthening institutions abroad. The International Cooperation Administration (ICA) was the predecessor agency to AID, responsible for administering foreign aid. Its philosophy of sister university relationships was a creative invention for institution-building, but suffered in its implementation. It was sometimes plagued by misunderstandings, mediocrity, and inflexibility, but the heart of the idea was sound. There are by-products of university-to-university cooperation that serve both institutions and their personnel.

The Rockefeller Foundation in this spirit made approximately twenty-five university grants to institutions in Great Britain, France,

Canada, Switzerland, and the United States, patterned after the arrangements described in the Gardner Report—but with a difference. First, the universities concerned extended assistance to developing institutions with visiting professors and cooperating junior colleagues in specific disciplines. For example, the Yale Growth Center, the Williams College Institute of Economic Development, and Northwestern University gave help in economics. Princeton, Notre Dame, Cornell, Duke, Michigan, Wisconsin, and Minnesota Universities sent visitors in the social sciences, as did Toronto, Sussex, and McGill Universities. Second, the developing universities themselves played a determining role in the selection of cooperating Western universities and the choice of individual professors. Third, a schedule was worked out of visitors for successive academic years so that both the developing and developed universities could plan for the years ahead. Fourth, the professionals concerned, including career service personnel at the developing universities, played an active role, not only in selecting visiting professors but in defining their role and working out the most meaningful assignments before they arrive. It would be impossible to exaggerate the pivotal role of the senior foundation representative in planning, consulting, and paving the way for visitors and assuring they have a serious piece of work to do without wasted time and effort. Fifth, the watchword was flexibility. A particular Western university, principally engaged in strengthening university X, was not precluded from assisting university Y. Equally, university X could receive help from more than one source, if appropriate. Sixth, the role of visitors was part of a total university development plan and their contributions were made to mesh with the overall design.

Phases I-IV

The machinery for assisting developing universities is of course less important than its purpose. Once an institution has entered into a cooperative program with the foundation, the first step for those who come to help is to make themselves expendable. Through fellowships and scholarships—for study both locally and abroad—the training of national educational leaders is facilitated; counterpart relationships between visitors and emerging national leaders are integral to the process. The foundation's fifty-four year fellowship program, under which over 10,000 fellowships were awarded, proved an indispensable factor in this aspect of the University Development Program. (See Table A.) As scholars returned, key academic departments come under local leadership and there was a magic moment of change to which visitors had to be sensitive and alert. There is a time for visitors to leave or move to the background—but when is it?

TABLE A

Study Awards 1963–1971

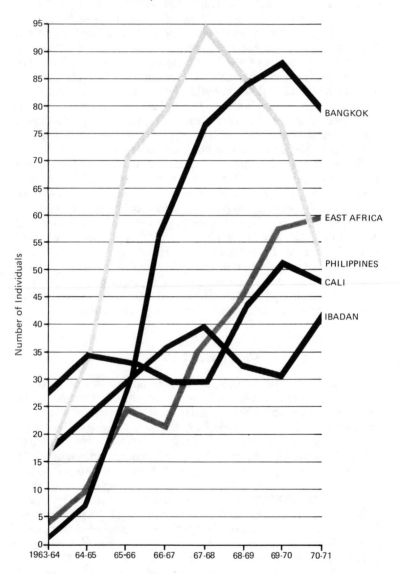

Is it when three Ph.D's have returned to a department, when one is serving as departmental chairman, or when two-thirds of the departments are under local leadership?[2]

The tests for the ending of Phase I are at best rough and ready and the developmental phase, even for disciplines with initially favorable prospects, may vary from a period of five to ten years. But at some point, cooperating institutions must assume that the first chapter is complete. It is time to change the form and substance of cooperation. Phase II signals the emergence of national leadership. However tempting it may be to protest that the transfer of responsibility is premature, the issue at this point is not negotiable. No one should expect that the new leadership will be carbon copies of the old. The type of person sent abroad to assist in Phase II should be more an advisor than an institution-builder, patient and responsive rather than visibly aggressive, willing to work through others. If Phase I requires a critical mass of outside institution-builders, Phase II calls for a very few, low-profile advisors. The time required for Phase II may be anywhere from one to three years.

Phase III is a period of consolidation, of putting new capacities and institutions to work. It involves planning for graduate programs, serving the community, and turning emergent human resources toward the solution of national and regional problems. Phase III is a period of reaping the harvest of earlier developmental efforts. The application of trained intelligence to problem solving is for the first time fully possible. Not by accident, each of the International Agriculture Institutes is located next to a university development center. Equally, an attack on unemployment problems profits from economics, engineering, and agricultural resources in university centers.

Phase IV is a time for giving back by those who have received. It involves first-generation university development centers helping second-generation centers. Thus, leadership in the newest UDP center at the University of Bahia was provided by men such as Gabriel Velazquez of Universidad del Valle, at the University of Zaire by leaders from the University of East Africa, or by Philippine economists such as Dr. Jose Encarnacion teaching and directing research in Thailand and Indonesia.

To be effective a plan must be flexible, taking its cue from the strengths and weaknesses within each institution and adapting its timetable to changing needs. Because institutions differ, forms of assistance vary. The university centers which were assisted fell into at least four broad categories or models. The foundation in the 1960s gave some form of assistance to approximately ten institutions or complexes of universities but major support was concentrated in five centers, namely, the Universidad del Valle in Columbia; three national universities making up the University of East Africa originally Makerere College in Kampala, Uganda; The

University of Dar es Salaam in Tanzania, and the University of Nairobi; the University of Ibadan in Nigeria; the University of the Phillippines; and Kasetsart University, Mahidol University and Thammasat University in Thailand.

Universidad del Valle

Model I is university development in which the foundation had been virtually a co-equal partner over a sustained period, sharing a major part of costs and manpower needs. The Universidad del Valle was a provincial university in Cali, Colombia, with a student body of 5,000 in the 1960s and a new concept of a university for a developing country. Its goal was to keep the university close to the community, addressing itself to urgent social needs. It was a leader in medical education for all of Latin America, directing the interests of students toward rural peoples through mandatory clinical residency in the Candelaria Rural Health Center, and teaching preventive medicine, child care, and family planning. In the early 1960s, the Medical School, which had enjoyed assistance throughout the 1950s, towered over the rest of the University, but a concerted effort was made to help raise the level of engineering, economics and agricultural economics, university administration, the humanities and the basic sciences. The proportion of foundation support to the total university budget is indicated in Table I.

East Africa

Model II found the foundation—as in East Africa—playing the role of catalytic agent, helping to initiate change or, in Raymond Fosdick's graphic phrase, providing the "extra engine put on to help . . . over a stiff grade." As indicated in Table II, the foundation's contribution was always minor, first to the three independent national colleges, then to the federated University of East Africa, and thereafter to the three national universities bound together by numerous functional ties and a common Inter-University Committee. However, Table III shows that sixty-six percent of all East African faculty were Rockefeller Foundation scholars or holders of Special Lectureships established with foundation funding for returning national scholars for whom an established post was not yet available. If the sample is limited to East Africans who were full professors and deans, eighty percent had assistance. The agricultural faculty at Makerere College in Uganda reoriented its curriculum with greater emphasis on crop production during the leadership of Dean John Nickel, Rockefeller Foundation staff member. The Institute of Development Studies in Nairobi reached maturity in the same period. For a far-flung multinational university in these countries, help at crucial points affected the entire university even through the total resources provided from outside were small relative to the overall educational budget.

TABLE I

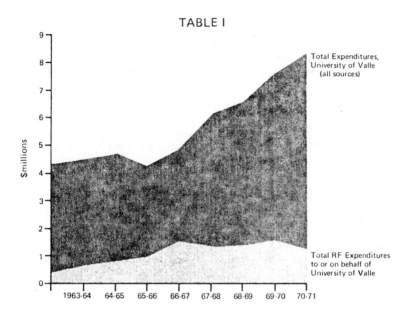

University of the Philippines

Model III involved help to more fully developed universities to complete or round out institutional development, or some aspect of that development. At the University of the Philippines, the application of this approach was illustrated in a dual sense. When General Carlos P. Romulo became president in 1963, he declared he would seek help for fields other than agriculture, engineering, and medicine, which had been strengthened through outside assistance over the years. Unless other areas, including the social sciences and humanities, could be developed, Romulo was convinced the University would not be worthy of the name. At the same time the University pressed ahead to bring the graduate program in economics to the Ph.D. level and to establish the agriculture faculty as a regional center for graduate studies. In both instances, the foundation provided supplementary fellowship funds and visiting professors to fill gaps until local faculty returned from study abroad.

Bangkok

Model IV involved help to strong points in a complex of universities within a city or region or to independent but cooperating universities. Institution-building in agriculture, the biomedical sciences and economics was fostered in three separate universities: Kasetsart, Mahidol, and Thammasat, respectively, in Bangkok, Thailand; the strategy was one of building on existing strength at the three centers (Table IV traces the Mahidol program). The goal for each was the building of institutional strength capable of serving a wider geographical region (nine young Indonesian scientists did their Ph.D. study at Mahidol University). While ideally university development should go on within the walls of a single institution, practically differing forms of institutional cooperation are possible with aggregate effects similar to the strengthening of one university. Once again, imagination and flexibility are of the essence. Table V depicts the total efforts of the foundation in UDP and traces the phases of help at each institution.

Universities and National Development

The two lessons of greatest moment that derive from a decade's experience with the Rockefeller Foundation's UDP model were: (1) the need for scientists and educators working abroad to operate within a framework reflecting the interrelatedness of human problems and knowledge; and (2) the need for continuity within a broad strategy or design having definable stages of development and looking toward points of completion.

With regard to the first, the very successes of foreign assistance can create new challenges and problems, some more exacting and perplexing than the failures. The work of development too often has been a "catch-up" operation. It is probably unfair to say that the success of the International Health Division created the population explosion, but surely it was a contributing factor. Improved health, lower mortality rates, and longer lifespans thereby add to a nation's problems. We see now some of the hazards in pursuing health or agricultural programs in isolation. The unique opportunity that university development presents is that advances on one front can be coordinated with determined and concentrated efforts along other fronts. Programs in improved health delivery systems can go on simultaneously with population control. Efforts to increase food production can be accompanied by inquiries into the economic and social consequences of the "green revolution." Instead of "catching up," the developing countries can be assisted in preparing for the problems that lie ahead three, five, or ten years down the road.

On the second lesson—the need for continuity within a broad design—there was a striking difference with the approach of the International Health Division or the cooperative agricultural programs and many undertakings in international cooperation. It is sometimes noted that foreign assistance often involves the struggle to meet twenty-year needs with a three-year program, two-year

TABLE II

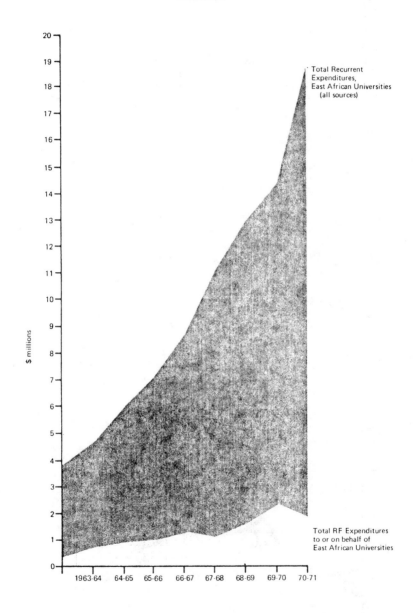

Total Recurrent
Expenditures,
East African Universities
(all sources)

$ millions

Total RF Expenditures
to or on behalf of
East African Universities

1963-64 64-65 65-66 66-67 67-68 68-69 69-70 70-71

TABLE III

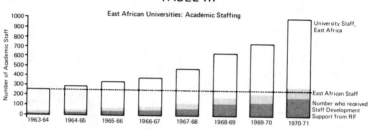

East African Universities: Academic Staffing

TABLE IV

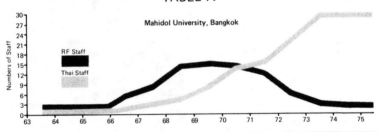

Mahidol University, Bangkok

TABLE V

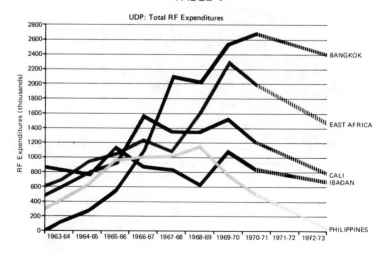

UDP: Total RF Expenditures

personnel, and one-year appropriations. By contrast, the Rockefeller Foundation's Mexican Agricultural Program was inaugurated in 1943. It evolved from a limited exploratory effort, through a national program carefully housed in the Office of Special Studies within the Ministry of Agriculture, to an International Maize and Wheat Improvement Center. More than forty years later, a handful of the original team of Rockefeller Foundation agricultural scientists continued to serve as participant advisors in a fully Mexican international agricultural program, aiming to share with others the accumulated knowledge developed over the past three decades.

There is a time to give assistance and a time to withhold it or bring it to an end. The University of the Philippines, under the vital and dynamic leadership of General Carlos P. Romulo, reached the stage, particularly in the arts and sciences, where strategically placed assistance could enable it to move to a new level of excellence. How shortsighted it would have been for agencies that had faithfully provided fellowship help in other periods in its history to have terminated aid at that point. With the growing nationalization of the university the possibilities and need for aid became more restricted and more sharply defined. But continuity of effort was essential if enduring institutions were to be developed.

The ultimate goal of institution-building is of course national development—to widen the range of choice open to the general population, improve the quality of life, and serve the most urgent needs of the people, As nations undertake this complex and many-sided task, they must rely to a large degree upon the strengths and involvement of their universities, with the necessary concentrations of talent. The universities, to be effectively involved, must understand the nation's needs and how best to meet them; this requires that universities participate with other agencies in the planning and execution of national programs. In this way the university faculty and students can contribute to national progress as they teach and learn. Course offerings must become increasingly relevant, as new information related to national need is developed. University graduates should be much better equipped with both the knowledge and skills required for participation in accelerated national development. Faculty must increasingly teach from a basis of understanding derived both from a study of efforts of others (past and present) and from experience gained through involvement in meeting real needs of the region and people served by the university. Nor should the study of the humanities and social values be ignored, for these are determinants of the ways knowledge and skills will be used.

As universities demonstrate their usefulness not only as centers of scholarly effort but as institutions capable of joining scholarship with effective action, appreciation of them and support for them can be expected to follow.

As the late Dr. Sterling Wortman, speaking of agriculture, declared in a conference at Bellagio, Italy:

What, then, should be the nature of the activities of an agricultural college, and how should its success be measured? It would seem that at least two criteria would be useful: (a) the student's proficiency in the use of the knowledge and understanding gained through his university experience; and (b) the impact of the college's research program on the nation's economic development.

Each central agricultural college should have on its staff a number of specialists who, through years of dedicated experience, have emerged as authorities in their fields. At a good college in the tropics, one should expect to find authorities on each crop or animal species of major importance or potential importance in the region served. One should also find specialists on the major animal and plant diseases and on major insect problems, as well as specialists in economics, agricultural engineering, and other fields.

Each crop or animal specialist should be providing leadership for important components of the overall research program for the area served, whether this be a province, a region, or a nation. His program should be closely integrated with those of the action agencies of the ministry of agriculture, and with extension agencies that may be administered separately. There must be a minimum of administrative barriers between the central experiment station and the farmer. If leadership of major research activities has been vested in a different research organization, then university personnel still must contribute significantly to the total effort. . . .

The medical profession usually requires that a candidate for the M.D. degree spend a substantial period of time as an intern under the guidance of qualified professionals. Agricultural colleges might well require a year's internship in a dynamic research program as a prerequisite to graduation. This, however, would require crop- or animal-oriented research programs— well-equipped experiment stations with staff members working on critical problems in the region served—which in turn would require the presence of effective and continuing scientific leadership.[3]

It is of course difficult to measure quantitatively the influence of universities on national economic, social, and cultural development but clearly significant inputs were made through the UDP effort. For example, the Development Economics training program, undertaken by the School of Economics in the University of the Philippines for members of the government economic civil service, made a significant difference in the quality of operation of the economic secretariat. The School of Economics' research program, with its focus on Philippine development problems, led to far-reaching governmental policy changes. A faculty member served as chairman of the National

Economic Council and drew heavily on his colleagues for relevant policy-oriented studies. Clearly the university made a difference.

The emphasis on a better understanding of African history, under the leadership of a succession of outstanding Nigerian historians at the University of Ibadan, helped develop a better understanding of Nigeria's history and cultural heritage—a most important element in nation-building but one with a delayed impact. Ibadan faculty members served on a wide variety of state and federal government panels and study commissions, including very substantial participation in creating successive Nigerian development plans. The Bureau of Resource Assessment and Land Use Planning of the University of Dar es Salaam geared its total research efforts to priority needs as outlined in the Tanzanian development plans, with a significant impact in the rural areas.

In Kenya, the Institute for Development Studies in the University of Nairobi was created as a multidisciplinary organization in response to a strongly felt need for organized, full-time research on urgent social and economic problems of development. It was concerned with basic, long-term development problems as well as more immediately pressing policy issues. Research projects reflected national needs with a focus on rural development, urban and industrial development, employment, and education. In the 1960s and 1970s, the Institute was deeply involved as a partner in the International Labor Organization (ILO) employment studies in Kenya.

The Vice-Chancellor of the University of Nairobi, Dr. J. N. Karanja, who was the first East African scholar to be appointed to the post of special lecturer with Rockefeller Foundation support, wrote:

As a major national institution the University of Nairobi has a duty, an opportunity and a determination to contribute significantly to all aspects of Kenya's national development. In co-operation with our Government, with other departments and institutes of the University, and with all other agencies concerned with development—national, regional and international— the Institute for Development Studies is responsible for initiating, co-ordinating and directing its own programme of applied and interdisciplinary research on high priority social and economic problems of development of Kenya in particular and of Eastern Africa in general. This broad mandate includes the provision of research opportunities, facilities and professional guidance for the study of problems of development to a rapidly expanding number of Kenyans interested in academic or other careers in the service of the nation; the accelerated Africanization of university teaching and other instructional materials based on research on the development problems of our own society; and the maintenance of a centre of intellectual stimulus and productivity with which visiting scholars from all over the world can be associated and to which they can make their own contribution to human knowledge as well as to the development of our nation.[4]

The participation of the biomedical sciences in the University Development program ranged from minimal, as in East Africa, to a maximum effort, as in Bangkok. In each instance, two factors were taken into consideration: first, the university's view of its own needs in medical education; and, second, the actual needs of the communities as estimated by outside evaluators. Many medical faculties expressed a desire for an organ transplant team, whereas the simplest community evaluation indicated that their primary need was in the less glamorous area of control of infectious diseases.

From these experiences, the most significant health effort occurred in the realm of community health education. The program at Candelaria received international recognition, and US-AID undertook to expand the work to include a large urban segment as well as the rural communities already involved. The program at Bay in the Philippines represented a success that continued under government sponsorship even after the withdrawal of all Rockefeller Foundation personnel. The program in Bangkok, while newer, achieved a record of equal success. Each of them served as a demonstration model in immediate health problem-solving. Thus, physicians from Central and South America were sent on fellowships to study the program at Candelaria and, hopefully, to return and implement similar ventures in their own countries. The physicians involved in the community health teaching in Bangkok were invited to present two different training sessions in different universities in Malaysia. These programs contained elements of family planning and prenatal care with whatever additional features the health of the community demanded (nutrition, control of infectious diseases, etc.).

In many ways, these community health programs, which represented but a fraction of the biomedical science participation in University Development programs, constituted one of the most lasting contributions of University Development. They were action programs and tended to refocus the curriculum and the student's thinking toward local health needs rather than toward the emulation of the super-specialized medicine of the developed countries.

Countless other examples could be given of ways in which universities—their staff and students—responded to economic, social and cultural developmental needs in the various countries. The pace was uneven, and impatient observers may say the responses are always too slow and not on a large enough scale. However, as one views the changes which occurred over past decades, the transformation has been deep and profound. Many universities are developing into institutions capable of adapting existing knowledge and creating new knowledge and technologies more appropriate to the social and economic resources of the less developed countries. An impressive impact has been made but a great challenge remains.

Ten years of experimenting with university development made it clear that national development was no simple one-dimensional process. It is more than industrial growth, increased food production, or preparing economists or engineers. The values by which men live, the social structures within which they make choices, and the political systems they espouse may be as crucial as material advances. A university development approach helps donors and recipients to recognize the multiple dimensions of national development and make some modest contribution wherever possible.

CHAPTER FOUR
NATIONALISM, INTERNATIONALISM,
AND THE GLOBAL ENVIRONMENT
Soedjatmoko

I am most pleased and honored at the opportunity to address this session of a Special Character of the Governing Council of the United Nations Environment Program (UNEP). We are met here to mark the Tenth Anniversary of the Stockholm Conference on the Human Environment which brought UNEP into being. . . . As one who was fortunate to attend that conference as a delegate, I am doubly honored to be here today.

The Stockholm Conference, at the time the largest United Nations conference ever convened, was a signal effort to focus the attention of the governments and the peoples of the world on the growing threat that the human endeavor, collectively and individually, posed to our planetary life-support systems and the finite supplies of air, earth, and water on which they function.

The conference came at a time when perceptions about the importance of environmental issues were already changing—more and more people were coming to realize that the state of our forests, lands, and waters was not a diversion for a few ecology enthusiasts, but a deadly serious urgency for the whole world. Stockholm undoubtedly helped to accelerate that change. So too did a series of jarring environmental shocks that marked the early 1970s—in the drought-stricken Sahel, in the suddenly fished-out Peruvian waters, and, above all, in the ending of the era of cheap oil, an event with immense and far-reaching environmental consequences for the globe's forests and croplands.

As we look at the economic and political problems and difficulties we now face today, it is difficult to recall that it was Stockholm that made the concept of the environment a concrete and living reality at the local, national and international levels, and set in train many developments and action programmes and institutions, apart from

UNEP, that have made environment a household word the world over. To this extent, then, much progress was made and continued to be made over the decade in man's relations to the environment.

Yet for all the environmental lessons which the past decade should have driven home, the realist is forced to conclude that few were. However much awareness and knowledge of environmental problems might have increased in the ten years since Stockholm, it has not resulted in much effective or concerted action that even remotely match the magnitude of these problems. One hard question that must be asked then, in evaluating the impact (or lack of it) of Stockholm, as well as other major UN conferences, is: why have the action programmes adopted by these conferences not been as successful as they could have been, when measured against the goals that were set, and the resources that were made available?

The knowledge that was generated about the environment in the last ten years has left major gaps—evidence of the degree to which we have become prisoners of our habitual academic inclination to approach something as immensely complicated as the environment primarily along single disciplinary lines. Such narrow approaches—however much they might deepen understanding of one particular area—will avail us little in trying to unravel the tightly-knit web of social, political, economic, technological forces and ecological balances, that are involved in most environmental issues.

The difficulties that hindered the effective implementation of plans of action at the national level have proven much greater than were expected. Among these, one may mention the inadequate data base and lack of analytical tools with which to clarify the different trade-offs, not only between the economic and environmental imperatives, but also to reconcile the differential impact of environmental intervention on different regions of the country, and on different segments of the population, or to work out the technological or other solutions which might turn such conflicting interests from zero-sum games to plus-sum games. The most crucial and difficult problem has turned out to be how to deal with the profound and complex linkages between environmental deterioration at the national and global levels and the persistent deep poverty in the poor countries of the world, thereby resulting in the failure of environmental policies that do not take into account the food and energy needs of the poor, and generally their economic and social interests. In addition where separate ministries or agencies for the environment were established, they have often proved to be incapable of dealing with the indifference and hostility, or of reconciling conflicting policies and bureaucratic interests, as well as equally powerful commercial and vested interests.

All these problems testify to the failure to identify adequately the critical management issues in the policies adopted and the failure to develop suitable management tools for the task. They also highlight the failure of the educational systems to develop the necessary manpower and the management expertise for the purpose. As a result, our collective capacity to monitor environmental change has proven incapable of keeping up with the rate of environmental deterioration in many areas. Especially many Third World countries can make only the crudest guesses about the extent of exploitation, depletion, and deterioration of their natural resources. Without this capacity, their ability to develop sensible and appropriate resource—and environmental—management policies is sharply limited.

Neither have we been able to arrest environmental deterioration on a global scale. We all know the figures. Some eighteen to twenty million hectares of the world's forests disappearing each year, six million hectares lost annually to desert encroachment, another million or more paved over or otherwise lost every year to urban sprawl, thousands of species disappearing whose resistance to crop disease and blight might have been priceless future weapons against hunger. I need not take up this group's time with further elaboration of a picture of continuing global deterioration of earth, air, and sea.

Another sort of deterioration is equally disturbing—in the recognition that sensible and sensitive management of the environment is an essential partner of development. Instead, we are witnessing once again the emergence of the view of the environment and development as rival players—the one as the guardian of virginal wilderness, the other as the champion of human advance.

Ironically and sadly, the view is gaining adherents not so much in the Third World (where it was once widespread) as it is in the First, in evidence among those policymakers who hold that environmental concern and control are all well and good so long as they do not interfere with the progress of business and industry, and efforts to overcome the economic recession.

This point of view completely misses the recognition that production patterns which pay little heed to environmental degradation or resource depletion are ultimately doomed and in their dying may create enormous and irreversible ecological havoc. The desolate wastelands in various river basins in the world which once were the locations of great ancient civilizations, are mute testimony to this.

Thus environmental crises are not new. What is unique about the current one, however, is its rate and scale. What might in the past have been a deterioration over some centuries is now compressed into a few decades and it is happening everywhere on the planet. This stresses the particular folly in seeing environmental problems only in national terms. We cure one country's smog by building taller smokestacks only to find that the increased height helps to feed another country's acid rains. In such cases, Erik Eckholm asks: Who speaks for the biosphere?

I fear the answer must be: fewer today than at the time of Stockholm. For, most disturbingly in my view, what improvement there has been in environmental awareness and support over the last ten years has pretty much been confined to the national level—interest in international cooperation has actually declined. Yet in the waning of this interest, we could well be ignoring, and at our own peril, some of the most serious environmental concerns of this or any age—the irreversible damage that we could be wreaking on those regions of the earth's crust and atmosphere in whose protection and preservation all living creatures have a stake. These global commons—our climate, our tropical rain forest, our seas, our soils and other essential components of planetary life support—can only be efficiently monitored and managed on an international and on a regional basis.

The commons of the English country towns in the eighteenth and ninteenth centuries suffered destruction from decisions by individual farmers to enlarge their herds with no heed to the consequences for the grazing needs of neighboring farmers. The ultimate result was exhaustion of a common resource by overuse to the detriment of all users.

So too it could be with the global commons. If individual nations continue to overload the atmosphere with CO_2, over-fish the seas, or recklessly destroy tropical rain forests—with little heed to the larger international interests—it will only be a matter of time until these commons suffer irreversible damage.

This points up what I believe to be the most fundamental and important environmental challenge that must be met in the second decade after Stockholm: the development of improved ways of managing the global environment, i.e., the global commons. In many ways, the most important "breakthrough" on the environmental front would be the creation of innovative and imaginative new management tools. In his 1980s tool kit, the national and international policy-planner needs no more notice of new committees or new agencies formed. He needs rather to know about ways to respond more flexibly, to adapt to the unexpected, to cope with the uncertain, and to break down bureaucratic rigidities.

The management strategies that are developed need particularly to recognize how intimately interlinked are environment problems and the problems of the poor. Much of the environmental degradation we are witnessing today—in soil erosion, deforestation, encroachment of deserts, loss of genetic strains—is a result of the widening and desperate search by the poor for food and fuel. They simply have nowhere else to go but deeper into forests, higher up slopes, farther into grazing lands, pushing cultivation onto ever more fragile soils.

The future shape of the global environment will, among others, also be determined by countless millions of decisions by poor individual farmers and villagers. Our ability to manage this environment will hinge on our capacity to cope with such decisions and incorporate them into our scientific and technological planning.

There are three particularly important dimensions to the development of appropriate environmental management policies at the global and regional levels.

The first should be the recognition that we need to prepare planners and decisionmakers for the management of complex interactive systems. Environmental issues cannot be taken up one at a time—such attempts in the past have too often triggered other, often more stubborn problems. There is essentially no one single entry point into complex environmental issues; the approach therefore must be able to take many different aspects and levels of the problem into account simultaneously.

One thing that can stand in the way of the management of complexities at the national and international levels is single-issue politics—which can divert valuable human and material resources away from broader and more complicated issues. Whatever their other merits, we have to recognize that at times single-issue politics can be essentially a "cop-out," and abdication of broader and more complex sets of interrelated responsibilities to humankind requiring responses at different levels and different degrees of sophistication. In each of our countries we will have to develop the political constituencies capable of doing so, as an essential element toward the enhancement of our environmental management capacity. The development of new forms of public education—of global learning—will have to be an important element of global environmental planning.

A second important consideration is the demonstrated incapacity to date of both governments and intergovernmental systems to cope with new conflicts of interest. The examples are legion.

In the field of communications, for example, there have been extreme difficulties and much inconclusive debate over the establishment of criteria for assigning priorities among legitimate but conflicting interests for the use of limited resources. In regard to satellite use, for example, who decides and on what basis the relative weight and importance to be assigned to the needs of meteorology? Of navigation? Of broadcasting? Of remote sensing? Obviously, we need management systems to cope with these kinds of conflicting demands in ways that are equitable and most beneficial to society and to the end users.

A third management consideration should be of the international legal instruments that might be available to help regulate and enforce sounder environmental practice on a global basis. Ways need to be found to extend international law to cover a variety of human users of the biosphere. The effort to codify the law of the sea marks a valuable beginning, perhaps, but it is significant that it has really very little concern with some of the broader and more long-term environmental considerations of marine resource use.

Given the reluctance that so many governments have displayed to date in establishing legal measures to enforce environmental practices, it may be that we have no other choice but to start at the international level first in establishing standards and agreements—in anticipation that national governments would then eventually follow suit.

I say this in no degradation of the sovereign rights of nation states. It is rather in recognition of the fact that there are certain pressing environmental problems that are too global in their implications and potentially capable of too disastrous an impingement on the lives of all humanity to be left untended.

In particular, therefore, we need to begin to design global and regional management mechanisms that can come to grips with problems such as those whose consequences threaten irreversible change and damage. By their very nature, these are the toughest and the most complex problems. But to put them aside—in favor of the more immediate or the more solvable—would only mean that they would still be there, grown larger, more cancerous, and less likely to solution, during the lives of our children. Surely this would be a shameful abdication of responsibility to future generations.

To be able to take up such responsibilities, however, and to cope with the complexities they imply, may mean that we need some sort of institutional response that goes far beyond the present international bodies that now exist. We need to ask ourselves, in all candor, whether our present intergovernmental bodies have proved sufficient to the task. But even if there is more focused cooperation among the United Nations and other international agencies than is now the case, perhaps we need in addition to think about kinds of institutions, and mechanisms that would represent not just the interests of governments, but also those of concerned publics along with the perspectives and values of scientists and other experts. Institutions, in other words, capable of representing and helping to manage the affairs of the many constituencies of the global commons.

Such institutions will need to encourage the kind of thinking that seeks neither the ideal or the possible solution—but rather the most desirable one. Insisting on the ideal can be a futile exercise, settling for the possible a timid one. However, finding desirable solutions to our environmental and resource needs will be a challenging task. This could require serious re-examination and rethinking where a country's sovereign rights regarding its own natural resources end, and responsibility and accountability for the transnational and global impact of the manner in which these resources are used begins. Certain pollution abating policies and massive interventions in river-flows for irrigation purposes, with significant transnational and even global impact on climatological conditions or legitimate access to shared resources will force us to face up to these problems from a heightened awareness of human solidarity on the one hand but also from the recognition of the importance of the sovereign nation state in the process of decolonization, development, and of the establishment of a more viable and just international order. We have to do this also if we are to develop an overriding sense of responsibility to the needs of future generations and a notion of transgenerational unity.

In the foreword that Barbara Ward wrote just before her death for the book *Down to Earth,* that she would have co-authored with Erik Eckholm and which Erik Eckholm completed himself, with her usual unforgettable eloquence and perspicacity, left us this invaluable message:

> No matter how much we try to think of ourselves as separate sovereign entities, nature itself reminds us of humanity's basic unity. The vision of unity shared by so many of the great philosophers and so central to all the great religions is recognized now as an inescapable scientific fact. Could it be the vocation of this generation to give the planet the institutions of unity and cooperation that can express this insight?

Her words most amply define the institutions we are after in the closing years of this century, and sets the vocation of all of us who wish to work together to save the environment and humanity's share in its benefits. We at the United Nations University stand ready to turn our hand to this task, in cooperation with the United Nations Environment Program and others of like dedication.

II. AMERICA AND ECONOMIC AND SOCIAL WELL-BEING

In international conferences and world organizations, the socialist countries have challenged the United States to demonstrate its concern for economic and social well-being. The issue has often been joined in terms of liberty vs. social welfare. Debates of this kind which stir national emotions are likely to obscure the genuine commitment to economic and social needs within those Western societies in which freedom is defended. A vast array of programs have evolved to meet such needs including unemployment insurance, social security and medicare and medicaid. The methods, economic organization and social structure differ from east to west but free societies including the United States are engaged across a broad front in giving expression to their values and responding to social needs.

The purpose of the four chapters which follow is not to continue the debate which has gone on at the United Nations and other international bodies. It is rather to stimulate thought and discussion in three broad areas which illustrate commitments in the United States to economic and social needs. From the earliest days of the republic, America has provided a haven for refugees from famine, natural disasters and political persecution from countries around the world. With the onset of the Cold War, this historic role, symbolized by the Statue of Liberty, has grown more complex of realization as illustrated in the chapter by Valerie Sutter. Nonetheless, the willingness of Americans to open their shores to the world's "tired and poor" and to accord economic and social opportunities to the "homeless and tempest tossed" persists. Not only America's "huddled masses" but refugees from around the globe are cared for because of an American value the lamp of freedom depicts.

Corporations and notably multinational corporations at work abroad are another expression of the American pursuit of economic well-being. Writings on the American corporation have tended toward the two extremes of uncritical defense or irresponsible criticism. Mary E. Cunningham, a Vice President of Joseph E. Seagrams and Sons, Incorporated, traces the need for shared values within the corporation. Dedicated to the concepts of international economic order, multinationals involved in the extension of American economic ideals and practice abroad must recognize and adapt to the economic values of other peoples. Professor Joseph Grieco provides an even-handed evaluation of the possibilities and limitations of multi-nationals. He is a political scientist at Duke University.

Thomas R. Donahue completes the section on economic and social well-being with a remarkable evaluation of the underlying values of American labor. As Secretary-Treasurer of the American Federation of Labor, Donahue would be the first to acknowledge his partisanship but in relating the values of the American labor movement to certain more universal values he helps us understand the core values of American labor.

CHAPTER FIVE
AMERICAN VALUES
AND INTERNATIONAL REFUGEES
Valerie Sutter

. . . [a] refugee is a person who is unable to return to his or her homeland because of a well-founded fear of persecution because of race, religion, nationality or political beliefs.[1]

Introduction

The poignant story of refugees fleeing from Indochina has been dramatically chronicled by the media since the fall of Saigon, April 1975. Photographic accounts of the "boat people" leaving Vietnam in leaky sailing crafts will be etched on the mind of the world for years to come. An estimated 1.4 million people are said to have left Vietnam, Kampuchea, and Laos, seeking asylum in other countries. To date, approximately 600,000 have found their way to resettlement in the United States. With the coordinated assistance of the U.N.H.C.R., (United Nations High Commission for Refugees) other voluntary organizations, countries of first asylum and nations of final resettlement, refugees continue to be looked after. Although the Indochinese exodus that peaked in 1978 and 1979 is showing signs of diminishing, refugees continue to arrive in the Association of Southeast Asian Nations (ASEAN) countries and in Hong Kong. The consensus seems to be that any further upset in an already volatile region could generate as many as three million additional refugees. Although the program for refugee resettlement is reasonably organized, internationally little has been done politically and officially to address the problematic causes of why refugees leave their homelands.

The policy of the United States has been to offer asylum to refugees who seek an alternative to a life of oppression under Communist domination. This strategy was developed after World

War II when the world was arbitrarily divided between Communist and non-Communist nations. Applications of the policy occurred, historically, when refugees from Hungary and Cuba were granted asylum in the United States. Today, this same policy is applied to refugees from Indochina and, most recently, from Poland.

It is the intention of this discussion to describe and analyze those factors related to the foreign policy of the United States that affect and are affected by the Indochinese refugee issue. Factors to be considered include the conflict between humanitarian and strategic interests; the power struggle in Southeast Asia among the Soviet Union, China, and the United States; Vietnamese-American relations; Vietnamese-Chinese relations; ASEAN considerations; and the conflict between American foreign policy and domestic economic and political realities. The complexity of the refugee issue is made evident by multiple, related factors.

Humantiarian Values vs. Strategic Interests: A Dilemma

An assumption is often made that American foreign policy *vis-à-vis* Indochinese refugees is based solely on a strong, moral, humanitarian commitment. In some sense, we almost need to believe this is the case, given the human tragedy involved. Without a doubt, the fact is that the United States accommodates compassion and magnanimity. It is well within the Judeo-Christian tradition and American democratic ideology to assist those oppressed by extending opportunities for freedom and liberty. This is evident in the culturally pluralistic nature of the American population. Addressing a congressional subcommittee in August, 1977, when asking for an increase in Indochinese refugee admissions, then Assistant Secretary of State Richard C. Holbrooke eloquently declared: "The motivation is simple: the deep humanitarian concern which has for so long been a distinctive part of our national character."[2]

With all due respect to Mr. Holbrooke, his assessment of American motivation is too simplistic, if not self-righteous. He may have been appealing to the heartstrings of Congress, but both Congress and the administration probably had additional motivations in mind. Contrary to the popularity of Skinnerian behaviorism's penchant for single cause and effect relationships, the human condition has a vast repertoire of behaviors that often work simultaneously. While many believe human beings are in the image of a creator, the policies of people are not entirely divinely inspired. Rather, theological anthropology tells us that man's dual nature includes man as creatures as well as man as divine. Taking a leap to the issue of refugees, it is probably reasonable to assume that the American response includes some elements of vested interest. Risking the accusation of sounding cynical, but with respect for realism, it may be appropriate to quote a paraphrase of Reinhold Niebuhr: "Original sin is the only Christian doctrine based on empirical evidence."[3]

The inherent conflict in an approach by nations to an issue like the refugee crisis involves idealism and realism. Concerns for human dignity and rights related to natural law conflict with national, political realities. Dr. Thompson indicates the importance of considering and incorporating idealistic and realistic factors in decisionmaking in international relations.[4] An exclusively idealistic approach is often incapable of finding feasible solutions to political problems. This approach can deteriorate into moralizing that becomes hypocritical. This seems to apply to the human rights policy of the Carter administration. At the other extreme, policies devoid of values, that do not reflect a nation's principles and beliefs, become calculated strategies that can be dehumanizing. Some critics of American policy toward refugees claim the United States is too self-serving. Machiavelli warned: "The final temptation is to do the right thing for the wrong reason."[5]

In reference to culture, an anthropologist explained that each society has a story to tell about itself that constitutes truth for that culture. This ideal embodies the society's ethical beliefs. The story can only be told if the culture has provided the appropriate conditions. Certain realities present in the culture can prevent the story from being told properly. This conflict between an ideal and reality can be discerned at times in American society as the inspiring rhetoric of democratic principles clashes with realistic considerations.[6]

The Indochinese refugee issue may be viewed with an awareness of the tension between idealism and realism. Neither extreme is solely responsible for policies and decisions. Rather, an interplay between humanitarian concerns and national vested interests acts itself out, as Hans Morgenthau suggested.[7] The complexity of the refugee issue with its tensions and conflicts make solutions difficult to come by. Dr. Thompson warns that the balance between realism and idealism is not easy. Yet, the seriousness of the dilemma, involving the fate of millions of human beings, makes it imperative that nations assume responsibility to try to reach a solution that includes humanitarian concerns.

When discussing any international issue, a realistic assessment of the capabilities and functions of nations must be kept in mind. Reinhold Niebuhr said: ". . . nations are not particularly generous; a wise self-interest is usually the limit of moral attainment."[8] More recently, appearing at a press conference to respond to accusations that his country had turned away refugees, Malaysian Home Minister Mohammed Ghazali Shafie said he was weary of humanitarian hand-wringing by Western nations. "This government is responsible first and foremost to the people of this country . . . please write that down."[9] With this philosophy, no wonder the refugee problem is difficult to solve.

Prior to the Refugee Exodus

Refugees are the innocent victims of the strife that has plagued China for nearly forty years. Although direct involvement of the United States ended in 1975, instability still characterized the entire region. Unresolved issues involving the quest for a balance of power in Southeast Asia find nations still jockeying for positions that are in their interests.

The first notice taken of refugees from Vietnam came in 1975 when 130,000 were airlifted out of Saigon, along with American military and diplomatic personnel. But, three instances of refugee movement prior to 1975 may have set the scene for the later exodus. First, after the Geneva Conference in 1954, 40,000 sought asylum in Thailand as Ho Chi Minh consolidated his power in the north. Second, at the same time, an estimated one to two million Catholics, led by their clergy with assistance from the U.S. Navy and the Voice of America, fled potential persecution in the north and found their way to Saigon in the south. Third, an estimated one fifth of the population of South Vietnam became refugees within their own country. Making use of previously classified materials, Guenter Lewy in *America in Vietnam* reports that thousands of people were shifted about for humanitarian, political, and military reasons.[10] Villagers were often dislocated to avoid civilian casualties in the difficult effort to discern the enemy, who often used the tactic of clinging to the people. People may have been deliberately encouraged to seek safety with military forces of South Vietnam and the United States, thereby "voting with their feet" in support of the war effort. Pacification programs moved citizens from traditional homes to new villages for political reasons.

These instances of refugee movement pale by comparison with the later exodus. Yet, it is possible that these early experiences of dislocation psychologically influenced the possibility for flight after the United States withdrew in 1975. Refugees continued to follow U.S. and South Vietnamese personnel beyond Vietnam's borders much the way they had followed these same units inside Vietnam during the war. This is largely speculation, and it should be remembered that conditions within the new Socialist Republic of Vietnam as it tightened its hold on the south were and still are the major reasons for the exodus.

A Power Struggle: U.S., China, and the Soviet Union

After the withdrawal of the United States from Indochina in 1975, American policy was to avoid substantial involvement in the area. Disengagement was needed to attend to the psychological fragmentation the war experience had caused at home. In 1976, the United States removed its forces from Thailand, aid was reduced to Asian countries and consideration was given to withdrawing from bases in the Philippines. This withdrawal of the United States created a power vacuum in Southeast Asia. The Soviet Union appeared interested in lessening the impending influence of China in the area, while China warned of the ". . . Soviet tiger coming through the back door as the American wolf was driven from the front door."[11]

At this time, refugees were leaving Vietnam by boat but without much notice. By the end of 1976 the number of refugees had reached 5,619.[12] Those 130,000 refugees who had come to the United States in 1975 were symbolic reminders of Communist tryanny. But, there was no alarm yet about refugees. Many were thankful that the expected bloodbath predicted after the takeover of the south by Hanoi did not materialize. By 1977, ominous signs were evident. Severe drought, cold, and then typhoons caused shortages of rice. Border disagreements between Vietnam and Kampuchea increased. Nearly 15,000 refugees were generated in 1977.[13]

By 1978, certain factors led the United States to change its involvement in Southeast Asia. First there was the escalation of rivalry between China and the Soviet Union as the exodus of refugees from Vietnam increased dramatically and as Vietnam prepared to invade Kampuchea. Southeast Asia would figure in the role of the United States as tensions between China and the Soviet Union increased. Second, the security of sea routes through Southeast Asia bringing oil from the Middle East to Japan and the ASEAN nations was threatened by the expansion of Soviet naval and air power in the region that utilized base facilities in Vietnam. ASEAN, China, and Japan advocated a more active U.S. involvement in the area. Third, ". . . the publicized plight of Indochinese refugees brought Southeast Asia back into the consciousness of Americans."[14]

The administration of President Carter and Congress responded to these events by retaining bases in the Philippines, increasing the activity of the Seventh Fleet, expanding foreign military sales to Thailand, airlifting arms to Thailand after Vietnam's incursion over the Thai border in June, 1980, and through direct assistance to Indochinese refugees. Significantly, the United States' foreign policy in Asia began to rely heavily on increased cooperation with China to confront the challenge from the Soviet Union.[15]

The Reagan administration's policy appeared to continue to involve a relationship with China to meet the continued threat posed by the Soviet Union. This was evident in the reaction of the United States toward Vietnam's occupation of Kampuchea. The administration of President Reagan re-emphasized the significance of Southeast Asia, especially Thailand, in policies related to security.[16]

It seems that humanitarian concerns for increasing numbers of refugees combined with strategic interest factors involving a balance of power conflict led to a decision by the United States to reactivate its foreign policy in Southest Asia. If the United States was unwilling to resume a posture of direct involvement to the degree it had during the Vietnam War, the new relationship with China left no doubt that the

United States was back in Southeast Asia, to some degree at least. More questions than answers are offered in regard to the refugees. Would the United States have pursued the policy it did had no refugees appeared on the scene? To what extent do refugees legitimize an American role in Southeast Asian politics? Realistically, the answers may lie in an acceptance of the interplay between values and beliefs and vested interests. Perhaps neither motive can be identified and isolated as the sole cause. Rather, the complexity of the issue belies single factor analysis.

The Socialist Republic of Vietnam

Recent criticisms of American foreign policy emphasize that the United States may be influencing the decisions of many Vietnamese citizens to leave Vietnam. Voice of America broadcasts and the assistance of U.S. naval vessels have been cited as factors that encouraged people to leave. The existence of resettlement camps in ASEAN countries and easy assignment to permanent asylum in Western countries are mentioned as "pull factors."

Hanoi has maintained that those who left and continue to leave Vietnam are "soft," spoiled by years of exposure to American capitalism and materialism and the corruption of South Vietnam prior to takeover by the Communists. It is reasoned that those who leave are not committed to the noble cause of rebuilding a new social and economic order. Supporters outside Vietnam praised the absence of a bloodbath in the wake of the Communists' victory as evidence of the lack of vindictiveness of the Socialist Republic of Vietnam. The exodus of the opposition has been cited as a natural occurrence after a revolution. All of these accusations are beginning to influence the arguments of those critics who perceive those fleeing to be economic migrants in search of opportunities instead of bona fide political refugees.

All of these "pull factors" that encourage people to leave Vietnam are not to be summarily dismissed. The complexity of the issue demands the inclusion of a multitude of factors related to the exodus. However, a consensus is developing that conditions within Vietnam and policies of the regime have constituted the major "push factors" that cause people to leave. Even if forces outside Vietnam influenced departure decisions, it should be remembered thousands risked all they had, endured theft and rape at sea and even lost their lives. A conservative estimate puts the deaths at sea by-mid 1979 at 40,000 lives.[17] Intolerable political and economic conditions apparently compelled many to leave; these include ethnic Vietnamese and overseas Chinese.

The regime of the Socialist Republic of Vietnam faced enormous tasks after the war. Some experts say more destruction occurred than has been admitted by Hanoi. Natural disasters of severe cold, drought, and flooding in 1976 and 1977 compounded the problems. Contrary to expectations, postwar Vietnam experienced large population growth, mainly in already overcrowded urban areas, where unemployment was high. To these conditions were added the harsh measures usually associated with totalitarian regimes. The existence of re-education camps, where many refugees were incarcerated, have been cited as especially cruel. By 1977, the Political Committee decided to go ahead with plans to implement a full-fledged economic system in the south by collectivizing agriculture and abolishing all private business. Coincidental with these measures, refugees in large numbers began appearing on the shores of ASEAN countries and in Hong Kong.[18]

Refugee accounts tell of escapes from re-education camps that have been labelled Vietnam's gulags. Even those less critical of Vietnam are uncertain about these camps where a reported one million people have been forced to live.[19] Some reports indicate incarceration for long periods of time still affect as many as 300,000.[20] Surveillance by party cadre continues not only for those associated with the pre-1975 South Vietnam regime but also for more recent opposition groups. Surprisingly, religious groups are still allowed but activities have been limited to religious ceremonies.[21] Other refugees, spared the re-education camps, left because of their forced assignments to new economic zones in remote, rural areas. While Hanoi justifies this policy because of the real need to increase land cultivation acreage, many refugees have reported the perceived punitive aspects of the policy that finds citizens moved to barren lands without adequate assistance to ensure survival.

In the debate over the reasons why people left and still leave Vietnam, whether the causes be pull or push factors, one ardent supporter of the refugees underlines the influence of conditions in Vietnam. Journalist Barry Wain reported the story of one refugee who escaped a re-education camp after three years, fled by boat and lost his wife and son at sea. Mr. Wain said " . . . Mr. Ngar's misfortunes accurately mirror those of his country. His book should be read by all those who think most refugees leave Vietnam because they want a double-door refrigerator and a new Honda motorbike."[22]

It seems that refugees from Vietnam have escaped but many have also been deliberately "pushed out" with the knowledge and assistance of the regime. The large exodus would appear to be a source of embarrassment to Hanoi, especially as countries like the United States use this as evidence of gross violations of human rights in Vietnam. Reports of harrowing escapes indicate that at times the regime has tried to restrict the flow. But, other accounts, especially in 1978 and 1979, indicate that Vietnam willingly allowed and even forced many to leave. Large payments in gold taels to minor officials by refugees have increased the treasury's coffers considerably. This trafficking in refugees may have produced needed monies while ridding an already overpopulated country of dissidents, real and potential. The flow of refugees to the ASEAN countries, particularly Thailand, Malaysia and Indonesia, may have been a calculated policy to undermine ASEAN unity.[23] Indeed, these countries have undergone considerable stress as a result of the influx of refugees.

If Vietnamese refugees genuinely escaped more than they were pushed out, it is the consensus that a half million Chinese living in Vietnam were systematically driven out. Constituting the entrepreneurial stratum of Vietnamese society for centuries, the ethnic Chinese could not exist as private businessmen under the new regime. In the north, the nationalization of most businesses had already been accomplished before the war ended. But in the south, the Chinese could either go to the new economic zones or leave Vietnam. Added to this economic factor in the exodus of many Chinese was a political dimension. Increasingly, since 1975, China posed a threat to Vietnam. By 1978, growing hostility reached a point of open conflict.

Vietnam and China

Traditionally, Vietnam has lived with the threat of Chinese domination. Vietnam's strong sense of independence is attributed by some to its long-standing opposition to China. At times in its history, Vietnam was a part of China. At best, it often retained a tributary status to its powerful neighbor to the north. A common political ideology, Communism, has been undermined by nationalistic forces.

In the power vacuum left by the withdrawal of the United States from Indochina, China became more assertive in its foreign policy against Soviet expansion, Vietnamese expansion, and Vietnamese-Soviet relations in general.[24] In January of 1978, China launched a campaign, soliciting the support of overseas Chinese. The large Chinese minority in Vietnam had failed to assimilate into Vietnamese society. Vietnam was alarmed that China would support the Chinese in Vietnam, who were disgruntled over the new economic reorganization. The Chinese in Vietnam, constituting a fifth column, might support China in any conflict with Vietnam.

By mid-1978, Vietnam dubbed China its main enemy, planned an invasion of Kampuchea, expanded its military, revamped the economy along military lines, sought closer ties with the Soviet Union and reconsidered its relations with the United States and ASEAN. The threat of impending conflict generated thousands of refugees, especially among the Chinese. It is possible that China encouraged refugees in northern Vietnam to flee across the border into China in order to build support for an incursion into Vietnam that occurred in February of 1979, two months after Vietnam invaded Kampuchea.[25]

After the border between Vietnam and China was sealed and after 160,000 refugees had fled to China, refugees continued to leave

Vietnam. Vietnamese authorities arranged for boats and exacted huge amounts of gold and other valuable possessions from those departing. Nearly 250,000 eventually resettled in China. By the middle of 1979, the number of boat people not included in the numbers who went to China reached over 300,000.[26]

An ironic twist finds many refugees on state farms in China, perhaps similar to those they might have been assigned to had they remained in Vietnam. A few have fled from China, making their way to Hong Kong. But, they do not qualify for resettlement because China has been designated as their permanent asylum. This predicament is further exacerbated by the friendly relations between the United States and China. Although U.S. foreign policy after World War II was intended to provide asylum to those seeking alternatives to persecution under Communism, that policy has been difficult to implement. The current political interests of the United States makes that policy cumbersome. If the policy ever involved humanitarian concerns, apparently Sino-U.S. relations takes precedence over those motivations.

The Socialist Republic of Vietnam and the United States

As might be expected, postwar relations between Vietnam and the United States were and unfortunately still are characterized by strong, mutual distrust. Vietnam has accused the United States of promoting the isolation of Vietnam from other nations, especially the ASEAN countries. During the Ford administration, the United States blocked Vietnam's admission to the United Nations. The issue of U.S. MIA's (servicemen Missing In Action) has been a constant source of ill-will between the two nations, with the U.S. demanding an account of these missing servicemen. During 1975 and 1976, the United States repeatedly demanded to know what Vietnam's intentions were in the south. Vietnam continued to ask for postwar aid from the United States.

In 1977, President Carter called for " . . . healing the Vietnam war scars."[27] Some trade restrictions were lifted, ships and planes bound for Vietnam were allowed to refuel in the United States, travel restrictions expired, mailings resumed and Vietnam was admitted to the United Nations, July 20, 1977, without an American veto. An impasse was reached, however, when Vietnam continued to demand aid as a condition for normalizing relations.[28]

As the threat from China grew, Vietnam changed its position by dropping aid as a precondition for normalizing relations with the United States. This new policy was perceived to reduce impending Sino-U.S. ties, limit China's role in Vietnam's conflict with Kampuchea, improve Vietnam's image with ASEAN, improve the Vietnamese economy, and provide leverage in Vietnam's relations with the Soviet Union.[29] But, by this time, the United States had changed its mind. The possibility of diplomatic ties with Vietnam was unpopular in the United States. Some felt Vietnam had designs on other countries in Southeast Asia. The increased refugee exodus, especially the expulsion of ethnic Chinese, was definitely a negative factor. Importantly, the United States decided to pursue better relations with China, not Vietnam, as the key to stability and a balance of power in Southeast Asia.[30] With secret negotiations with China occurring at this time, some critics have accused the United States of deliberately stalling any rapproachment with Vietnam.[31]

In December of 1978, the United States agreed to establish diplomatic ties with China. The Sino-U.S. relations coupled with ASEAN-U.S. relations became the United States foreign policy strategy. Just prior to the announcement of normalization, Vietnam signed a friendship treaty with the Soviet Union in November. In December, Vietnam invaded Kampuchea. By February, 1979, China had invaded Vietnam, with the cooperation of the United States, according to Hanoi. "Meanwhile, the exodus of refugees from Vietnam grew and was seen in the U.S. as one of the worst violations of human rights in the 20th century."[32] The Reagan administration seems to be following the same foreign policy course, playing the China card in the power struggle with the Soviet Union. The continued occupation of Kampuchea by Vietnam and the Soviet invasion of Afghanistan reinforced the validity of U.S. policy.

It appears that dramatic increases in Indochinese refugees during 1978 and 1979 were related to foreign policy decisions made at about the same time. Refugees may have been an impetus to Sino-American reconciliation as well as a source of increased Vietnamese-American estrangement. But refugees may also have been generated as a result of these strategic policies. Vietnam stood accused of deliberately pushing out ethnic Chinese and Vietnamese, causing undue human hardships. Tensions increased in ASEAN countries receiving the refugees, prompting the call for an international meeting in Geneva, July 1979, to discuss the crisis. If the United States had been less shortsighted and vindictive *vis-à-vis* Vietnam, could the massive exodus been avoided? Did refugees serve to validate the new Sino-American relationship? Was it necessary to look at China and Vietnam as either/or choices? Or, through delicate negotiations could both countries have been included in a reconciliation? Did China encourage agitation over the ethnic Chinese in Vietnam to the point that Vietnam was pushed to expel them? Could a solidifying of Soviet-Vietnamese relations have been avoided had not China and the U.S. promoted a threat to Vietnam? The questions could go on and on. Unfortunately, definitive answers may never be forthcoming. However, it seems clear that refugees figured in deliberations and decisions related to strategic interests. Humanitarian concerns may have been an important factor. But, refugees may also have been pawns utilized in the power struggle in Southeast Asia.

Foreign Policy Interests Versus Domestic Realities

In October, 1979, former Senator Richard Clark, representing the Carter administration, said: "Refugee programs are an important element in our foreign policy."[33] Refugees from Indochina are a dramatic reminder to the world of the tragedy of Communism. They enhance the image of the non-Communist world, led by the United States.

The first waves of refugees entering the United States were families headed by urban, educated, elite professionals, for the most part. They quickly demonstrated their ability and willingness to work hard, help themselves and keep off the welfare rolls. But, four factors contributed to a change in the favorable initial response to refugees. First, the influx increased dramatically during 1978 and 1979. This upsurge led to fears of uncontrollable numbers in the future, from Indochina but also from other unstable regions. The arrival of Haitians augmented the fear. Second, the American economy continued to experience high inflation and unemployment. Third, later refugees were less educated, rural, and unskilled in contrast to those who arrived prior to 1978. Fourth, the cost of social services associated with resettlement reached one billion dollars per year.

While President Carter was pressured by interest groups to take in more refugees on humanitarian grounds and while refugees may have served foreign policy interests, there was growing concern about how many refugees the United States could reasonably be expected to take. This concern coincided with the tensions experienced and expressed by ASEAN that culminated in a meeting in Geneva, July, 1979. In addition, political motivations found a variety of individuals and committees in Congress ". . . jockeying for position in the boat people campaign which has become a popular issue."[34] In Geneva, the Carter administration was successful in deflecting pressure on the United States by calling for other countries to increase their quotas and financial support of resettlement. This made the refugee issue more of an international responsibility. The *New York Times* wrote: "President Carter, mindful of Senator Kennedy's activities on behalf of the refugees, is expected to take a more active role, pressing European and Asian nations to accept more refugees."[35]

In Geneva, Hanoi agreed to try to curtail the exodus of refugees from Vietnam by implementing an orderly departure program. Many were significantly impressed with this offer of cooperation. The program seemed to serve the interests of those suffering from refugee problems. The program was disbanded within a year by Vietnam apparently because of the inability (or unwillingness) of the U.S. and Vietnam to work out the logistics involving the matching of names on lists of eligible refugees kept by both countries. It appears that those at the conference may have been genuinely worried about the fate of refugees who were being lost at sea, robbed and raped by pirates, and denied entry at certain ports. However, there was a fundamental conflict inherent in the proposed solution of orderly departure. How could a refugee be designated as such when he was no longer an escapee but one who made application and arrangements for departure with the very government whose tyranny he was trying to flee from? There was a conflict of interests in Hanoi's involvement. Prior to this time, refugees were perceived to be victims of human rights violations in Vietnam. Now, Hanoi could further repress its citizens by stemming the exodus with the sanction of the non-Communist nations. Although Hanoi stood accused of deliberately expelling the ethnic Chinese, thousands of other refugees were genuine escapees. Unfortunately, the Geneva Conference never dealt with the basic causes of the exodus, the situation within Vietnam and the political maneuverings among those nations with special political interests in Southeast Asia.

With increased opposition to admitting large numbers of refugees to the United States, attention is being given to addressing "pull factors" that encourage refugees to leave Indochina. There is growing evidence that more and more refugees may be economic migrants. The House Judiciary Committee in August, 1981 indicated that the flow should be curtailed, refugee laws needed to be revamped, and closer congressional scrutiny was called for.[36] The idea of repatriation for those arriving in ASEAN countries is more acceptable now than previously. Congress is at work on immigration and refugee legislation, directed by Senator Alan Simpson, a longtime critic of liberal admission policies.

A conflict between foreign policy motivations and domestic interests led to a confrontation between the Department of State and the Immigration and Naturalization Service (I.N.S) in 1981. The Department of State accused the I.N.S. of unwarranted interference with the processing of refugees for resettlement in the United States. The I.N.S. claimed the State Department was deliberately allowing economic migrants to enter for foreign policy purposes. Others joined the I.N.S. in the criticisms. Senator Huddleston accused the State Department of ". . . recruiting refugees to fill unused quotas set by Congress."[37] Finally, a special panel, led by State Department official Marshall Green, was sent to Southeast Asia to assess the refugee situation.

One journalist summed up the results: "The panel found no grounds for charges that the United States is seeking to continue the flow of refugees in order to destabilize the regime in Vietnam."[38] The panel's report indicated larger proportions of refugees were economically motivated, not politically persecuted, especially those from Laos and Kampuchea. Fewer refugees had family ties with the United States or ties with the United States dating back to the Vietnam War. The high costs of resettlement was a factor to be considered, a direct reference to domestic concern. The report emphasized that boat people from Vietnam were still legitimate political refugees.[39]

As domestic realities affect a change in attitude toward Indochinese refugees, certain ethical questions should and do surface. What happens to refugees who are pushed back across borders or at sea?[40] Is it possible to determine categorically if a person is a bona fide political refugee? Are the latest definitions of eligibility for asylum merely a demonstration of American penchant for legalism that obscures or rationalizes away responsibility for other human beings? Journalist Don Oberdorfer writes about American responsibility based on guilt: "How long lasting should the American special obligation toward the Vietnamese be, resulting from heavy United States involvement in the 1960's and early 1970's?"[41]

In April, 1982, H. B. Cushing, director of the Office for Refugee Admissions at the State Department confirmed that the admissions policy had changed in view of the pressures from Thailand to discourage refugees from leaving Indochina. Presently, the United States considers refugees for resettlement only if ". . . they can demonstrate close links with the United States." This policy is expected to eliminate by forty percent the numbers entering the United States. This new policy along with ASEAN's deterrents are expected to reduce the exodus considerably. In April, 1982 alone, 700 arrived in Thailand, compared to 7,600 in April, 1981.[42]

What remains to be learned is whether conditions in Vietnam have also contributed to the curtailment of refugees. To what extent do the new limitations imposed by the United States and ASEAN curb access to asylum for those truly in need? Although the new American policy is related ostensibly to pressures from Thailand and to the reduced numbers of refugees in recent months, it seems that domestic realities led to the questioning of foreign policy motivations in the refugee issue. Did American policy change because refugees do not serve foreign policy interests as they once did? Are the new refugees really different from their predecessors or does the United States find it less convenient these days to accept responsibility for these people?

Conclusion

It has been the intention of this essay to present and discuss the salient factors influencing the foreign policy of the United States that appear to be related to the exodus from Indochina, from 1975 until the present. Consideration has been given to humanitarian concerns for refugees based on a code of values as they coincided and conflicted with the realistic and strategic national interests of the United States. The power struggle that characterizes Southeast Asia, involving Vietnam, Kampuchea, Laos, China, ASEAN, the Soviet Union, and the United States was found to determine American foreign policy in the region. To some extent, this policy affected and was affected by the exodus of refugees. Domestic economic, social, and political concerns in the United States also seemed to be related to American reactions and policies toward refugees.

The complexity of the refugee issue is evident by the numerous, interrelated factors involved. More questions may have been asked than answered, with the tendency at times to be judgmental in response to certain actions of the United States. However, it may be more important to attempt to come to an understanding of how and why certain policy decisions were made. The tragedy still remains that over a million refugees left Indochina and sought asylum. Instability in Southeast Asia could result in additional refugees at any time. Looking at events described in this study, it might be asked if anything can be learned to help solve the dilemma as it now exists and to avoid further expansion of the crisis. A less strident anti-Vietnam policy by the United States could conceivably lead to a more conducive atmosphere to address the problem. If any reconciliation between the United States and Vietnam is forthcoming, its repercussions *vis-à-vis* China, the Soviet Union, and ASEAN would need to be anticipated.

The United States seems to have been involved in refugee assistance for both humanitarian and special interest reasons. Each motivation influenced the other. The Socialist Republic of Vietnam appears to be primarily responsible for generating refugees, unintentionally at times and at other times deliberately. The United States' response capitalized on its own humanitarian gestures for propaganda and strategic purposes to the point of increasing the exodus beyond "push factors" operating within Vietnam. It is possible a less vindictive attitude by the U.S. toward Vietnam might have curbed the flow by permitting aid from abroad to assist in postwar recovery. Instead, the polarization of China and the U.S. against Vietnam posed a threat that contributed to a military preparedness in Vietnam with funding that might have been used to improve living conditions for the Vietnamese population. The new alignment with China and the strategic importance of ASEAN, especially Thailand, resulted in less concern for refugees from Kampuchea. The Sino-U.S. friendship also found the United States playing down human rights violations within China at the same time U.S. policy toward Vietnam was rationalized by the refugee exodus.

The refugee issue demonstrates the difficulty in balancing ethical dimensions and strategic interests in international relations when the primary consideration is power. Machiavelli may have been right to say the right things are done for the wrong reasons. Sharing an abundance is relatively painless. When the level of refugees in the United States reached a point where true charity was called for involving self-sacrifice by American society, the attitude toward refugees became less generous.

CHAPTER SIX
THE CORPORATION AND THE SEARCH
FOR SHARED VALUES
Mary E. Cunningham

Productivity is a central concern of corporations and the nation. And that word will probably be found in the title of more workshops, retreats, senior seminars and planned doctoral theses than even the words "access" and "interface" from earlier years. I have a friend who claims you can get by at most corporate executive meetings this year by using—judiciously, of course—the words "productivity," "macro," and "hands-on."

But cliches or not, these words are telling us something. They fit very appropriately in a discussion of historical trends, trends that alarm people who take the state of business seriously.

Consider a simple index of productivity growth: the United States as compared with Britain, West Germany, and Japan.

Between 1870 and 1950, our annual growth in productivity was approximately 0.7% higher than in those other countries. And that relatively small but decisive difference contributed to making us first the economic, and subsequently, the political leader of the world.

But since 1950 and particularly since the mid-60s, those numbers have been reversed. In 1979 and 1980 we actually had a net decline in productivity and the differential of last year is substantially in favor of West Germany and Japan.

Can anyone imagine—would anyone care to imagine—what this will mean in terms of our standing in the world in 1990 or 2000, and how other nations will perceive us?

Those productivity statistics rest on some ominous facts—facts that tell us that other countries have produced better products than we have, and have done so at lower costs, with fewer people, with fewer layers of management, with far fewer job classifications, with higher quality—and with a far more stable work force.

We business people will be making a mistake if we think that the election of pro-business people to the Congress and the Senate, and a President committed to balancing the budget and "freeing business from government," will solve these problems. It is, of course, essential to improve the investment climate in a variety of macroeconomic ways—whether through a more equitable tax structure, selective decontrol and deregulation, or the encouragement of savings.

But I suggest that we may have become somewhat mesmerized by all those macroeconomic plans.

It is not enough, I believe, for us to become cooperative spectators as the administration institutes a series of broad macroeconomic reforms. In fact, I believe that even if every tax reform and proposed budget cut were implemented in full we would still remain at a competitive disadvantage with other industrialized nations.

This is because the battle against declining productivity must be fought bilaterally, both at the macro-level of government policy and at the micro-level of organizational reform.

The present administration is doing its job by creating a blueprint that emphasizes savings, investment, monetary prudence and fiscal restraint. Our corporations must also do their part by examining what I will call the corporate culture, and instituting the necessary changes in that culture that will make them more competitive and more productive than they are at present.

I invite you to examine three concepts with me.

First. The absence of a shared system of values has a measurable impact on the bottom line.

Second. A less-than-humane working environment shows up as a concealed cost on the profit and loss statement.

Third. Prejudice is an expensive luxury.

Let me start by admitting that I am not very pleased with my phrase "a shared system of values." Not that it doesn't say precisely what I mean. But it sounds so impractical and lofty that it might provoke a few yawns.

I can just hear you say, "Does she expect every member of a corporation to be a soul-mate of every other?"

I'm not that naive.

But I do know, as every observer of the human condition knows, that a culture is defined in a very important sense by the ethical system that binds it. Not that everyone in a society practices right and wrong in identical fashions. But in a fundamental way there is a shared notion of ethical behavior.

A sub-society, like a corporation, is equally devoid of cohesion if it has no common values.

Today, the members of society at large, and of the institutions within it, including corporations, are yearning for that sense of meaning that comes from a well-developed system of values. We need this value system as individuals to give purpose to our work and therefore satisfaction to our lives. And the corporation needs it to create unity out of diversity, loyalty out of selfish opportunism and cooperation out of internally directed competitiveness.

Unfortunately, when you talk about ethical systems in the corporate realm—and that is another reason I hesitated to broach this subject— the word "ethics" suddenly shrinks to puny proportions. All it seems to mean to most people is improper payments and pilferage. Oddly enough, those infringements of ethics, while important, are likely to do much less financial damage than the violations I have in mind.

When I think of ethics in regard to a corporation, I see something with wider repercussions than the usual feeble Corporate Code. I envisage a common value system that causes the members of the organization to function together as a loyal unit. You need only to look at the Japanese to see that where there is unity, there is a tremendous increase in productivity.

You are familiar, I am sure, with Quality Circles in Japan—those weekly meetings where automobile workers, with absolutely no supervisors present, discuss assembly-line problems, quality control, and any other subjects relevant to their work—and look for solutions to present to management. Attendance is absolutely voluntary. The motivating force is precisely the shared sense of values that I say has bottom-line results.

Indeed, the results are measurable. Japanese management receives six to eight suggestions per employee per month. And a measure of the seriousness accorded this exercise is that over fifty percent of the suggestions are adopted. Is it any wonder that, as the flip side of the coin, management regularly rejects courses of action on the grounds that they might "hurt" the employees. . . ?

In the United States, joining an organization is like being born into a family or taking on a citizenship. With that joining, you take on new responsibilities, the most serious of which is to work for the good of the organization. This does not absolve you from adherence to principle. Nor does it deny your individual rights. It just amends them. It is not responsible to do what is akin to reneging on a contract—not a written one, to be sure, but one that has the same moral force.

I am convinced that as this notion of common purpose takes hold, we will find that we are building a new kind of cooperation. The organization will become more humane, more like a family—and this is the second condition I believe is required in order to reverse the trend toward indifference, and create, instead, a climate for increased productivity.

The analogy to the family is a risky one for a woman to make—it evokes sentimental, non-businesslike stereotypes. But families have functioned as economic units throughout the history of our species. And because the members had to pull together to survive, cooperation became a necessity—and skills were not wasted.

This kind of organizational framework will, I believe, bring a new humaneness and stability to the corporation. And none too soon, for our corporations have become bureaucratic and overly dependent on systems. It is true that sheer size, new technologies, complex government regulations, social pressures and other factors present extremely difficult challenges. But our reaction—indeed, over-reaction—to complexity has been to impose a system, and the result has been an artificially satisfying sensation that order has somehow been restored to our universe.

As a result, we have become the victims of the systems we have created. Computers, forecasting models, organization charts, and new methods of quantification have been idealized as solutions. Business has become austere and stifling.

Am I suggesting that we abandon all systems, models, and computer printouts? Not at all. If I did, I would be out of a job. Used appropriately, they can contribute to efficiency. What I am calling for is a return to balance—not a swing to the opposite extreme, to seat-of-the-pants decisionmaking. As our respect for numbers grows, our regard for judgment must not diminish.

I am suggesting that in the future, if the organization chart does not fit the person, we may well decide to change the chart, not the person.

I would hope that the business schools would sense the need for change and take a leadership role in bringing it about. What I would hope to see is the same emphasis placed on courses in Business Ethics, Organizational Behavior and Human Resource Development as has been traditionally placed on Marketing, Finance and Production. And in giving these subjects their due they should be presented to students not as electives but as part of the core curriculum.

Once again, if we refer to the Japanese example, we will see that this humanizing of the corporation is a major factor in their high level of productivity. I will draw from an industry I became very familiar with during my two years in Detroit. The evidence was gleaned from a Japanese automotive plant—not in Yokahama but in one of *this* nation's cities. There, the same figures on productivity, the same differentials in cost, quality, and reliability that I mentioned earlier are beginning to appear as though the plant were in Japan. But this time, there is a Japanese management with *American* workers.

A recent study by a large U.S. corporation tells us that "absenteeism" in Japan runs at only 4-5% annually, and those figures *include* sick leave and vacation time. If you take out those elements, the statistic drops to 1%. Furthermore, the average Japanese worker, entitled to fifteen to twenty vacation days a year, takes only an average of five days, because to take more would "inconvenience" his fellow-employees. We need to understand the far-reaching consequences of this spirit.

We could start by asking why Japanese auto workers have only six job classifications at a plant while one of our major producers, for example, has more than two hundred. Or explore why Japanese and German industry impose less than one half the number of management layers that we do between the chief executive officer and the workman at the machine.

The answer to our competitive disadvantage is not to copy the Japanese but to adapt the best from their style and stamp it Made in America.

I come now to the third of my basic themes: Prejudice is an expensive luxury.

Much of what I will say about prejudice in business represents personal observations—not scientific research. And because it depends on observation, it will focus largely on prejudice against women, the situation with which I am most familiar. I know, as you do, that prejudice is not directed exclusively or even primarily at women. Jews, Italians, Irish—virtually every ethnic or religious group—have been victims in the past, and to some degree still are. Blacks, women, Hispanics and other minorities are more common targets today.

So if I talk largely about women, it will be essentially as examples. I will not repeat each time that I am including in my thoughts other victims. I have not forgotten them and I hope you will not, either.

Prejudice takes many forms. And it changes with time. Five years ago the problem was getting women on to the corporate ladder. Now the problem is moving them up. If the move is exceptionally rapid or involves a very high level appointment, the bewilderment, skepticism, jealousy, and resentment are even greater.

It would seem there are no norms for people's minds to rest on when they see a woman set a record in business—so they turn to the very shopworn explanation that she used her sexual charms to get there.

The inability in some people to accept a woman's advancement is only one form of sexist prejudice. The other is the failure to promote her at all. In both cases, the observers simply refuse to see merit where it exists. A variant on this is where they see the merit, but, heeding the signs of resentment around them, fear the consequences that might result if they reward it.

The power of the press either to further prejudice or to combat it is awesome. The temptation to capture ratings and wider readership must be very tantalizing.

But when the press engages in irresponsible and sexist journalism, it cannot offer in its own defense that it has no norms for people who have broken the age barrier. It has—but they have been men. Faced with a woman with a similar record, they feel obliged to describe the color of her hair, her shape, and assign an overall 10-point rating. I am still waiting to hear a detailed physical description of David Stockman who directs our Office of Management and Budget and was a congressman at age thirty.

Or Samuel Armacost, the young chief executive officer of Bank of America, who first became an officer of his bank at age thirty.

By consistently focusing on the biologically female side of a woman's success, by sensationalizing events, the media does more than hurt the individuals involved. They deny their readers the formation of vital new symbols needed to undo old stereotypes. In short, they perpetuate false notions and betray a public trust.

I have said, and I believe it is worth emphasizing, that American management indulges its prejudice at great economic cost. This statement is not subject to the kind of cost/benefit analysis performed on a calculator. But every good manager knows that our greatest natural resources is human creativity. It is only a small step from that knowledge to the realization that corporate attitudes which systematically place the filter of preconception between the potential candidates for important corporate posts and the eyes of the personnel decisionmaker must necessarily cost the organization untold earnings.

Beyond the obvious opportunity cost, there are other direct costs associated with a corporate culture that does not include women as a normal part of organizational activity, particularly at the highest levels of decisionmaking. The loss in productivity as a result of resentment or frustration is not obvious but nonetheless real. If such rejection ultimately causes the woman to leave, the time and money spent on her training is an obvious waste.

There has been no more consistently sounded theme recently in this country than the need to recognize that our resources are limited and that we must exploit them with maximum efficiency and minimum waste. Oil, coal, water, timber—yes. . . . Why not people?

In my opinion, people are our most underutilized resource in America today. And to the extent that we continue to accept barriers which prevent certain talented individuals from achieving the most responsible levels of corporate power, to that extent we are wasting our greatest resource, the intelligence, creativity and judgment of our people. Can this country really afford to pay such a price for discrimination? Is American industry really willing to provide the receptacle for such waste?

Prejudice is a moral failing in the souls of the people who harbor it. But it is also an error in logic—a particularly expensive one that takes the form of overgeneralization. It is a flaw that has practical consequences, for unless we free our minds of the generalities that preconceptions represent, we cannot make room for the exceptions. Yet, it is the exceptions throughout history—in business, in medicine, in politics—that have made the breakthroughs and moved us forward—not by inches—but by leaps. Bigotry is not only foolish, but destructive—destructive of the contributions such people could make to the greater group, whether the corporation, the university or the hospital.

Human creativity is the resource we can least afford to waste. And while the creative talent, working in isolation, will always survive and find some means for expression, we have not yet tapped the special creativity that could emerge from bringing together people who have not, in the past, had the opportunity to exchange ideas or attitudes or values. It is not enough just to give a woman or a black or a young person a job. They must be made part of the process at all levels of problem solving to which they can meaningfully contribute.

I maintain that the continued underutilization of certain segments of our work force in America is morally unjust, politically unsound and commercially stupid. If we do not overcome this tendency, we will resign ourselves to creating a group of second-class corporate citizens who are less informed and therefore less effective in the business world, and we will accept a corporate America that is less dynamic, less creative, and less competitive worldwide.

As for my other two themes—the importance of a shared value system and the need to humanize the corporation—I believe there is a lot of educating to do. Nonetheless, in many ways, great and small, the individual has the power to take action personally right now. You can look for opportunities to speak out—and if you do, I hope you will agree that it is not only possible but necessary to infuse a practical note into what are normally considered soft themes. Emphasize that a corporate culture will ultimately be played out either as an asset or a liability.

Even more important, you can apply the principles that would guide a new corporate ethic and a more humane organization to your own spheres of influence. This will not only bring direct benefit to those immediately affected but it will also become part of the process that will cause those principles to permeate the entire organization.

CHAPTER SEVEN
AMERICAN MULTINATIONALS
AND INTERNATIONAL ORDER
Joseph M. Grieco

Introduction

To understand the variety and significance of international activities of American institutions, it is clearly worthwhile to pay attention to the multinational operations of American business enterprises. These United States-based multinational firms have become vital elements in the national economies of many countries around the world. By 1977 United States-based enterprises operated almost 25 thousand subsidiaries, branches, and other types of affiliates in over 140 countries. Over seven million individuals outside the United States received compensation in excess of $78 billion for their employment by these U.S. enterprises, and these enterprises produced goods and services abroad valued in excess of $680 billion.[1]

This essay explores a possible consequence of interactions between American multinationals and foreign elites which to date has received little scholarly attention, i.e., their impact on international order. Before exploring this question, however, it may be useful to note how American political-economic values contributed to the tremendous expansion of U.S. business operations around the world. While U.S. firms had limited operations abroad from the beginning of the 1900s, the dramatic expansion of U.S. overseas business activities took place during the 1950s and 1960s. A variety of factors unrelated to American political-economic values per se were necessary conditions for the outward expansion of U.S. enterprises. First, American political military power made it clear that, however the international economic order would develop after the Second World War, it would be the preferences of the United States which would determine that course of international economic evolution.[2] Second, technological and managerial comparative advantages of American enterprises, which in turn were the result of the factor endowment of the United States economy, allowed American firms to be highly successful as they entered new foreign markets.[3]

American political-military and techno-administrative assets thus were necessary conditions for the outward thrust of American firms after World War II. However, a last condition, which together with these two factors constituted the conditions sufficient for the internationalization of U.S. business, was the particular set of values embedded within the vision of American policymakers in the postwar period. This vision had two key components. In recent years immediately following the war, American policymakers firmly believed that poor international economic conditions and statesmanship had clearly contributed to the rise of fascism and the onset of World War II. At the same time, these U.S. national leaders believed that they could contribute immensely to the prospects for international peace and security in a context of gradual, non-violent change, i.e., international order as defined by the American national political-economic experience, through the creation of new international economic institutions and practices.[4]

Drawing upon the American national experience, the United States policymakers believed during and after World War II that one element of a successful strategy for the pursuit of peace was to establish an international economic order that would be conducive to the growth of all nations. These policy officials believed that maximum opportunities for growth would be generated by an international economic order facilitating free as opposed to state-regulated international exchanges of goods, services, and capital. Relatedly, the American policymakers believed that these exchanges would be most extensive and would grow most quickly if they were executed by private, and not state-owned, enterprises and parties.[5]

Finally, while private-sector actors would be the primary generators of international economic growth, and therefore indirectly of international political order and peace, American policymakers recognized that some state regulation and intervention might be necessary from time to time to offset the downward periods associated with business cycles, or to spur growth in underdeveloped regions or countries. Hence American and British diplomacy leading to the Bretton Woods international monetary system and the trade regime associated with the General Agreements of Tariffs and Trade, as well as the international development work of the International Bank for Reconstruction and Development, all permitted limited forms of state regulation and intervention in national and international economic activities.[6] However, for the most part these regulatory-interventionary activities, in the minds of U.S. officials, were to result most significantly in facilitating privately generated international economic exchanges. Hence American political-military and political-economic power combined with American values in such a way that American enterprises faced a markedly favorable international environment for their overseas expansion after World War II.

Attention has been focused to this point on explaining how a particular U.S.-inspired international system allowed for the overseas expansion of American multinational enterprises. With this background, attention may be redirected back to the central concern of the present essay, i.e., to the problem of how the operations of American multinationals currently affect the level of order in the international system. The concept of international order cannot be given exhaustive analytical treatment in the present brief essay.[7] However, the United States after World War II was able to generate a consensus among many countries that international order involves, at a minimum, efforts to facilitate peaceful resolution of conflicts among nations, gradual change in international relationships and institutions, and an avoidance of violence as an instrument of national policy. Moreover, the United States was successful in persuading many countries outside the Communist bloc that an open international economy is basically helpful to the maintenance of international order.

The present discussion restricts itself to an analysis of how U.S. multinationals might affect only one major element of international order as described above. This single element is the degree to which national governments ascribe legitimacy (i.e, moral and practical approval) to the basic structures of the contemporary international order. These structures, such as the General Agreement of Tariffs and Trade and the remnants of the Bretton Woods system, differ significantly in their level of legal and institutional form and strength, but they share a common quality of seeking to promote relatively unhindered international flows of goods, services, capital, and technology. If several powerful national governments ceased to ascribe legitimacy to these liberal economic structures, then the resulting breakdown in international policy consensus and coordination would be a powerful force leading the international community toward instability and disorder. The central question is whether foreign elites are more or less likely to ascribe legitimacy to the contemporary international economic order as a consequence of their relations with American multinationals, which are both major beneficiaries and vital instruments of the present world economic system.

The discussion below is presented in four parts. Two sections describe how American multinationals affect the level of order which characterizes relations, respectively, among developed countries, and between developed and developing countries. A third section then examines an especially new issue involving U.S. firms in both developed and developing countries which could affect prospects for future international order. This is followed by a concluding section which summarizes the discussion as a whole.

American Multinationals and Developed Countries

The total book value of U.S. foreign direct investments exceeded $213 billion at the beginning of the 1980s. Almost three-fourths of these investments were located in other developed countries. Canada and the United Kingdom alone served as hosts at the beginning of the decade to approximately one-third of all U.S. foreign investments by book value, and these two countries plus Germany, Switzerland, and France were the hosts to one-half of all U.S. investments abroad.[8]

Given this intense visibility of American multinationals in the societies of Europe, Canada, and to a much lesser degree, Japan, one might have expected ample opportunities for U.S. enterprises to come into conflict with the various elites of these countries. Complaints have in fact been made periodically about the harmful effects of U.S. firms in terms of contributing to the "Americanization" of Canadian and European consumer tastes. Another criticism of American multinationals has been that their geographic mobility has weakened the bargaining power of unions in any particular advanced country.

However, for the most part U.S. enterprises have been considered generally a positive force in Canada, Europe, and, to some extent, Japan. American enterprises have been recognized as having contributed to an important degree to the postwar reconstruction of Europe, to the industrialization of Canada, and to the acquisition of important technological capabilities by Japan. Also, the inter-affiliate trade of U.S. multinational enterprises has been viewed as one important means by which Europe and Canada made their postwar thrusts into the American domestic market. American multinationals are recognized in developed countries to be important generators of employment and of high-technology research and development. Finally, American firms have constructed a good track record with regard to adapting their industrial relations programs to be in accord with those practices in many developed countries which sometimes differ substantially from practices in the United States.[9]

Thus social-cultural problems arising from the operations of U.S. firms in other developed countries are moderate in intensity and, for the most part, are overshadowed in the minds of national elites by the concrete economic benefits American enterprises deliver to the advanced societies. However, political and economic problems have arisen in developed countries as a result of the presence of U.S. enterprises, and these problems may tend on occasion to tear at the consensus among the advanced countries as to the legitimacy of free trade. The basic political-economic issue is that national elites in developed countries (and in developing countries) sometimes fear that their openness to U.S. firms limit their autonomy in key industries, and therefore in vital areas of national policy.[10] For example, during the early 1960s, the United States government limited the computer sales by one and perhaps two U.S. data processing companies to France in order to restrict the latter's nuclear weapons program.

In this and other cases, developed host countries have viewed U.S. firms as inappropriate instruments of U.S. national policy, and have taken actions to try to limit the ability of the U.S. government to so influence their national policies. It is these nationalistic responses to U.S. governmental attempts at transnational influence which have been harmful to an open international economic order. For the most part European countries have sought to escape possible dependence on U.S. firms through the creation of government-favored national firms. These are so-called "national champions"; in the data processing field examples include Britain's International Computers Limited (ICL) and France's Compagnie Internationale pour Informatique (CII). Given the perception by some developed-country national elites that economic openness has led to efforts by the U.S. government to exercise influence through American multinationals, the national elites have responded through the creation of indigenous firms which rely on anti-free trade programs such as direct government-mandated preferential purchasing programs. Thus American firms themselves may not have triggered the nationalistic responses in other developed countries, but their responsiveness to U.S. governmental pressure has led to economic policies in these countries that are manifestations of a weakening in the belief that economic openness is the preferred course of action.

Other conflicts harmful to free trade may emerge if a national champion is formed but is unable (even with massive government aid) to withstand competitive pressures from U.S. enterprises operating in the developed host economy. An example of this was the failure of France's CII to compete successfully with IBM/France, and its eventual need to establish equity ties with another American firm, the Honeywell Corporation.[11] A third way in which U.S. enterprises could destabilize relations between the U.S. and other developed countries is by contributing (without apparent intent) to the failure of efforts by developed countries other than the U.S. to cooperate in industrial ventures. In the early 1970s the French, German, and Dutch governments agreed to cooperate in fostering a European-wide computer company (Unidata, to have been formed by CII, and units of Siemens and Philips). This venture was aborted when CII decided in 1975 to join forces with Honeywell-Bull. For many in Europe, this event was seen as proof that, in data processing, only nationalistic strategies, such as those of Britain and especially Japan, could succeed in meeting American competitive pressures. Hence an unintended consequence of U.S. corporate success in open developed countries may be to generate a distrusting of economic openness and actual policy moves on the part of America's major economic partners toward protectionism.

Yet, it is unlikely that protectionist tendencies arising from a fear of U.S. multinationals will grow so strong that the basically open economy among the developed countries will be fundamentally threatened. U.S. enterprises are seen by developed-country elites as clearly contributing to their respective societies. Also, developed-country elites recognize that in many respects they can make U.S. firms accommodate their interests and concerns to those of the host country. For example, sophisticated observers of French electronics policy have shown that the French government has not felt defeated by the linkage between CII and Honeywell-Bull, but instead they have come to view the linkage as a means by which France has gained significant control over the local and indeed the international operations of a major American high-technology multinational.[12]

Hence conflicts involving sovereignty and national autonomy may erupt periodically between elites of developed countries and U.S. multinationals. Yet it is likely that the national elites will respond only with limited forms of protectionism, and will engage in direct bargaining campaigns with the U.S. firms with levels of success sufficient to assuage basic fears on the part of the elites. Indeed, as we shall see, the "power" of U.S. multinationals *vis-à-vis* developed country governments and elites may not be nearly as disruptive of the international economic order as their actual weakness and willingness to comply with developed host country policies. However, before pursuing that line of analysis it is necessary first to examine the consequences for international order of relations between U.S. firms and developing host countries.

American Multinationals and Developing Countries

The total book value of U.S. foreign direct investment in all developing countries was in excess of $50 billion by 1980, and accounted for one-fourth of all U.S. direct investments abroad. One-half of all U.S. investments in the developing world (in terms of book value) were concentrated in ten developing countries. Brazil and Mexico alone accounted for more than one-fourth of the total of U.S. investments in all developing countries, and indeed these two countries ranked among the top ten national hosts of all U.S. investments abroad. Five of the top ten developing country hosts as of 1980 were in Latin America (Brazil and Mexico, plus Argentina, Venezuela, and Peru), four were in Asia (Hong Kong, Indonesia, the Philippines, and Singapore), while one was in the Middle East (Egypt).[13]

Controversies about the operation of U.S. multinationals in other developed countries pale in comparison to those surrounding the presence of American firms in the developing world.[14] American multinationals are viewed in Marxist and *dependencia* scholarship as being the key instruments by which the United States exploits developing countries and keeps them in a subservient position in the international system. Early analyses (such as those by Andre Gunder Frank) suggested that the operations of U.S. firms in the developing countries of Latin America actually led to the absolute impoverishment of these countries. Foreign natural resource enterprises were seen as creating within these countries a narrow "comprador" class which essentially served as a collaborator in the exploitation of the countries. The "comprador" class was thought to lack any desire to develop an autonomous national base of power. The class was thought by early Marxist-*dependencia* writers to have taken on the cultural and consumer tastes of the "metropolitan" country from which the foreign enterprises originated, and therefore its only desire was to assist in the exploitation of the country in exchange for access to the luxury goods and cultural attributes of the metropole.[15] This view was held not only by early Marxist-*dependencia* writers; non-Marxist critics of American (and other) multinationals such as Johan Galtung (with his concept of "structural imperialism"[16]) basically argued that multinationals were an instrument of capitalist exploitation and a force for underdevelopment in the Third World.

These views still have attraction in some academic circles, and they are often used in intergovernmental meetings (especially those sponsored by the UN) by developing country delegates as debating points. Yet the continuing aggregate growth of developing countries (combined, however, with the simultaneous persistence of widespread unemployment and poverty of large segments of the population in these countries) have encouraged a restatement of Marxist-*dependencia* analyses of the multinational corporation. More sophisticated discussions were presented by writers such as Fernando Herique Cardoso and Engo Faletto in Latin America and by Peter Evans in the United States.[17] The "new" Marxist-*dependencia* position is that American multinationals do contribute to some extent to the aggregate growth of many developing countries, and this growth is distributed beyond a narrow comprador class. However, Marxist-*dependencia* writers continue to maintain that the growth is restricted to relatively small portions of developing countries, and they also maintain that the operations of multinationals may harm the economic interests of the lesser income groups of developing countries.

Also, Evans recognizes that developing country elites do have national interests which conflict with those of multinationals and which result in bargaining. However, Evans maintains that these conflicts and bargaining encounters take place within a "triple alliance" (involving the multinational, the local capitalist class, and the host country government) in which the multinational is the senior and dominant partner. Especially because American multinationals control sophisticated technologies of keen interest to host country governments and business groups, the former are able to keep the latter in a subservient (albeit negotiated) position. Developing countries are not in as hopeless a position in "new" Marxist-*dependencia* analyses as in "old" Marxist-*dependencia* writings. However, in terms of basic relations, the argument of even the most sophisticated "new" Marxist-*dependencia* writers is that multinationals still fundamentally hold the balance of power over developing governments.

If this analysis were correct, then one would have to view American multinationals not only as a force harmful to the development prospects of Third World countries, but also as a profoundly destabilizing factor in relations between developed and developing countries. Nationalistic governing elites in the latter countries would view relations with American multinationals as involving not only economic costs but also the loss of national control over vital industries in which the American enterprises were active. Moreover, these elites might conclude, if the Marxist-*dependencia* analysis were correct, that there was no hope to change unfavorable relations with American and other international firms. Nationalistic elites would be unlikely to accept such unfavorable and unchangeable relations. They might decide that, given the intrinsic inequity and inflexibility of an international economic system which involved (and to a great extent is based) on relations with multinationals firms, it would be better for the country to terminate relations with these firms and indeed to withdraw from other forms of participation in the capitalist international economy. This, indeed, is the policy prescription of Marxist-*dependencia* writers and other analysts who recommend that developing countries "delink" or "decouple" from the international economy and instead pursue a strategy of "national self-reliance" until the country is powerful enough to manage its relations with advanced capitalism more effectively.[18]

This prescription can be challenged from an economic viewpoint, but this essay is more immediately concerned with the international disorder that would result from pursuit by several large developing countries of a strategy of "delinkage" and "self-reliance." Of course, there would be a host of conflicts between these countries, and advanced capitalist societies concerning issues such as the nationalization of corporate assets and the breaking of contracts. More disturbing would be the likelihood that delinkage might lead not only to changes in the external relations of developing countries, but also to rapid and drastic changes in internal political and economic relations. Such changes could become uncontrollable and, as has occurred in the past, could result in the coming to power of domestic groups sympathetic to the international adventurism of the Soviet Union.

Hence the impotence of developing countries with regard to relations with American multinationals could lead to the eventual destruction of those relations and to the producing of international disorder. Yet events in the past two decades suggest that the Marxist-

dependencia (both "old" and "new") viewpoint on power relations between American multinationals and developing countries can be strongly challenged. Work by what may be termed the "bargaining school" on such relations has shown that developing-country elites can increase their power over multinationals over time, and thereby attain greater levels of effective sovereignty over their countries and extract greater economic benefits from foreign enterprises for their economies.[19]

Studies by the "bargaining school" indicate that multinationals do indeed begin their relations with developing countries with superior bargaining assets in the form of capital, technology, and managerial expertise. However, once investments are made, several processes come into play which lead to a shifting in the balance of bargaining power in favor of the developing host country. Most obvious is the fact that the company's assets in the country become a kind of hostage to good relations with the host government. However, other, more subtle, dynamics also are at work. First, the developing country may devote resources to the acquisition of expertise so that the country can have a better understanding of the technology and economics of the industry in which the enterprise is involved. Second, once the initial foreign entrants into a developing country indicate that operations there can be profitable, other foreign firms from the U.S. and other advanced countries are likely to seek entry into the country. The host government, more aware of the industry's potential in the country and of the heightened international interest in the country, can use that knowledge to strike more favorable bargains with both the new and the original entrants. The result of these domestic and international dynamics is that developing countries can be confident that control over their economies cannot be maintained by multinationals over sustained periods of time.

Empirical examples of the phenomena described above were first observed in relations between developing countries and international firms in the natural resource industries. Comprehensive empirical studies have shown the balance of power shifted during the 1950s and 1960s to Middle Eastern and South American countries in their relations with foreign enterprises in the petroleum and copper industries.[20] More recent research suggests that the same dynamics observed in relations between developing countries and low-technology natural resource sectors may also begin to characterize relations between at least the more advanced developing countries and high-technology manufacturing industries. For example, both India and Brazil have been shown to have exerted substantially greater levels of control over multinationals computer enterprises during the 1970s compared to the 1960s.[21]

In sum, it is likely that developing country-elites can be increasingly confident that they will be able to increase their power over multinationals across a wide spectrum of technologies and industries. Hence, they probably recognize that, over time, they can expect to attain greater sovereignty over their countries and extract more economic benefits from the enterprises. As these countries so increase their power over multinationals and extract more benefits from them, it is likely that they will be more willing to accept such relations with foreign firms and to grant higher levels of legitimacy to the broader economic system of which multinationals are an important component. Indeed, it is not the power of American and other multinationals over developing countries which can be a source of international disorder. On the contrary, it is their long-term pliability in the face of increasing host developing country pressures which could lead to international instability.

American Multinationals, Host Country Power, and International Conflict

As noted above, both developed and developing countries have been able to formulate strategies through which they can increase their control over, and extract greater benefits from, U.S. multinationals operating within their economies. Most frequently host country strategies in this area include policies which serve as incentives coaxing U.S. (and other) multinationals to take on activities of interest to the host country, as well as other policies designed to compel certain U.S corporate actions through the imposition on them of performance requirements.[22] Investment incentives over a wide range of instruments, include preferential tax and tariff treatment, cash grants and subsidized loans, and preferential access to land and other local resources. Performance requirements also are diverse in nature; they include equity-sharing requirements, targets for minimum local value-added and exports, as well as limits on repatriation of earnings and payments on technology transfers and the use of trademarks. Sometimes an incentive acts like a performance requirement. For example, from the viewpoint of any one of several international firms contemplating entry into a country, the granting by the host government of incentives (such as low-cost loans) to any of its competitors in exchange for specific corporate operations would place it and all other non-participating firms at a competitive disadvantage. Hence it and the other firms might feel compelled to shape corporate operations to the desires of the host government in order to obtain the "incentive" that the competitor (or competitors) had already received.

In all three cases the effect is the same: U.S. and other multinational enterprises seek to tailor their operations to be in accord with host country interests. The problem from the viewpoint of international order is that such pliability on the part of U.S. enterprises in foreign countries is seen by the U.S. government and by key American labor and business groups as hurting the already soft

American domestic economy. Local value-added requirements in foreign countries lead U.S. firms operating there to increase their use of local vendors and manufacturers, thus decreasing U.S. exports. Export requirements may lead to a diminution of U.S. sales to third countries and perhaps even to an increase in U.S. imports. Perhaps over time the increase in economic activity in the host countries may lead to an increase in their imports from the United States to the extent that the resulting expansion in U.S. employment arising from exports matches the contraction in employment stemming from foreign host country requirements and incentives. However, in an already weak U.S. economy such expectations for future adjustment may not be sufficient to contain current pressures on the American government to "do something" about foreign host country policies concerning American multinationals.

Already the U.S. government has indicated that it intends to challenge certain performance requirements imposed on U.S. firms by Canada's Foreign Investment Review Agency. Less dramatically, the current U.S. administration has taken the initial steps toward calling for an international convention aimed at controlling and reducing host country performance requirements and investment incentives. It is possible that this effort for a "GATT for Foreign Investment" could be accomplished in a manner that does not lead to international instability.[23] However, if the U.S. economy remains soft, and if the U.S. government believes that "quiet diplomacy" is ineffective in this area, then it might be tempted to take actions that could be harmful to international stability. For example, the U.S. might put forward its own requirements and incentives, or it might devise policies penalizing foreign countries which have especially extensive requirements and incentives applicable to U.S. enterprises.

In these instances the foreign countries might consider U.S. government actions as being an infringement on their legitimate interest in economic sovereignty and development. They also might conclude that the U.S. no longer was the leader of an "open" international economy (a role requiring it to take on some of the costs of "cheating" by others). In the light of other aggressive actions on the part of the U.S. in the trade and money issue-areas, foreign countries might conclude that the U.S. was taking on the behavior of "an ordinary country." In the absence of effective leadership, the international political economy would very likely be plagued by the increasingly extensive use of "beggar-thy-neighbor" national economic policies. Such a development could only be very harmful for international order and stability.

It is unclear that concern in the U.S. about requirements and incentives will become so intense that the unfavorable scenario sketched above might actually be set into motion. Recovery from the current recession in the United States and other developed countries surely would lessen American sensitivities about host country policies affecting American multinational corporations. However, even if economic recovery removes the present dangers in this issue-area, it still might be worthwhile to investigate ways in which the international community can regulate requirements and incentives, if for no other reason than to avoid conflicts during future economic downturns. An international regulatory regime concerning host country policies would be difficult to formulate and to monitor, and much research and consultation is needed before specific terms of such a regime can be articulated. However, at least two basic principles appear to be appropriate for inclusion in and guidance of a host-country foreign investment policy regime. First, greater latitude should be given to developing countries than to developed countries; this of course is in keeping with international agreements in the trade issue-area giving preferential treatment to countries facing massive problems of poverty and underdevelopment. Second, all host-countries should try to avoid creating permanent (and inefficient) distortions in the international division of capital and labor. For this reason efforts should be made to attach specific time-limits on the operation of requirements and incentives. Host-country performance requirements and investment incentives should be viewed as instruments of questionable economic value and as forces clearly harmful to the smooth operation of the international economy. Hence for the sake of economic efficiency and political order it would be prudent to develop long-term agreements aimed at limiting, and in time perhaps eliminating, their usage by national-hosts of American and other multinational enterprises.

Conclusion

This essay has examined how the operations of American multinationals abroad might affect the degree to which foreign elites ascribe legitimacy to the contemporary international economy, and therefore how U.S. enterprises might affect levels of order in the international system. The first major argument of the essay is that, for the most part, developed and developing host-country elites view American multinationals as contributing in positive ways to their respective economies. This probably contributes to a belief on the part of these elites in the legitimacy of the international economy and of the broader international political order in which the economy is embedded. Second, host-country elites may on occasion fear that their power positions are threatened by U.S. enterprises. However, elites in both developed and developing-country contexts have strong reasons to believe that, over time, they can establish mutually beneficial relations with American enterprises in which national sovereignty is preserved. This ability on the part of national elites to reconstruct their ties with American firms removes a potentially dangerous source of national resentment about participation in the international economy. Indeed, the ability to reform ties with U.S. enterprises probably leads national elites to ascribe even greater legitimacy to the international economic system, and this is a positive force from the viewpoint of international order.

Growing power on the part of national elites in their relations with U.S. enterprises is therefore something to be desired *up to a point.* However, American (and other) multinationals actually have shown themselves to be relatively easy prey to host country pressures. American enterprises have in part been so pliable with regard to host country requirements and incentives that the U.S. government and key American societal segments are beginning to believe that the enterprises are serving as channels through which unacceptably high levels of economic activity are being transferred out of the U.S. and to the foreign host countries. Thus if there is a destablizing loss of legitimacy taking place with regard to the contemporary international economy as a result of the operations of U.S. enterprises, this loss is perhaps taking place most rapidly at the present time in the United States itself. In the 1970s it was thought by many that international order would be well served through the creation of international agreements aimed at regulating the operations of American (and other) multinational enterprises in host countries. Ironically enough, in the 1980s it may be recognized that, in fact, international order would be served more through the development of an international consensus leading to constraints on the ability of host countries to exercise their formidable power over these foreign enterprises.

In contributing to the development of such consensus, the United States needs to face the fact that the problem of international regulation of host country policies brings into acute tension the two strong American values concerning international economics noted at the outset of this essay. On the one hand, the United States has a firm belief in the utility of open international economic exchanges, and host country investment incentives and performance requirements violate this belief. On the other hand, the United States also has intellectual and practical sympathy for indirect, limited forms of state intervention to guide private economic actors, and compared to other economic instruments (such as state-owned enterprises), incentives and requirements are in fact relatively indirect forms of state regulation. Perhaps the proposals discussed above (of distinguishing between developed and developing countries, and of placing time limits on the operation of host country investment policy instruments) allow for some movement toward striking a balance between these two values. It should be realized that the United States was successful after World War II in striking just such a balance (both domestically and in international negotiations) in the fields of trade and money, and the successes of that period should lead Americans to have high standards for evaluating current U.S. efforts in the field of international investment.

EDITOR'S INTRODUCTION TO CHAPTER EIGHT

Thomas R. Donahue's paper differs from other essays in this volume becaue it takes as its subject certain papal encyclicals relating to labor. It was presented as part of a symposium held on May 3-4, 1982 at the University of Notre Dame and titled "Co-Creation: A Religious View of Corporate Power." It is included in the volume because Mr. Donahue, AFL-CIO Secretary Treasurer, addresses himself directly to the core values of the American labor movement by associating its history and its principles to the encyclicals. He relates the particular history of American labor to the universal values of the encyclicals. His paper is published substantially as delivered with only a few paragraphs omitted.

CHAPTER EIGHT
AMERICAN LABOR AND UNIVERSAL VALUES
Thomas R. Donahue

Father John Coleman, S.J., in a paper delivered on May, 1981, at a convocation commemorating the anniversaries of *Rerum Novarum, Quadragesimo Anno,* and *Mater et Magistra,* stated his view that "the foundation for such a unitary view is the legitimate understanding that social encyclicals form an interconnected social charter and tradition."
He continued:

> In that sense, as the various popes—despite . . . different historical contexts . . .—built on one another, so it is legitimate to show the particular Catholic teaching on social issues captured, for example in key principles and concepts such as human dignity, solidarity, subsidiarity, the right to integral development participation, the ultimate subordination of economics and politics to human fulfillment.
> As social charters, the encyclicals tended to be read, absorbed and commented on mainly by socially involved Catholics who generally gave them a more progressive interpretation than their location in historical context might have warranted. The encyclicals, then, represent in some sense a genuine unified tradition of sane and humane social thought which we both celebrate today and try to bring forward into the future.
> . . . [T]hey have formed over the past ninety years men and women who have found in them a charter to become concerned about institutional and structural reform, to support organization for justice, to heed the papal call to respect human dignity and to go to the poor. These men and women and the Catholic movements they have spawned are the best exegesis of the documents.
> Ultimately, the future of this tradition will depend less on our

ability to parrot its significant terms such as subsidiarity, a just wage, socialization, or to define in precise ways social charity, social justice or the common good, and more on our ability to read the signs of the times in fidelity to the Gospel of human dignity as Leo, Pius XI, Pius XII, John XXIII, Paul VI—with all their historical limitations, biases and failures—tried to do in their times.

John Paul II has given us an excellent reading of the "signs of the times in full fidelity to the gospel of human dignity," but more, has given us a soaring hymn in praise of that dignity, triumphant over all else.

The American Federation of Labor was formed a decade before Pope Leo XIII issued *Rerum Novarum.*

Indeed, the labor movement in the United States hardly survived its infancy. In those early years, giant American industries such as Carnegie Steel Company and the Pullman Railway company decided to ignore their workers' just claims, and when those workers went out on strike, the companies stopped at nothing to break those strikes.

But bolstered by the encyclical teachings, great Church leaders such as Cardinal Gibbons and Archbishop Ireland came to the defense of the trade unions, supporting them as free associations seeking justice for their worker members.

In the early part of this century, Archbishop Ireland, in a famous Labor Day address, referred to the days when an economic school of thought "authorized capital to see in the laborer only his output of labor and to purchase that output at the lowest possible price." He went on to say:

> Then it was that the operators of the 'black fields' of England reduced their miners to the level of beasts of burden and as, even at that level, men seem to cost too much, put women in their stead, and later, for similar reasons, substituted children for women.
>
> How very different is the situation today. The change is due to an improved public opinion and an enlarged Christian humanitarianism; but it is due very largely also, and facts could easily be adduced to prove, to the intelligent self-assertiveness of labor itself, and to the new strength coming to it from the aggregation of its scattered units into well-organized societies. Labor unions have a noble mission and are entitled to the sympathy of all intelligent men.

Rerum Novarum and Its U.S. Implications

The enduring message that Pope Leo XIII conveyed in *Rerum Novarum,* the cornerstone of Catholic social thought, was that call for a new order of things, for a new relationship between workers and employers in the new industrial society. With superb Christian charity he pointed out the injustices that had occurred in the development of this new economic order, while reminding men of their common origin and destiny in Almighty God, and their universal brotherhood, despite any class or economic difference.

Protesting against the despotic power of accumulated wealth, he called upon owners of industry to recognize not only the rights of their employees to press their just claims for a share in the wealth they produced, but to recognize as well their natural right to associate in workingmen's associations or unions.

This encyclical greatly influenced many American Catholic labor leaders and provided new support for them in their opposition to Marxism and its class warfare theories. Indeed, in 1895, Daniel DeLeon, a Socialist leader, attempted to form the Socialist Trade and Labor Alliance as a rival to the AFL. This not only failed, but caused a great split in the Socialist movement itself, with Socialist trade unionists rejecting dual unionism and returning to the American Federation of Labor.

But support by Pope Leo XIII and other outstanding religious leaders did little to diminish the opposition of industry to the labor movement.

Professor Carroll Dougherty described the mood of many employers early in this century in his book, *Labor Problems in American Industry.* "The more powerful employers," he wrote, "believing that unionism was getting too strong and fearing further encroachment of their control of industry, decided to break off relations, and the years 1902 to the War [World War I] were characterized by increasing anti-unionism."

During this difficult period, the labor movement in the United States found aid and succor in those who were exploring the implications of Leo XIII's encyclical. Monsignor John A. Ryan, a moralist and economist at Catholic University, published two notable studies on "The Living Wage" and "Distributive Justice." And Monsignor John O'Grady busied himself with the encyclical's implications as they bore on the government's obligation to care for the disabled and needy citizens beyond their working lives. . . .

Quadragesimo Anno—Part of the Heritage of Social Teaching on Human Rights

When Pope Pius XI issued *Quadragesimo Anno,* he continued the great tradition of his predecessor Leo XIII and gave strength to the interpretations of encyclical teaching by the American bishops. In the next half-dozen years, the United States went through a fairly peaceful social revolution, enacting into law practically all of the points contained in the two encyclicals and the bishops' program of 1919.

In the last fifty years, many of the encyclical concepts have found their way into the fabric of non-Communist Western societies. Much, of course, needs to be done, not only in our own nation, where social inequities and social injustices continue to persist, but in an over-whelming sense in what is called the Third World. . . .

Laborem Exercens

Before I treat of *Laborem Exercens*, let me make clear that I have not ignored, nor do I lack appreciation of, the tremendous impact of the other modern encyclicals, but I have confined my remarks to those encyclicals directed to the labor question. I have no credentials to explore the theology of *Laborem Exercens* nor to offer a scholarly examination of it. Rather, let me concentrate on an examination of its reception in the United States, of the issues it raises (against the background of the current level of development of trade unionism in the U.S.), and of its implications for the future development of the struggle for social justice for workers and its directions.

When it first appeared, the encyclical was hailed in the United States as a major social pronouncement, but the secular press concentrated on two of its subsidiary notes rather than on the major issues raised.

Early attention in my country centered on the discussion of the political activities of unions and of the right of public employees to strike. The former issue obviously was raised in the context of the struggle of Solidarnosc with the Polish government, and the latter issue was of great interest because of the encyclical's publication during our air traffic controller strike.

Only to a lesser extent, and in later analysis, was thoughtful attention given to the principal points of the encyclical relating to the centrality of man in work, the conflict between capital and labor, the rights of workers and (largely in the Catholic press) to the elements of spirituality in work.

In the Catholic press, the headlines noted "New Encyclical Warns of Evils of Capitalism, Marxism," "Encyclical Offers No Easy Answer to Complex Labor Problems," "New Encyclical Presents Teaching on Work and Ownership," "Papal Labor View Focuses Agenda for U.S. Workers," and "Workers, Not Capital, Key to Moral Order."

All of those lines heralded the publication of what is, for the American labor movement and particularly for Catholics in that labor movement, a document which is a great comfort and a great challenge.

The themes of the dignity of labor and of worker rights, of the need for a just wage, and of the duty of the state to protect the worker's natural right to enter into workingmen's associations, are all carried forward from *Rerum Novarum*.

They were echoed in *Quadragesimo Anno* in its treatment of the unjust claims of capital and labor, the principle of just distribution of wealth and property, and the need for a just wage. Indeed, it was there that we found the first call for workers sharing in some way in the ownership, management, or profits of the enterprise.

The same themes, of course, reappeared in that part of *Mater et Magistra,* on the subject of labor, where we found the reaffirmation of the right of workers to organize with the extension to the view that organization of workers is not only desirable but necessary, and where we found, to the great pleasure of trade unionists, praise for labor for having developed "a more responsible attitude toward the greater socioeconomic problems of the day."

In *Mater et Magistra,* we found the statement of the themes later echoed in *Laborem Exercens* that labor must try to reconcile its rights with those of other workers in the community; a repetition (albeit in far more forceful terms) of the instruction that workers should share in ownership as well as management of the enterprise; and the introduction of the concept that traditional collective bargaining should be supplemented by new institutions which will make it possible for workers to exert their influence effectively, beyond the limits of the individual productive units.

Pope John XXIII also clarified that which had been a difficult concept for American Catholic trade unionists—namely, the view of *Rerum Novarum* that the truly appropriate associations of working men were those organized along religious lines. For us in the United States, this was a concept totally outside of our experience. Pope John XXIII, while praising "associations of workers of Christian inspiration" gave equal praise to work performed with a Christian spirit by other groups and associations or workers.

Mater et Magistra had great importance in the United States and was described by Monsignor George Higgins, then Director of Social Concern of the United States Catholic Conference, as "positive and constructive in tone." "The encyclical," he noted "takes it for granted, almost as self-evident truth, that unions are absolutely indispensable and the scope of their activities should, if anything, be expanded." Monsignor Higgins' comment finds its echo in the use of the word "indispensable" in this latest encyclical in describing the role of unions in modern society.

While *Mater et Magistra* clearly placed a man as a worker at the center of the economic order, and affirmed the view that "the economic order is the creation of the personal initiative of private citizens themselves," *Laborem Exercens* goes quite beyond that point when stating the fundamental thought that "human work is a key, probably the essential key, to the whole question," and noting that "the principle of the priority of labor over capital is a postulate of the order of social morality."

"Indispensable" Unions and the Church as Employer

Monsignor Higgins noted in one article on *Laborem Exercens* that while "previous encyclicals strongly favored the organization of workers into autonomous unions, none had made the point so forcefully as this one. To say, as the earlier documents did, that unions are legitimate or even necessary is one thing, but to say they are indispensable takes the argument one step further.

> Many Americans will gag at this, [he continued] even though the preamble to the basic statute governing labor relations in the United States comes close to saying the same thing . . . [and] powerful forces in the U.S. opposed to unions are prepared to go to almost any length to return to the bad old days of the so-called open shop.
> The new encyclical will probably have little or no influence on people who hold this view, but it will give new hope and encouragement to the labor movement. Eventually, it may be a positive influence on public recognition of the right of workers to organize.

The U.S. Labor Movement in Struggle

To understand fully the new hope and new encouragement which this encyclical gives to the labor movement in the United States, one must see that movement, as it sees itself—facing the unrelenting opposition of the nation's employers to every single expression of desire on the part of workers to enjoy the "indispensable" union affiliation of which the Pope speaks.

In our system of labor relations, a union either exists or not at each workplace depending on the majority expression of the workers at that workplace. The union either enjoys "exclusive recognition" as the collective bargaining agent for a defined group of employees or it is not recognized at all.

This fact seems to have encouraged the view of U.S. employers that almost any tactic is permissible in their struggle to convince a majority of their employees that they do not need, or do not want, a union to represent them.

Consequently, our unions struggle every day for recognition, for their right to exist at a particular workplace or in a particular plant, hospital, or establishment or whatever kind. The exercise by workers of their right to associate freely with one another is challenged by the employer as if the effort to assert that right could properly be treated as the subject of a contest, of a game. The workers who attempt to form or join a union are arrayed on one side with the employer on the other. The employer's advisers, people who in the U.S. are called "labor-management consultants," mount a campaign of propaganda, pleas for loyalty to the employer, and often, intimidation and coercion. Arrayed on the other side are the union adherents, their professional staff and their campaign—intended to offset the employer's propaganda, to attract new adherents to the union cause and to minimize any intimidation or coercion.

The inevitable result of these struggles is the maintenance of a climate in which cooperation is difficult and coexistence is more the norm.

I do not claim that all virtue in such discussion and contest is on the union's side but only to point out that what the Pope takes for granted as a right of association freely exercised, guaranteed in a democratic society, is often trampled upon in my country and others. And one must conclude that it is trampled upon in pursuit of the profit motive and in an effort to exclude workers from any voice in ownership, or management, or, indeed, from any effective participation in the fixing of the conditions under which they will labor.

The struggle of our unions is, as the Pope points out, a "struggle for the good which corresponds to the needs and merits of working people." We do not see it as a struggle against others but as a struggle against their ignorance and their pursuit of the ultimate maximization of profit. It is never, for us, a struggle "for the sake of struggle" or "in order to eliminate an opponent," since the first is wasteful of human effort and the latter carries with it the elimination of the opportunity for employment—always too scarce in our country. . . .

U.S. Collective Bargaining System

The labor movement in this country has long insisted on a written collective bargaining agreement with each employer as the fundamental protection of workers on the job and has always regarded our collective bargaining system as the cornerstone of labor-management relations and, hopefully, as the basis for labor-management cooperation.

We believe in a conflict theory of collective bargaining as the soundest basis for worker representation, worker participation, and worker gains, in the current labor-management climate, because we see no real or broad evidence of acceptance by employers of the concepts of just remuneration, protection of worker interests or of the participation of workers in the ownership, management or profits of the enterprise.

We accept fully the view that all capital is the product of past labor, that labor is not a commodity and that nothing has been created in the human realm except through labor. Consequently, we seek a redistribution of the wealth of our nation and an enlarged share in future wealth. Workers properly want, and are entitled to, a larger share of the wealth they produce. It is our almost universal experience that the employer—individual, corporate or non-profit organization (both secular and religious)—does not want to give workers their fair share, and we are therefore in essential conflict over this issue. It is, hopefully, a conflict which always "aims at the good of social justice."

Since our relationship with our employers remains at this primitive level of struggle, it has always been difficult for us to regard seriously, for ourselves, the forms of participation in the enterprise generally grouped under the heading of co-determination.

For so long as the attitudes of U.S. employers remain unchanged, we shall continue to advance a theory of collective bargaining rooted in the conflict between trade union efforts to advance social justice and what we regard as the employers' efforts to maximize profits and maintain "management prerogatives"—(a euphemism for unadulterated control of work rules or work process with the least possible "participation" of workers in management).

I would note, however, that we do believe that our adversarial role, appropriate to the conflict of collective bargaining, should be limited to the period of negotiation. During the lifetime of a contract so arrived at, it ought to be replaced by the period of cooperation aimed at maximizing the potential of the joint enterprise to advance the company's business and the workers' satisfaction.

For that reason and on that premise, many of our unions are participating in "labor-management committees" and other cooperative programs, where those programs have their base in collective bargaining. Much attention is now being paid to the question of worker satisfaction on the job and the quantity and quality of his or her work output. These two subjects have been joined under the title of "quality of work-life" and a great deal of experimentation is now going on, seeking to find new and better ways to give to workers a sense of pride in their work, a sense of their involvement in the production process, and through this sense of involvement, to draw forth from workers a greater personal interest in the quantity and quality of the product of work. All of this effort is to the good and is an implementation of the encyclical's view that through work man achieves fulfillment as a human being and, indeed, in a sense becomes "more a human being."

Unfortunately, in many instances non-union employers are introducing such programs or giving the appearance of real participation to their employees in an effort to dissuade those employees from joining together in a union. For the most part, such programs will fail in the long run since while they appear to manifest a real concern for worker fulfillment they are, in fact, based on a less admirable desire to maximize profits, and when a conflict between the two eventually arises, as inevitably it will, that conflict will be decided in favor of maximizing profits.

The Dignity of Work

In our country, as in so many other industrialized nations, there has been a drifting away in recent years from the long accepted view that work is necessary, noble and fulfilling, and that the virtues of work are to be enjoyed. As our society focused more on the individual and his comfort, as materialism has grown, and as the perception has become more widespread that hard work is neither any longer necessary nor desirable, there has been a wandering among ideas in search of some value.

For some—generally, the young of the middle and upper economic class—this became a more personalized search for an elusive self-centered fulfillment, or, the pursuit of radicalism in search of some seemingly more noble goal. For others, there has been a confusion and a bitterness about a "work ethic" they don't share. *Laborem Exercens'* statements that work must provide "fulfillment as a human being" and must be arranged so that it is not only worthy of man but also "corresponds to man's dignity . . . expresses his dignity and increases it" challenge us to spread this view of work and ensure that it pr~·~ls.

Worker Solidarity

The encyclical's emphasis on greater worker solidarity gives trade unionists great heart. We were pleased with the call for the extension of worker solidarity to "social groups not previously included in such movements" which are "undergoing what is in effect proletarianization," and the note that this can be true "of certain categories or groups of the working intelligentsia." This call for extending worker solidarity to new groups parallels our recent efforts to bring the benefits of trade union organization to scientists and engineers, teachers and nurses, as well as to agricultural, service, and industrial workers.

The call for new movements of solidarity on an international level is a call for the labor movement to "go to the poor" in various parts of the world and assist in their development. We note proudly that our recent return to the International Confederation of Free Trade Unions is an expression of our solidarity with workers throughout the world and a reflection of our belief that we can best work with, and cooperate with, other unions through such an international organization.

Worker Rights as Human Rights

The encyclical examines workers' rights within the broad context of human rights and notes that "respect for this broad range of human rights constitutes the fundamental condition for peace in the modern world." U.S. unions have argued unceasingly in international labor forums and international political forums that respect by any nation for the right of association of its workers is critical to the exercise of all other rights in that society and can be used as the yardstick for the measurement of other rights. Convention 87 of the International

Labor Organization sets forth this right of workers to associate freely in their own interests, but it is violated with impunity in Poland, Czechoslovakia, Chile, South Africa, and dozens of other nations, while nations (including my own) which respect that right mount feeble protests but draw back from the application of trade sanctions or embargoes which might make that right a reality.

The AFL-CIO has always been in the forefront of those who argue for the application of the strongest sanctions against those nations which trample on the right of association, or any other right, and we intend to continue in that course. Because we do so, we are in conflict with our government at this time over its failure to take the strongest sanctions against the Soviet bloc for its role in the crushing of free trade unionism in Poland and to embargo the export of grain, goods, and factories to the Soviet Union.

"The Indirect Employee"

The concept, first introduced in this encyclical, of considering "all of the agents at the national and international level that are responsible for the whole orientation of labor policy" as "the indirect employer" is startling in its imaginativeness and brilliant as a way of grouping all these forces and thereby forcing upon us a recognition of the need for national and international planning. Such planning would require a level of national selflessness and international interest and cooperation which we are currently incapable of reaching. But, it nonetheless provides the concept as a goal and the term "indirect employer" as a helpful and informative shorthand phrase for describing those "persons and institutions of various kinds and also collective labor contracts and the principles of conduct which are laid down by those persons and institutions and which determine the whole socio-economic system or are its result."

"To Act Against Unemployment"

The section of the encyclical on "The Employment Issue" is central to the document and central to the solution of the industrialized nations.

"The role of the agents included under the title of indirect employer is to act against unemployment, which in all cases is an evil and which, when it reaches a certain level, can become a real social disaster." In my country with a current unemployment level at 8.8%, or 8.5 million workers unemployed, with an additional 1.5 million no longer counted because they are too discouraged to seek work and with 5 million workers working only part-time, we believe that we have already achieved the level of a real social disaster, with the economic, social and moral consequences becoming more apparent daily.

In the United States, the indirect employer-government is not acting against unemployment and, in fact, has made it clear that it sees unemployment as an essential element, if not a tool, in bringing down inflation and reordering the distribution of national wealth. Our government, like other governments which describe themselves as conservative, is determined to avoid any degree of central planning or coordination on employment issues and leave these matters to the so-called "free markets" which have failed us so badly in the past. In addition to failing to act against unemployment, the current administration is also, by reducing the role of the national government in education and employment and training matters, failing to make provision for the "overall planning" the encyclical urges "with regard to the different kinds of work by which not only the economic but also the cultural life of a given society is shaped . . . and to organizing that work in a correct and rational way."

The "just and rational coordination" which the encyclical calls for would require a degree of national and international planning which "conservative" (i.e. liberal capitalist) governments reject. Nonetheless that national and international planning is essential if the good which we pursue is to be achieved.

On Work And Ownership

In an earlier section of the encyclical, "On Work and Ownership," the Pope affirms the Church's support for "various proposals for joint ownership of the means of work, sharing by workers in the management and/or profits of businesses, so-called shareholding by labor, etc." He continues then to note that "merely taking these means of production out of the hands of their private owners is not enough to ensure their satisfactory socialization."

The further suggestion that a way toward the goal of "socializing" property "could be found by associating labor with the ownership of capital, and by producing a wide range of intermediate bodies with economic, social and cultural purposes . . . enjoying real autonomy with regard to the public powers and pursuing their specific aims in honest collaboration with each other and in subordination to the demands of the common good," seems, in the context of current conflicts between contending forces in society, a wildly utopian dream—but perhaps there are mechanisms in current society which at least lead in that direction.

To some extent labor-management committees which have been formed at plant or industry level can be regarded as resembling these "intermediate bodies." In cases where these committees deal with the problems of a national industry they have enjoyed a certain autonomy and have pursued aims jointly shared by the two parties.

In exploring the employment issue, the Pope returns to this theme in speaking of the need for just and rational coordination, within the framework of which the initiative of individuals is respected, in bringing about a measure of overall planning.

For us, the labor-management committee is a natural vehicle for problem resolution or for the advancement of common interests. At various times in our history both labor and management in the United States have joined together with government to try to bring about some "overall planning" or to meet some special problem of the time. During World War II, the National War Labor board enjoyed this status. At several points in the last twenty years Presidents have called labor and management to work together with government. Most recently, in the United States, during 1979, we negotiated with the government a "National Accord" establishing a mechanism to provide for labor's involvement and cooperation with the government on important national issues. Out of that accord developed consultation and agreement on an incomes policy and a good deal of participation by labor in the overall planning process. Business leadership did not formalize its relationship with the process in a written accord but they were party to the same discussions with the administration. For a time it appeared to the American labor movement that we might be able to develop and hold together the kind of cooperative approach to national economic issues which is essential if we are to succeed on the employment issue. In the last month of 1980, as the Carter administration's term was ending, the President established a joint labor-management government committee on the revitalization of American industry, with a broad mandate for "overall planning."

Unfortunately, the election interceded and President Reagan's election ended the process because his administration's deeply held conviction is that no overall planning is necessary or appropriate and that free market forces will produce economic success and ensure employment.

We obviously do not agree with this theory and continue to be available for the consultation with business and government which is necessary if we are to have an agreed set of goals for our society and for our economy, and if we are to be able to relate those goals to international economic conditions.

Unions' Political Activities

The Papal analysis on political activities of unions seems to require particular consideration in terms of its relation to this need for governments "to act against unemployment" and to carry out some role in the "overall planning" for work. We in the AFL-CIO are quite comfortable with the formulation that "unions do not have the character of political parties struggling for power, and should not be subject to political parties or have too close ties with them," but we are equally sure that it is only our involvement in politics that enables us to work for a government which will "act against unemployment" and plan for providing work for all.

The encyclical's treatment of this subject is obviously far too short to warrant too much speculation about its application in individual countries. It would give substantial discomfort to the trade union movements or political parties of a number of industrialized nations if it were literally applied, and some writers have questioned its pertinence as a moral issue.

In the United States, on the other hand, it fits our present and past policies very comfortably. We have always insisted upon our independence of government and of political party, while maintaining a strong involvement in the political process. We have seen our role as one of encouraging the participation of union members in political activity and we have always insisted on being guided by the instruction of the first president of our federation to "Reward your friends and defeat your enemies" in politics. In the past year, while we have undertaken an enlarged role in the Democratic Party we have made clear that we are trade unionists first and party members second and that we would be guided accordingly. We have specifically reserved our right as trade unionists to support candidates of other parties where we deem it to be in the best interest of our members to do so. Similarly, we have made clear to the Republican Party our willingness to provide the same sort of coordinating role among those of our members who are adherents of that party.

The concept of a Labor Party or of a political party dominated by the labor movement has never had strong attraction for U.S. trade unionists. It has been raised from time to time as an expression of frustration with the extant parties and there have been some efforts to create such a party at various past times but each has foundered in a relatively short period.

Nonetheless, it is our participation in politics and in the political process, which is the only sure protection of those interests of workers which are dealt with by "the indirect employer." Consequently every success which we have in increasing and enlarging our political power enlarges our ability to defend workers' interests.

The Right to Strike

That small section of the encyclical which deals with the protection by government of the workers' right to strike, and the injunction that essential community services must be ensured, received a great deal of attention in the United States because of the coincidence of the issuance of the encyclical with the nationwide strike of air traffic controllers whose right to strike had been infringed upon by government legislation. While the section was obviously not intended to have that effect, it was much-cited as defending the actions of the President in discharging all of the striking employees.

Aside from abrogating government responsibilities, disrupting government functions, and demoralizing government employees, the administration by its intemperate and vindictive response to the strike of the air traffic controllers, established a climate of fear and resentment that puts unreasonable strains on public employees at every level.

The fact is that workers, as a last resort, after all other avenues of redress have failed, will strike even where that action is regarded by the state as a form of civil disobedience. And what is needed is the legal recognition of that right to strike along with special provision for the maintenance of essential services on an emergency basis.

It is unfortunate that the encyclical, while forthrightly noting that essential community services must be ensured, does not call with equal vigor for substitute mechanisms to ensure fair treatment of workers who, on the theory that there is no other way to ensure essential services may be deprived of their right to strike. It may be argued that the concept is included within the phrase "appropriate legislation" or that "appropriate legislation" includes the concept of mediation, cooling off periods, the availability of binding arbitration, or the specification of certain categories of workers as "essential" while protecting the right to strike of others in the work unit. However, in the circumstances of the current debate on this issue in the United States, the concentration on ensuring essential services was unfortunate and gives the impression that no special consideration is due to workers whose right to strike the state seeks to abridge.

The Immigrant Worker

The encyclical's examination of the position of the immigrant workers is a particularly timely one when some nations, in recession, must determine how to treat the immigrant or guest workers they once needed and when other nations are beset either by illegal immigration or by the necessity to receive large numbers of economic or political refugees—often with the additional difficulties attendant on making that distinction.

While the encyclical limits its instruction to the point that the immigrant worker, seasonal or permanent, "should not be placed at a disadvantage in comparison with the other workers in that society in the matter of working rights," it is interesting that this section and the sections on national planning are grounded in a respect for national boundaries and national identities and thereby avoid the pitfalls that await those who pretend that we have achieved some sort of world society.

If we are to deal realistically and rationally with immigration planning and with the need of nations to accept periodically the unexpected refugees from another nation's inhumanity, we must first recognize the serious employment effects of immigration and factor in those effects. The effort is not assisted by those who would pretend either that there is no need for immigration controls or that any nation can hold itself apart from necessary international efforts to accommodate refugees.

It is also obvious that increased international and national planning by "the indirect employer" must include assistance and aid to Third World nations so that the underdeveloped and less developed countries can grow and provide food and jobs for their own people with the resultant diminution of the pressure to emigrate.

Women Workers

Many people were particularly pleased with papal support for the theories of recompense for women who stay at home to care for children. There have been some efforts over the past few years to obtain social security (old age pension) coverage for homemakers because keeping a home and raising children are a form of work and should be recognized as such. The social re-evaluation of the mother's role advocated by the encyclical will support that effort.

Similarly, the thought that "the advancement of women requires that labor should be restructured in such a way that women do not have to pay for their advancement by abandoning what is specific to them and at the expense of the family" will provide additional support for those who have advocated flexi-time and part-time work for women who seek such work.

However, since such a large number of women are the principal or sole supporters of families in this country (nine million out of sixty-one million families), we would have preferred an additional emphasis on the equality of women in the workplace and on the impropriety of the historical low-rating of job classifications which have been regarded as "female jobs." Much attention has been given in this country to the question of equal pay for equal work and the re-evaluation of jobs so that those historically female occupations might be given equal status with jobs of "comparable worth" to society.

I am not one of those who finds the tone of the encyclical, or its use of the male pronoun, somehow anti-feminist, although that criticism has been made. I believe a more careful reading belies that description, but that is not to deny that a greater emphasis on the need for equal treatment of women, on the problems of women workers who are heads of families, and on the "comparable worth" issue, would have commended the encyclical even more highly to feminist leaders in the United States.

Profit Sharing

Profit sharing has never been a major factor in the remuneration of U.S. workers and unions have accepted the concept only when considered as a supplement to, rather than a substitute for, that "living, saving, family wage." In recent years there has been some renewed interest in profit sharing but the fact is that in good times most employers have shown no disposition to share profits and it has been most advanced as a substitute for a normal wage. Now that difficult days are upon industry there has been more employer and less union interest in it. However, in some of our most depressed industries where workers have agreed to pay reductions or to stand-still contracts, the promise of future profit-sharing has had renewed consideration.

Implications for Corporate Policy

The most immediate challenge posed by the encyclical is to the holders and managers of capital. The national, transnational or multinational corporation based in any of the Western industrialized nations is a corporation organized around the profit motive, seeking to pay the cheapest price for labor, the cheapest price for raw materials and to obtain the highest price for its product. The measure of success is "the bottom line" in accounting terms, the amount of profit returned to the shareholders.

In *Laborem Exercens* the Pope forthrightly states that the entire structure must be revised, the principle of the priority of labor over capital must be respected, and the employment process must be recast in the service of man. When he speaks of joint ownership and profit sharing or shareholding by labor, he notes that "even if these proposals cannot be applied concretely, it is clear that recognition of the proper position of labor and the worker in the production process demand various adaptations in the sphere of the right to ownership."

How much more, then, does that recognition require adaptations of corporate policy to workers? Is it not required that a corporate balance sheet give at least as much attention to the number and quality of jobs it has provided during the year as it does to profits? Is it not required—if the worker is to be the center of corporate planning and thought—that allowing one facility to deteriorate through inadequate reinvestment, and closing that facility with resultant unemployment, be considered a wrong that must be avoided and redressed? Is it not required that greater attention must be given to safety and health measures than to increased output—where that increase is achieved by diluting those measures? Is it not required that the transnational corporation be a force for social improvement in Third World nations, bringing with it a willingness to pay not just the going rate of an underdeveloped wage system but rather installing itself as a leading employer not only in pay and conditions but equally in terms of its management and its recognition of the dignity of its workers?

*   *   *

The encyclical has given both comfort and challenge to United States unions, employers, to political and economic analysts and to the Church itself. The condemnation of rigid capitalism and of collectivism presses us toward some middle course as yet insufficiently defined.

The applications which flow from the recognition of the proper position of capital and labor are considerable. They are surely immediately present for the non-profit institution, and particularly the religious non-profit institution, as employer.

For corporations or other employers who accept the concepts of the encyclical, the same consequences flow, but only time will tell how many of such employers and corporations will accept. There is, undoubtedly, a major teaching role ahead for the Church and its institutions, particularly in industrialized nations—an uphill struggle to reeducate those who have too long accepted the view that capital has priority, that capital buys labor, and that without a profit motive there can be no industry.

In such quarters, the encyclical's instructions that the means of production cannot be isolated "as a separate property . . . set up in the form of 'capital' in opposition to 'labor'," that they "cannot be possessed against labor" and "must serve labor and thus by serving labor make possible the achievement of the first principle of this order, namely the universal distribution of goods and the right to common use of them," will find tough going.

For our part, as trade unionists we will go on pressing for the individual elements of worker rights that the Pope has defined and worry not at all about the system's appropriate title. We will continue to struggle for workers' rights, for fair compensation and all that goes with it, and above all to struggle for the recognition of worker dignity that flows from employment, under decent conditions, in a fulfilling toil about which the worker has a say and through which he participates fully in the management, ownership and profits of the enterprise.

III. AMERICA AND INTERNATIONAL COOPERATION

The most important fact of the postwar world may well be the active involvement of the United States in the continuing drama of international politics. No longer can it be said of the United States that it stays its hand until the eleventh hour.

Its involvement takes the form of international cooperation within multilateral institutions ably discussed by Professor I. L. Claude, Stettinius Professor of Government at the University of Virginia. At the same time the United States conducts its relationship through traditional diplomatic channels assessed in this section by an experienced diplomatist, Emmett Ford. Perhaps the most explicit form of projecting values by Americans is in the ideological struggle. No one has defined this activity with greater clarity than Edward W. Barrett, former Assistant Secretary of State for Public Affairs. In the 1950s, Barrett published *Truth is Our Weapon* and has given permission to republish the chapter from his book, now out of print, dealing explicitly with underlying values, a chapter whose content Barrett considers as relevant as when it was published. Not content with official relations, Americans and particularly younger American have sought contacts with other people at the grassroots level through organizations such as the Peace Corps. Harris Wofford who was "present at its creation" contributes a chapter on the Peace Corps. Wofford's quotes are drawn from his book *Of Kennedys and Kings: Making Sense of the Sixties* by Farrar, Straus, Giroux, (New York: 1980); *Twenty Years of Peace Corps,* by Gerard T. Rice, published by the Peace Corps in 1981; *Point of the Lance,* by Sargent Shriver (New York: Harper, 1964), Peace Corps Issue; *Annals of the Academy of Political and Social Science,* May 1966; and *The Future of the Peace Corps,* by the Aspen Institute, 1977.

Chapters 10, 11 and 12 focus on four different institutional forms for international cooperation, raise important questions concerning the American values underlying such cooperation and analyze possibilities and problems in their transmission and projection.

CHAPTER NINE
AMERICAN VALUES AND
MULTINATIONAL INSTITUTIONS
Inis L. Claude, Jr.

No theme occurs more persistently in the literature about American history than the proposition that Americans have always regarded their society as the repository of a peculiarly precious set of political and social values. This assertion has sometimes taken exaggerated forms that ought to arouse skeptical reaction. One may question, for instance, whether a full consensus on values has ever existed in the United States, and whether the same values have prevailed throughout American history. It is unlikely that most Americans who have thought about the matter have believed that the values they esteemed were originally and exclusively American, failing to acknowledge the place of those values in the Western liberal heritage. The oft-heard claim that the United States has inveterately sought to impose its values upon other countries also deserves a critical reception; those who blithely read Woodrow Wilson's slogan about a "war to make the world safe for democracy" as meaning a struggle to impose democracy, American style, upon the rest of the world have some explaining to do. In short, society as a unique bastion of nationalistic universalism is to be resisted. While Americans may be no less self-righteous and arrogantly crusading in spirit than most other peoples, it is not self-evident that they have abnormally large quotas of those unlovely qualities. Indeed, the observer of present-day America might feel the need to coin an antonym for self-righteousness (self-wickedness?), and might be tempted to think that many of its people are aware of no values that they deem worthy even of defense, much less of propagation abroad.

Nevertheless, a qualified version of the theme deserves acceptance. Americans may have acknowledged their borrowing and sharing of values and they may not have agreed upon a systematic formulation of the values that constitute their special treasure, but they have been inclined to the view that their society derives a distinctive virtue from its enshrinement of political and social values that can be vaguely but meaningfully subsumed under the heading of constitutional democracy.

This view leads to the conviction that the United States bears a responsibility not only for achieving the progressive realization of those values at home, but also for promoting their realization in the world at large. If it would be imperialistic to impose American values upon the rest of the world, it would be, from the point of view of the true believer, selfish to deny them to the rest of the world. Even in their most fervently isolationist moods, Americans have never quite believed that their candle should be put under a bushel. That they have considered their values pertinent to foreign policy as well as to domestic affairs is indicated by the fact that Americans have generally been somewhat uncomfortable with the focus upon national interest in the doctrines and prescriptions of Political Realists; their notions of the proper place of values in international relations may have been ill-formed, but most Americans have not been content to concede the field exclusively to interests. The recent revival of emphasis upon human rights in United States foreign policy is evidence of this.

The aspiration to project American values into the outside world takes two forms. First, there is the urge to spread the essentials of constitutional democracy to other societies. Americans have hoped that other peoples, inspired by the example or induced by the admonitions of the United States, would adopt American values as their own. This hope no doubt reflects the altruistic desire that peoples everywhere should enjoy the blessings of what Americans regard as a good society. It also reflects the conviction that a world composed primarily of constitutional democracies will provide a safe and congenial environment for the United States. Wilson's formula for making the world safe for democracy was to create a securely peaceful order, and he was convinced that only democracies could be relied upon to maintain such an order; he gave expression to the American belief that a world safe *for* democracy must be a world made safe *by* democracy.

The second form taken by the aspiration to export American values is the effort to apply them to the foreign relations of the United States and to persuade other states to do the same. This entails the adaptation to the requirements of foreign policy of values originally conceived for domestic application. Constitutional democracy comes to be translated as the rule of law in international relations. The American ideal may be described as a world in which the values treasured by the United States suffuse both the domestic institutions of states and the institutions of the multistate system.

The promotion of this ideal is not an easy or simple undertaking. Other peoples have their own preferred sets of values, which they are loath to abandon. Many who share the values that Americans describe as their own are committed to the view that those values are irrelevant to foreign affairs, which are said to belong to a different moral universe. Even when the transplantation of American values is not resisted, it may not be genuinely successful; one might argue that values, like some wines, do not travel well. Perhaps the most troublesome problem is that of finding a way of spreading American values without violating them in the process. Freedom, consent, respect for the rights of others, and tolerance for differing views are values that cannot, without descent into absurdity, be imposed upon unwilling recipients. When men are forced to be free, neither those who are forced nor those who do the forcing are genuinely convinced of the value of freedom. Americans have seldom been content with the passive role of shining example, but their urge to do something to promote the global triumph of the values that they think the world needs has always encountered the question of what means are both effective and compatible with the values themselves.

The answer to this question has almost invariably entailed reliance upon international agencies of some kind. In the nineteenth century, Americans concerned about international relations turned with remarkable consistency to the idea of an international tribunal, a global approximation of the United States Surpeme Court whose very existence would symbolize, and whose operations would give effect to, the notion of the rule of law—fair play, justice, decisions based upon the merits of cases rather than upon the power of parties, equal treatment of all without regard to status, and the like.

In the twentieth century, emphasis has shifted from judicial to political institutions. First the League of Nations and subsequently the United States have been put forward as reflectors and carriers of American values. President Woodrow Wilson, as the principal architect of the League, clearly envisaged that organization as the embodiment of the principles of constitutional democracy on the international level and as an instrument for spreading the liberal values that he thought would be as good for the world as they were for the United States. Wilson did not succeed in convincing an adequate number of Americans of the accuracy of his view of the League; many of his critics saw it instead as a device by which the United States might be inveigled into complicity with essentially European regimes intent upon preserving a system of power politics that scorned American values. If Americans rejected the League on the ground that it expressed European values at odds with their own, many of the Europeans who entered it did so with skepticism derived from the belief that it embodied American values inappropriate to the realm of international relations; the conviction of Americans that Wilson had failed to put their imprint upon the League was matched by the conviction of Europeans that he had succeeded. I think that the Europeans were more nearly correct; it is impossible to read the

Covenant of the League without noting its American character, but its abandonment by the United States contributed to its failure to initiate the flowering of American values in the international system.

During World War II, the formulation of the plan for the United Nations system of international organizations was dominated by the United States, and the Charter of the United Nations negotiated at the San Francisco Conference of 1945 bears unmistakable signs of its American origins. From its opening words—"We the peoples of the United Nations"—onward, through provisions relating to human rights, self-determination, trusteeship, economic and social progress, peaceful settlement of disputes, and collective security, the Charter serves as a translation into the language of international relations of the political and social principles that constitute the American creed. Much of the same can be said of the constitutions of many of the Specialized Agencies that cluster around the United Nations. What could be more American, for instance, than the scheme for the independent participation of governments, trade unions, and employer groups in the International Labor Organization? The United States has obviously used its position of leadership in the creation of international organizations to put its ideological stamp upon those agencies. The basic documents of today's international organizations are to a considerable extent devoted to the formal endorsement of American values, constitutionally, of that value system.

It is evident that the United States regards international organizations as potentially useful carriers of its values into the workings of the multistate system and the domestic affairs of other states. Indeed, that vehicular function may be the most important one assigned to international agencies by the United States. This country's participaton in international organizations has seldom been inspired by the conviction that the United States has need of benefits that such institutions may be willing and able to confer upon it. Americans have, in fact, tended to be wary of the effects that international agencies might have upon their own society, and have concentrated on using these agencies to affect other societies. In this respect at least, Americans accept the biblical proposition that it is more blessed to give than to receive; they value international organizations as exporting rather than as importing agencies, and look to them not so much for support of American interests as for promotion of American values. The attitudes that pervaded American isolationism persist in American internationalism: the involvement of the United States in world affairs is a matter of choice, not of necessity; it is not a means of getting what we must have, but an optional method of giving to the world what we think it ought to receive.

This is not to say that the United States has conceived of international bodies as agents of American imperialism, even thought of them as providing an acceptable alternative to the morally repugnant course of imperialism, a hopeful answer to the question of how

American values can be made effective throughout the world without being betrayed and destroyed by the means adopted for their diffusion. The cynical view of the matter would emphasize the utility of the United Nations glove as cover for the American fist, with the implication that the United States has been less concerned to avoid than to conceal the imperialistic approach to the spreading of its values. Americans are by no means immune to the general human inclination to seek dominance and to deny that seeking, and it is no doubt true that they welcome the tactical advantage afforded by the affixing of the international label to American values. To suggest, however, that Americans want to impose their values upon the rest of the world while using international organizations to disguise the process of imposition is to deny that they really accept those values or wish to foster their spread. Insofar as the value commitment of Americans is genuine, they look to international agencies for something other than multilateral concealment of a unilateral quest for hegemony.

From the point of view of true believers who aspire to promote the global acceptance of American values, the creation and operation of international organizations provide legitimate occasions and opportunities for the United States to undertake the persuasion of other states. The constitutions of international organizations are, after all, freely negotiated and voluntarily ratified treaties, and their incorporation of the values advocated by the United States would appear to indicate that other states have found those values congenial. If multilateral agencies can be induced to serve the cause, they may be far more effective than the United States acting alone in encouraging the general adoption and facilitating the realization of the values that Americans believe essential to good societies at the national and international levels. For this purpose, international organizations are seen not only as institutions within which states may legitimately attempt to influence each other and to develop collaboration with like-minded states in pursuit of common objectives, but also as corporate entities capable of lending the prestige of a vaguely defined international community to a cause that might otherwise be regarded as the unilateral project to a self-interested state. Multilateral institutions offer the possibility of the certification of values advocated by the United States as internationally preferred values; they may be seen as transforming an American campaign into an international program for justice and order.

However much the United States may rely upon the United Nations and other international bodies for assistance in promoting American values, I think it is true that the American view of multilateral institutions has never been a purely instrumental one. Multilateralism is, in American thought, not merely a means of fostering the adoption and realization of values; it *is* a value, a good in itself, a part of the normative package that is to be sold to the world. In somewhat the same way that the church ranks for many Christians as the centerpiece of their religion, rather than merely as a useful device for propagating that religion, international organizations are regarded by many Americans as the heart of the message, rather than simply as the media. From this point of view, the creation, development, utilization, and support of multilateral agencies constitute an essential part of the *practice* of American values in international relations, just as attendance at church services and tithing are sometimes treated as essential parts of religious observance. International organization is the ecclesiastical component of the American political and social creed, as applied to the external realm.

This tendency to regard international agencies as ends, not simply as means to be valued according to their effectiveness, reflects the identification of multilateralism with such virtues as freedom of participation, rule by consent, and responsible consideration of the interests of all who may be affected by a decision. Multilateralists, if I may so designate champions of multilateralism, appear to offer a revised and expanded version of the title of one of Reinhold Niebuhr's best known works, *Moral Man and Immoral Society;* they convert it to *Moral Man, Immoral State, and Moral International Organization.* They do not disagree with Niebuhr's contention that the social collectivity, most notably the national state, tends to become the repository of the vices of its individual members. In the operation of multilateralism, however, they postulate some alchemy that transforms an aggregation of selfish, ruthless, and generally unenlightened states into an admirable society, the international analog of that all-too-rare phenomenon in the world of states, the constitutional democracy. It would appear that, in some mysterious fashion, states delegate their virtues to the collectivities that they form, or that multilateralism manages to filter the self-interested and antisocial qualities from the policy and behavior of states so that international organizations become morally superior to their constituent elements. This exalted view of multilateral institutions figures significantly in the tendency of the United States to give them a major role in its campaign for the diffusion of American values.

The American conception of the nature and the utility of international organizations, as I have described it, is a recipe for disillusionment. Multilateralism has no magic that transforms states or enables them to create composite entities better endowed than themselves with political virtue. Indeed, it may be that states tend to send their vices, not their virtues, to their larger groupings, so that Niebuhr's immoral societies spawn even more immoral super-societies. This view of the matter sometimes appears justified by the behavior of states in multilateral settings, where crowd psychology seems to produce ideological intoxication and where pressures for conformity overwhelm inclinations toward moderation and reasonableness. In any case, it is not obvious that the average moral quality of the proceedings of such a body as the General Assembly of the United Nations is superior to that of bilateral diplomacy. Moreover,

Americans have learned to their dismay that the ability of the founding fathers to embed their notions of the appropriate purposes of international agencies in constitutional documents does not imply the ability to determine the uses to which those agencies will be put by those who operate them as the years go by. The United States has also become acutely aware of the ephemeral quality of the prominence that it enjoyed in the management of international organizations during the first decade or so after World War II. One must question the assumption that the multilateral institutions of the international system are, or can be expected to become, expressions of American values and allies of the United States in the effort to imprint those values upon the world.

It should surprise no student of the world's political life in the twentieth century that in international organizations, as elsewhere, the outright repudiation of the values that Americans cherish and champion is exceedingly rare. No government is likely to describe itself as antidemocratic and contemptuous of human rights, or to present itself in the United Nations as committed to a policy of aggression and the extermination of small and weak states. Liberal values do receive tribute that goes considerably beyond lip-service; in what are usually the least noticed of the activities of multilateral agencies, those values are faithfully served by programs for promoting human welfare in a multitude of ways. Nevertheless, the commitment of multilateral institutions to the values with which the United States associates itself is highly selective, and those values are often, from the American standpoint, distorted or even perverted by agencies that purport to endorse and apply them. In fact, most global organizations today are dominated by states whose political and social values, practiced at home and impressed by them upon the organizations, are different from and even antithetical to those of the United States.

This situation creates puzzling problems for Americans. The first difficulty is to acknowledge the situation, to come to grips with the fact that international organizations may work against rather than for the ideals that Americans are likely to consider unchallengeably worthy of devotion—a discovery that for many is as traumatic as would be the discovery that churches were dens of atheism and iniquity or universities were the enemies of free thought and impartial inquiry. Confronted by the capture of the most prominent international bodies by political forces whose value systems have little in common with theirs, Americans are forced to question their attribution of value to multilateralism *per se.* Are adherence to the rules of multilateralism and respect for its results meritorious when multilateral institutions are exploited for causes that one finds morally offensive? Are the quasidemocractic aspects of multilateral procedure in international relations sufficiently weighty to offset the substantive evils that are multilaterally perpetrated? How ought the United States to react when it finds that multilateral institutions that it regards as valuable in principle are serving, in practice, to defeat

American values? If it would be petty of Americans in such a situation to pick up their marbles and go home, would they prove their magnanimity by acquiescing in the undermining of values in which they believe? In acceding to collective decisions of which they disapprove, do Americans demonstrate loyalty to multilateral procedures or disloyalty to their own values? Under existing circumstances, ought American resolve to struggle for a revived capacity to exercise substantial influence within and upon the United Nations and its associated agencies to be construed as evidence of courage and commitment or of unrealism and wishful thinking?

Such questions as these will plague thoughtful Americans for the foreseeable future, as they evidently plagued the leaders of the Carter administration who undertook to promote human rights throughout the world. The fact that President Jimmy Carter proposed American ratification of the major United Nations conventions dealing with human rights indicated his awareness that the legitimacy of his campaign would be strengthened by the involvement of the United States in the multilateral program, even though he never quite conceded the technical point that the United States had no legal standing to invoke those conventions against other states until and unless it became a party to them. Carter and his associates regarded active participation in the human rights efforts of international organizations as a useful supplement to activities carried on independently by the United States, but they were not inclined to emphasize the multilateral means to their objectives. Indeed, it may be less significant that Carter supported such participation by the United States than that his support was lukewarm and unproductive. He did not obtain the Senate's approval for ratification of human rights treaties, nor did he appear to regard this failure as a major setback for his program. His apparent indifference suggests that the Carter administration may have had misgivings about the multilateral approach; it may have entertained some doubts about the congruity of multilateral formulations with the American version of human rights, and about whether the United Nations was more likely to promote or to pervert the rights that occupy a central place in the American value system. It might be argued that President Carter's human rights program gave expression both to the traditional inclination to consider multilateral institutions as potential carriers of American values and to the more recent skepticism about those institutions' availability to serve causes favored by the United States.

The time has passed when one could, without the slightest discomfort or sense of incongruity, give allegiance both to the values of the American liberal tradition and to those of innovative and emergent multilateralism in the international system. The urge of the United States to use multilateral institutions to spread American values, and its tendency to make the flourishing of multilateral institutions one of its primary values, are on the agenda for reconsideration. The isssues of the exportablity of American values, the means by which they can be presented to the rest of the world, and the forms that they should take when applied to the international scene—all of these require fresh thinking.

CHAPTER TEN
AMERICAN VALUES AND
THE IDEOLOGICAL STRUGGLE:
TRUTH IS OUR WEAPON:
Edward M. Barrett

Laborers in the ideological struggle have long recognized that the free world suffered from one handicap: the lack of a dynamic appeal that would fire men's imaginations with a zeal and fervor approaching that of the Communists. Some have even yearned for Communist-like fanaticism, though others view fanaticism as a dangerous element incompatible with true freedom.

Volunteer advisers grope for the same sort of thing. They often talk confidently, if vaguely, of the need for "a new psychological crusade," of "starting an offensive that captures the imaginations of mankind," and of "mobilizing the vast spiritual forces of freedom." In their speeches and articles, they unfortunately neglect the matter of just how to do all this. Indeed, after reading a few of these clarion calls, one distinguished and wise friend recently put tongue in cheek and wrote me:

> Of course, we can always fall back on the recently proclaimed formula of acquiring a sense of mission and purpose which will unloose such moral and spiritual forces that the edifice of despotism will crumble into dust, without anybody having to work at it. Lovely work if you can get it, though some of our fellow citizens might find that building up their spiritual natures was about as painful as paying war taxes.

Of course, the free world's ideology needs—and deserves—more widespread, fervent, and enthusiastic support. Some slight and very gradual progress has been made in that direction. Certainly, however, in some years of work in the field I never found any simple formula. Nor did I come upon anyone else who had done so. At most we began vaguely to detect a few clues. Studies of the great fanatical mass movements of history have helped to clarify some of those clues—and have cast light on the whole problem, including the grave question of whether a truly fanatical counter-movement is really wanted. Analyses of the world's mass movements, particularly the extraordinary study of *The True Believer* by Eric Hoffer, have led to fascinating conclusions. Among them are these:

Frustrated souls have always provided the backbone for the truly fanatical mass movements. Most of these individuals come from among the intensely discontented poor, the misfits, the outcasts, the inordinately powerhungry, the bored, the temporarily frustrated youths, the resentful minorities, and the sinners seeking escape from a guilty conscience. All are trying to "get away" from themselves; all seek sweeping change.

By the time such frustrated characters are ripe for a fanatical movement, they are usually ready for any such movement without regard to particular doctrines or programs. The fanatic seems generally to embrace a cause not chiefly because of its righteousness or holiness but because of his violent need for something to hold onto. He wants to lose himself; in what cause he does so is relatively unimportant. In the 1930's it was a toss-up as to whether many discontented German youths would go Communist or Nazi. Moreover, the adult fanatic who deserts his holy cause can rarely return to normal existence. As Eric Hoffer put it, he is an "eternal hitch-hiker on the highways of the world, thumbing a ride on any eternal cause that rolls by." He is even ready to enlist in a fanatical crusade against his old cause, provided it is a full-scale crusade—strident, uncompromising, intolerant, and devoted to the one and only truth. Hitler recognized this when he ordered that ex-Communists should be admitted to the Nazi Party without delay. Communists are recognizing it today in proselytizing ex-Nazis in East Germany.

(The nature of the Communist fanatic, incidentally, makes one wonder about current tendencies to lionize American ex-Communists and put them on pedestals from which to lecture all citizens who had sense enough never to become Communists in the first place. Some of us suspect the typical ex-Communist—particularly the recent Communist—has great value as an informer and tipster but hardly any as a propounder of eternal verities.)

In their susceptibility to mass movements, both the extreme reactionary and the extreme radical have more in common with each other than with sober liberals or moderate conservatives. Both extremists loathe the present and both seek change. Though one seeks innovations and the other seeks what he considers glorious restitution, they often can wind up in the same cause.

Freedom is not a first-rank goal for fanatics in such movements. Those seeking to escape themselves usually want equality and fraternity far more than liberty. Equality provides the anonymity of being an equal part of a great whole; individual liberty and freedom of choice leave the blame for any failure on the shoulders of the individual.

Ingredients of the fanatical mass movement include extravagant hope for the future, symbols and make-believe, and a sense of great power growing either from an "infallible leader" or some powerful doctrine. The effectiveness of the doctrine generally depends less on its logic than on its certitude. The most effective doctrine usually is vague or unintelligible. At the least, it is unverifiable in that its truth can be proved only in heaven or in the remote future. In any case, it must be advanced as the one and only truth.

Religious faith and nationalism are often the sources of mass enthusiasm. But fanatical mass movements can rise and spread without belief in a god. They never do so without belief in a devil. Hatred of a devil, preferably a tangible one, indeed, appears the most universal and powerful force in such movements. Hitler said Jews would have to be invented if they did not exist, because "it is essential to have a tangible enemy."

One way to stop a mass movement is to substitute another movement for it, preferably a good one for a bad one. But the method is sometimes dangerous. The countermovements can get out of hand. As Hoffer pointed out, practical businessmen in Germany and Italy behaved logically when they encouraged Nazism and Fascism in order to stop Communism. But by so doing these practical people promoted their own liquidation. Again, Premier Mossadegh of Iran became the captive of the runaway nationalism he helped to arouse.

Viewed thus, the fanatical mass movement may well be an instrumentality the free nations do not want and should not attempt to use. In political fields, what attracts fanatical men often repels reasoning men. Most such movements can get out of hand. Moreover, the things in which Americans believe and for which they will fight are the antithesis of simple dogma and unreasoning conformity. Bascially, the free nations are struggling for an *absence* of rigid doctrine, restraints, and regimentation.

Nonetheless, there are degrees of zeal and fervor short of the type of dangerously fanatical "movements" dealt with above. Analysis of these movements, plus practical experience in combating them, at least provides clues to possible methods of generating enthusiasm of the sort too often missing from the free world effort. If there is no pat formula, at least four clues seem worth particular mention.

The Force of Religion

As one surveys the battle against Communism in various areas, he cannot fail to note that religious forces have been in the vanguard of effective opponents. The Catholic Church has proved a powerful deterrent in many nations. Father Keller's Christophers have aroused great zeal for the anti-Communist cause. The Moral Rearmament movement, whatever its critics may say on other scores, has shown notable anti-Communist efficacy in parts of Europe and in Japan. Buddhist priests have often been among the most effective exposers of Communism's flaws.

In my . . . [years] in Washington, my colleagues and I came to recognize that too little attention and too little support had been accorded to the great appeal of godliness versus godlessness, the spiritual appeal against the solely materialistic. We formed a Catholic-Protestant-Jewish advisory panel. With great help from that panel, the information program then began to emphasize appropriate religous matters far more than formerly. Materials stressing Communism's incompatibility with any of the world's great religions began to flow from the U.S.I.S. The government encouraged the production of Arthur Goodfriend's moving book, *What Can A Man Believe,* and facilitated its translation into eleven languages in Asia and the Far East. In words and pictures, it dramatically contrasted the faith and ideals of the world's religions with the cynical ruthlessness of the Kremlin gangsters.

Many other steps were taken. They were only a beginning. With Soviet Communism more clearly ranging itself against all religions each day, the potential of religious faith as a counterforce to Communism becomes enormous.

I will venture no simple "formula"; I doubt that any exists. It is now evident, however, that the spiritual content of America's Campaign of Truth deserves not only part-time help from a wise religious panel but full-time creative work over an extended period by a group of the ablest churchmen in America. And, as the great religions of the world chart their parallel counter offensives against the common foe, they will deserve all the support and assistance that free governments can properly give.

The "Devil's" Role

"We should stop being negative," say internal and external critics of government information efforts. "We should emphasize what we are *for* rather than what we are *against.*" The advice has become a truism in propaganda. Each time it has been heard, I and others have nodded our heads in thoughtful agreement.

With benefit of perspective, I am not so sure. The negative task of exposing the gigantic hoax of Soviet Communism is important and, in many areas, more persuasive than any honest picture that can be painted of democracy and freedom.

Americans and other champions of freedom cannot honestly promise that Arabs and Burmese and Pakistani will automatically partake of the Abundant Life two years, or even ten years from now, if they only will spurn Communism and follow the course of freedom.

The only honest promise is that free men working together, with mutual assistance, can slowly but steadily improve the economy, health, and well-being in their areas—and without enslaving themselves.

At the same time, it is possible, practicable, and persuasive to reveal the fraud of Communist promises and to expose the conditions actually existing in Soviet-dominated areas. Among the peoples of Asia, I know of no single item of persuasion that was more powerful than the authentic and credible story called "When the Communists Came." It told simply and authoritatively the story of Communist promises to a Chinese village, of the village's capitulation to the Communists, and then of the privation and brutality that followed. It was "negative propaganda." Yet, without it, the mild affirmative propaganda about the promises of freedom would have lacked appeal. "When the Communists Came" proved so persuasive that the United States Information Service reproduced it in twenty-odd languages, first as a booklet, then as a comic book, and finally as a film. When the U.S.I.S. assisted native groups abroad in obtaining and disseminating similar authentic material, the "negative" propaganda became even more persuasive.

As has been seen, the great mass movements have always had a devil. Hatred of the devil has usually proved more potent than any affirmative element. In the free nations' campaign of persuasion, no devil has to be invented. The Soviet tyrants already constitute one—more ruthless and more brutal than most men can believe. Perhaps the most important single step in enlisting zeal and enthusiasm for the free nations' cause is full revelation of the nature of Kremlin Communism. Particularly important is it to demonstrate that a people cannot just choose the Soviet path today and reverse the decision tomorrow; once in the clutches of Soviet tyranny, there is no easy turning back. When that realization has sunk fully into men's minds, the mild and hardly flamboyant promises that can be made in behalf of democracy begin to look pretty tempting. Berliners have been the most zealous foes of the Soviet in all of free Europe not because they have a more optimistic view of freedom but because they have had the closest view of Kremlin-style tyranny.

Precise methods of exposing the devil are another subject. Often exposes can be most effective when they are done by fellow citizens of the audience group. The blunt fact remains that portraying fully and accurately the bogey of what we are *against* is often more effective than any "affirmative" material in arousing determined resistance to Communist imperialism.

The Presidential Symbol

It is extremely difficult to create enthusiasm for a complex and intangible cause. It is much easier to do so when there is a dynamic personality to serve as a symbol. That has always been true. Woodrow Wilson acquired great symbolic importance in World War II; public squares and streets were named for him in much of Europe. Churchill and Roosevelt likewise became important symbols in World War II and made great psychological contributions to the eventual triumph.

In the past, political critics have been quick to pounce on the efforts of any administration to dramatize its own chieftain around the world. In the last war, many complained vociferously at O.W.I.'s "using the taxpayer's money" to publicize F.D.R. in other lands. One might have thought the citizens of Germany, Iran, and Thailand had decisive votes in U.S. elections.

There is no room for such nonsense today. Had the election of 1952 gone to the Democrats, Adlai Stevenson's personality and his deft, inspiring prose should have been dramatized around the world. As matters stand, Dwight Eisenhower's talent for leadership, his infectious smile, and his air of confidence were publicized to the hilt. Despite captious critics, the President and his subordinates should have no qualms about it. As a symbol of free-world confidence determination, and friendliness, he was a priceless asset. Overseas promotion of that asset will not swing a single precinct to Republicanism; it can help swing entire nations to democracy.

A "Creed of Freedom"

For some years, officials engaged in the propaganda of truth have looked for what might be called an "American Creed" or even a "Free World Creed." Paul Hoffman, in winding up his ECA stewardship, called for such a creed which would "walk up and down in the hearts of men." John Foster Dulles groped for it in his book *War or Peace*. Lesser lights, including myself, have attempted drafts—with discouraging results. One of the efforts in which I participated was designed to become a ringing declaration by the North Atlantic Council of Foreign Ministers. By the time that draft was modified to meet the criticisms of all the governments concerned, it deserved just the treatment it got: being buried in an official communique.

There can be interminable discussion of whether any ringing and reasonably brief creed is possible without resort to gross over-simplification. Some will argue that freedom-loving peoples who produced a Magna Carta and a Declaration of Independence, both drawing upon principles of Confucius, Plato, and Christ Himself, *should* be able to produce a rousing twentieth-century document. Others, including men of intellectual stature, argue that no simple, reasonably brief credo is practicable, that free men stand basically for diversity and resistance to rigid doctrine. They add that the best way to "sell" the cause of free nations is by continuous statement and restatement of the whole array of beliefs that differentiate the way of free men from the way of tyrants.

At any rate, many continue the quest, convinced that the effort to clarify basic beliefs will be a healthy force even if it does not produce a ringing document. The Ford Foundation has underwritten an effort by a panel of leading citizens to restate American principles and purposes. *Fortune* magazine has made efforts in the same direction. So have others. The U.N.'s Universal Declaration of Human Rights is a significant document, if not one that stirred men's hearts. It deserves renewed attention. Eisenhower's generally admirable Inaugural Address contained some elements of great international appeal. But the modern creed that is both fully honest and emotionally thrilling has not yet been produced.

The main principles are not too obscure or too controversial. They were embodied, clearly if not briefly, in a draft statement of foreign policy by members of the U.S. Advisory Commission on International Information in early 1953. Many individuals contributed to that draft, and a few fragments from it found their way into the President's Inaugural Address of 1953. It was hardly a ringing document. But, as an indication of content rather than as any stirring appeal, the opening paragraphs are worth printing here:

The foreign policy of the United States must be based on three universal cornerstones:

The first is the Principle of Self-determination. The second is the Fact of Interdependence of all peoples. The third is a deep and abiding faith in mankind under God.

Our nation, like many others, stands committed to the principle of self-determination. Our nations stands committed to it for *all* nations, and above all for *small* nations.

It is a principle upon which our own government is founded. But it is not something new and unique with the United States. It is an idea borrowed from the ages. It is a legacy from many lands. It is the common heritage of all freedom-loving people.

The Principle of Self-determination affirms, in moral terms, the privilege of all men to choose their own way of life, subject only to the condition that the rights of one individual shall not violate the rights of others. It affirms, in political terms, the territorial integrity of all nations. It means, in social terms, a concept that leads ultimately to government based upon the dignity and supremacy of individual man.

The second cornerstone is the fact that all free peoples are interdependent. This is a great and important realization of the twentieth century—that the political, economic, and moral well-being of all men relates directly to our own.

It involves the need for the full, free, and continuous flow of ideas across boundaries. Only through the interchange of ideas can the free nations progress together toward a common understanding, and a mutual plan of operation to achieve a common cause. There must be no iron curtain on ideas between the free nations of the world.

The third cornerstone is faith in our fellow men throughout the world—faith in the innate decency, honesty, and integrity of men in all nations and of all creeds who are guided by the God of their fathers, and not by any mortal man who seeks to destroy every God under which reverent men worship.

No universal brotherhood of man would ever be possible if the freedom to worship in the churches, the temples, the mosques, and the tabernacles of our ancestors were denied us.

These are the cornerstones. We gladly accept the duty to recognize and implement the Principle of Self-determination, the Fact of Interdependence, and to let faith in God and faith in our fellow men guide us in all of our policy making.

The formula for a rousing, yet meaningful, new "creed of freedom" may or may not be found. Any one-and-only document is unlikely. But constant, clear, and forthright restatement of principles like these can help produce, if not fervent enthusiasm, at least solid understanding, faith, and resoluteness.

CHAPTER ELEVEN
DIPLOMACY AND THE TRANSMISSION
OF VALUES
Emmett B. Ford, Jr.

"Diplomacy" is defined quite briefly in the Oxford Dictionary as the "management of international relations." It has also been described as the means by which foreign policy is implemented.

In the United States the institution charged with the management of international relations or with the implementation of foreign policy is the Foreign Service, which functions as the diplomatic and consular arm of the Department of State. Any analysis of the part which diplomacy plays in the propagation abroad of American political and social values must, therefore, be focused on the Foreign Service and the role which American diplomats and consular officers have played and still do play in the transmission of these values to foreign populations.

From the very founding of the Republic, the sort of men who served in the American establishment now known as the Foreign Service has reflected to an astonishing degree, the changing attitudes and values of American society as a whole. During the first thirty or forty years, for example, diplomats and consuls (like early presidents and Congressmen) were drawn from the ablest and best-educated segment of the population. Envoys and secretaries of state such as Benjamin Franklin, John Adams, Thomas Jefferson, James Madison, James Monroe, John Quincy Adams, and Washington Irving set a standard for excellence which has not since been equaled. Americans of that day seemed to appreciate the necessity for sending only the cream of their society to represent the young Republic abroad.

As the nineteenth century wore on, however, this Olympian standard declined precipitously. No longer did the continued security of the United States seem to depend so heavily upon the diplomatic skill and impressive stature of American representatives in London, Paris, and Madrid. As that peculiarly American type, the professional politician, began to supplant well-educated statesmen in Congress and the White House, the practice of handing out prestigious and/or lucrative foreign posts as patronage became the rule rather than the exception. The concept which underlay the spoils system—that any reasonably intelligent citizen is capable of performing any government job, whether it be that of postmaster or of ambassador—has, since the administration of Andrew Jackson, provided a rationalization for the routine distribution of diplomatic and consular posts in discharge of political debts or as rewards to personal friends.

According to that great British arbiter of diplomatic practice, Sir Harold Nicolson, the reputation of American diplomacy (and, implicitly, the foreign perception of American values) suffered as a result of appointments made under the spoils system. "A political supporter," he wrote, "who was accorded the perquisite of an Embassy or a Legation was all too often more concerned with maintaining his publicity value in his hometown than with serving the rights and interests of his own country abroad. The capitals of Europe and Latin America echoed with the indiscretions of these amateur diplomatists and much damage was done to all concerned."

An outstanding example of such political appointees was an unemployed former governor who was named American Ambassador to the Court of St. James. Although it was generally conceded, even by his friends, that the only qualifications he had for such a position were his presumed ability to communicate in English and his known ability to deliver votes in his home state, he eagerly accepted the honour bestowed upon him by a grateful president. Properly sensitive to the populist sentiments which prevailed among his constituents, however, he felt it necessary to explain to them that he had no intention of allowing himself to be seduced by foreign wiles and customs. In a hilarious newspaper interview which appeared shortly after agreement, he solemnly vowed that the Department of State would never force *him* to dress up in "funny knee britches" or "bow and scrape" for his presentation to the King of England or to any other foreign potentate. Unhappily for the governor (but fortunately for the United States), he died before he could assume charge of the embassy in London.

It was not until after World War I, and forty years after the passage of the Civil Service Act, that the Congress could finally be persuaded to regard diplomatic and consular service as a profession requiring special knowledge and training. In 1924, the Congress acted to establish the Foreign Service of the United States of America, based largely upon foreign service organizations which had long been in existence in England and France. Like its British and French prototypes, this new foreign service incorporated as essential features competitive entrance examinations, protected tenure, and merit promotion.

As a consequence of the tightened requirements of the Foreign

Service Act, especially the very selective screening offered by the competitive entrance examinations, diplomatic and consular ranks gradually began to be filled with well-educated and highly professional young men. The more-often-than-not incompetent dilettantes who had for so long misrepresented their country as vice-consuls and second secretaries were increasingly displaced by such budding junior officers as Charles Bohlen, George Kennan, Llwellyn Thompson, and Loy Henderson. For the first time in several generations, the quality of American diplomats, and hence, American diplomacy, began to earn the respect both of host country officials and of diplomatic colleagues throughout the world.

The quality steadily improved until the outbreak of World War II. Foreign Service officers were being inducted at the bottom, bringing with them solid grounding in the academic essentials for a diplomatic career—history, English, economics, and languages. A greater and greater proportion of ambassadorial and ministerial appointments were going to trained career officers and less to the amateurs. Nicholson noted that by 1938, career ambassadors were assigned to nine of the seventeen American embassies which then existed (most of these in Europe), and career ministers to the over half of the thirty-nine legations.

Yet, despite the fact that it was no longer necessary to have a private income in order to enter the Foreign Service, many, if not most, of those who passed the very stiff entrance examinations came from the upper middle class, and some were even wealthy. Many, if not most, belonged to what has been called "the Eastern establishment," and a majority had graduated from Ivy League or other top-ranked private universities.

Although this new and more professional foreign Service Officer was far better attuned to and equipped for diplomatic service than his politically-appointed predecessor, he certainly did not resemble the average American. As for the average American of the time, he pictured the diplomat as a distinctly exotic person who habitually dressed in morning coat and striped trousers, spoke with an affected British accent, and did nothing but attend teas and cocktail parties. Thus, while these new professionals were correctly perceived by the people of host countries and diplomatic colleagues from other countries as an American elite, they were regarded by their compatriots, including most Congressmen, as "unrepresentative," or, at worst, "unAmerican" in their lifestyles.

Unfortunately, the American people, as de Toqueville once observed, do not take kindly to being governed or represented by what they regard as an elite leadership, even if this leadership is distinguished only by superior educational attainment. Whether it be their elected officials, their bureaucrats, their diplomats or their president, they have always felt more comfortable with someone of ordinary talents and ancient republican virtues. Because of this attitude, the new professionals came increasingly under attack for being unable, by the very reason of their elitist qualifications, to represent American values abroad. Indeed, the vast majority of congressmen believed along with their constituents that the primary function of diplomatic and consular officers was to represent and "sell" the values of Middle America to the rest of the world.

There arose, as a consequence, a distinct bias against admission into the Foreign Service of candidates who were adjudged to be "atypical" or "unrepresentative" Americans. Some candidates, no matter how well they had performed on the exhaustive written exam, might be turned down by the examining board for being too suave, too precise in their speech, or too "European" in their appearance or mannerisms.

In this connection there is a somewhat apocryphal, but true, story told about a brilliant candidate who applied for the Foreign Service during this period of bias against anyone not fitting a "typical American" stereotype. Although this young man had graduated from one of the best universities in the country and had scored exceptionally high on the written examination, the examining board did not approve his immediate entrance into the Service on the grounds that his dress and mannerisms were too "European." Raising particular objection to his habit of carrying a cane, wearing doeskin gloves most of the time, and stuffing his handkerchief up his sleeve, the board told him to get a job in a filling station somewhere in the Middle West where he might familiarize himself with the manners and customs of real Americans, and to present himself for another oral examination the following year.

The candidate dutifully worked for a good part of the year pumping gasoline (which he called petrol) at a Texaco station in the heart of Illinois. When he appeared before the examining board the following June, however, neither his dress nor his mannerisms seemed to have changed in the slightest. Taxed by members of the board with his apparent failure to assimilate the tribal customs of Americans, he said he did not really see how his personal appearance and manners could reflect badly upon the country which he would represent. Then he added as something of an afterthought that, while *he* might not have changed much, several of the other lads at the filling station were now carrying canes, wearing doeskin gloves, and stuffing their handkerchief up their sleeves.

The advent of World War II marked the beginning of the end of the short-lived predominance of a professional elite in the Foreign Service. With the inevitable wartime increase in overseas responsibilities, the Service was forced to appoint large numbers of "temporary" diplomatic and administrative officers in order to staff expanded embassies, missions, and consulates throughout the world. Unfortunately, those temporary appointees who might otherwise have qualified as Foreign Service officers for the most part returned to private life at the end of the war, while a great many of the unqualified managed to move from temporary status to permanent tenure. Only the continued leadership of career officers, new as well as old, enabled the Foreign Service to maintain, for a time, its professional reputation and the respect of the foreign governments to which it represented.

Today, as the result of a variety of social and political pressures over the past twenty years, the Foreign Service enjoys neither a strong professional reputation nor the respect of foreign government and their populations. It has been integrated, democratized, and politicized to the point at which it resembles just another mediocre Washington bureaucracy, distinguished only by the fact that it has overseas branches. It is far surpassed in the professional competence of its personnel and the quality of its diplomacy by the British, the French, the Dutch, the Belgians, the Swiss, the Austrians, and quite a few others.

Why has this come to pass? First of all because latter-day presidents are reverting more and more to the spoils-system appointment of ambassadors and other senior diplomatic officers. Secondly because, in the name of sexual equality, racial equality, and general egalitarianism, the nation no longer seeks the best and the brightest of its young men and women for the Foreign Service, but rather those who are as good as possible so long as they represent all elements of a pluralistic society. "Elitism" has become a pejorative, if not an extremely dirty word.

If it is accepted as a premise that, in the ideal diplomatic establishment, all but an exceptional few ambassadors and other senior officials should be career diplomats (Britain usually has only two non-career ambassadors serving world-wide at any one time), the United States Foreign Service is currently in a deplorable state. Slightly more than half of President Reagan's ambassadors are political appointees—personal friends or the recipients of political grace and favor almost none of who has the slightest diplomatic training or experience. President Carter's record in this respect was almost as bad. What is truly disturbing in this day and age, however, is the trend toward the appointment of more and more amateur ambassadors. Presidents who would never dream of appointing a corporation lawyer to the bridge of an aircraft carrier or a real estate tycoon to command an army corps see nothing at all wrong with sending a doctor, a lawyer, or an Indian chief to manage the political, economic, and administrative complexity of a modern American Embassy.

In 1924, when the Foreign Service was established, it was confidently assumed by the Congress and the administration that eventually the vast majority of senior State Department and Foreign Service officers would be professionals and the virtually all ambassadorial appointments would be made from the ranks of the Foreign

Service. Now, almost 60 years later, the trend is running in the opposite direction. Indeed, the present situation in this regard approximates that described by Sir Harold Nicolson when he wrote: "The capitals . . . echoed with the indiscretions of these amateur diplomats and much damage was done to all concerned."

Much damage continues to be done, not only to the efficient conduct of American foreign policy, but to the image projected abroad of the American value system. The usual political appointee is instantly recognized as such by the foreign community in the capital to which he is assigned. Generally he speaks no language but English and knows little about the politics or culture of the country. Quite often he is privately regarded by the foreign minister and head of government with amused contempt as well as some feeling of being offended that the President of the United States of America could not send an accomplished diplomat, as, for example, the British and the French always do. Every foreign national who has contact with the typical American amateur has occasion to wonder whether this usually rather pleasant, but naive and ignorant, man really represents the governing elite in America. (Only the Russians seem to match the American in the number of unqualified or incompetent ambassadors they appoint.)

Until recently, however, despite any given amateur ambassador's lack of qualifications and experience, he could always count on having a well-trained and highly-skilled staff of career officers to do his work and to make him look good. His Deputy Chief of Mission or second in command was carefully selected by the Department of State from among those senior officers who had had fifteen to twenty years of experience behind them, and who could either serve as his close advisor or simply run the mission in his name. Even his junior officers—second and third secretaries and vice consuls—were very knowledgeable young men and could be depended upon to do their own jobs with a minimum of supervision and a maximum of enthusiasm. In short, the political appointee or amateur ambassador has customarily taken charge of a mission which could function very effectively under the leadership of his career deputy, whether or not he was actually at the helm.

There are disturbing indications, however, that no ambassador, amateur or career, can count any longer upon the support of a highly-skilled career staff upon taking charge of a mission. Foreign Service officers today are simply not as well trained or as highly-skilled as they were a generation ago. As the career officers of twenty-five and thirty years service retire, many posts overseas are left without even a leavening of the old professionals.

The progressive deterioration of the quality of the Foreign Service over the past generation can be directly attributed to fundamental social changes which have taken place in American body politic during that period. In the Foreign Service—as in many other

American institutions—reforms have been introduced and changes have been put into effect, not to raise the standards of performance of its personnel or to enhance the effectiveness of American diplomacy, but to meet some new social objective regarded as necessary for domestic political reasons. And, if such an objective comes into conflict with a professional requirement, the requirement has had to give way.

The first such objective during this period was the integration of the Foreign Service Staff Corps (mostly junior and middle grade consular and administrative officers who were not eligible for diplomatic assignment) and State Department Officers (junior, middle, and senior grade officers who were not required to do overseas duty) into the ranks of Foreign Service. This was done upon the recommendation of a presidential panel whose avowed purpose was to "democratize" the Foreign Service, thereby eliminating it as "a separate and elite caste" within the American foreign relations establishment. Predictably this mixing of apples, oranges, and bananas was a failure; not only did it create some monumental administrative problems within the Service, but it had the effect of filling many overseas posts with people who had no business dealing on a diplomatic level with foreign governments.

Next came the decision to lower substantially the educational qualifications required of entering Foreign Service officers. The competitive entrance examination was reduced from twenty-one hours to three, and from an exhaustive testing of general academic knowledge, including the ability to write well in the English language, to a true-false, multiple-choice, sort of test closely resembling the Scholastic Aptitude Test (which, strangely enough, is also the product of the E.T.S. in Princeton). While it is still a technical requirement that every candidate pass an examination in at least one foreign language, this requirement is waived more often than not, sometimes for years, sometimes indefinitely. Although this lowering of standards did have the desired effect of making the Foreign Service somewhat more accessible to so-called "minority" elements in American society, it has placed American Foreign Service officers at a serious disadvantage in dealing with their counterparts from other countries, most of whom are more intelligent, better-educated, and bi-lingual if not polyglot.

Several other undisguised efforts at social engineering have had a devastating effect on the morale and effectiveness of the Foreign Service as an instrument for the management of international relations. One such is the policy of setting higher admission threshold scores for white male candidates than for minority and female candidates. Another is a policy demanded by women's liberation activists encouraging the wives of Foreign Service officers to refrain from participation in that wide range of social and cultural activity which diplomatic wives (including even those from Communist countries) traditionally undertake in support of their husbands. Lastly, there has been the virtual dismantling of the selection-out system (promotion after a certain number of years in grade or dismissal from the Foreign Service)—which had always served to clear the way to the top for the most effective officers—mainly because a disproportionately great number of "minority" officers were being selected out.

It might be concluded from all this that those who have worked for the "democratization" of the diplomatic arm, and its recruitment from a broad spectrum of representative Americans have, on the whole, succeeded. But they have not succeeded in thereby fashioning a better instrument for the "selling" of American values throughout the rest of the world—that simply cannot be done and should not be done.

In this diverse world of sovereign and independent nation states, the primary objective of American diplomacy must be the security of the United States and the pursuit of those vital interests which ensure that security. It is basic to the security of all nations that no one nation shall interfere for any reason in the internal affairs of another. Any attempt to impose American standards or institutions on foreign societies or even to "sell" America abroad like some sort of magic elixir will invariably be resisted, resented, and counter-productive. Americans may deplore and denounce repression, brutality, and undemocratic regimes, but they have no right to expect their government to reward or punish a foreign government which does not happen to share the American view of what is right and what is wrong.

To extend the definition, "diplomacy is the management of international relations *among recognized governments*"—not among peoples. Diplomacy should deal with values only to the extent that values affect power relationships, e.g., the Shite revolution against the Shah of Iran. Accordingly, although diplomats should have a deep and comprehensive knowledge of the values of the foreign peoples among whom they work, they should rarely, if ever, be employed either as examples or as conveyors of American values.

Secretary of State Alexander Haig stated last year that "the President's foreign policy seeks to establish a world environment which is hospitable to fundamental American values—above all the freedom and dignity of the individual." The establishment of a hospitable environment deals with power relationships and is, therefore, the work of the Foreign Service. Explaining or exemplifying American values is someone else's job.

CHAPTER TWELVE
THE PEACE CORPS AND THE GRASSROOTS
Harris Wofford

The first Peace Corps Director, Sargent Shriver, liked to tell the story of how an African mother calmed her child who had fled in fear of the first white American to be seen in their village. "Don't worry," she said, "he's not a white man, he's not an American—he's a Peace Corps Volunteer."

A variation on that theme occurred during the 1965 crisis in the Dominican Republic. In the midst of an angry wave of anti-Americanism, a sign appeared: "Yankees go home—Cuerpo de Paz [Peace Corps] stay."

Many of the more than 80,000 Americans who have served in the Peace Corps—in 88 countries—since 1961 have enjoyed similar high moments of popular acceptance in their host communities. The primary experience of the Peace Corps, according to former Volunteer Michael Sellon, was "becoming in mind, and even more in spirit, those very people we had come to help—we *felt* like Dominicans, and *reacted* like Tanganyikans." Speaking on behalf of the first 5,000 Volunteers to return from service, Roger Landrum declared, "We are sons and daughters of America but we are in a sense also sons and daughters of a thousand towns and villages scattered around the world."

Nevertheless, in spite of this international or supranational spirit emphasized by former Volunteers and by people in the countries where they served, the Peace Corps was indeed very American. The Volunteers were never more American than in their determination to be accepted as more than just American.

The bold promise in the very name "Peace Corps" is an example of the kind of ambition—and presumption—the world associates with America. In the years after the launching of the U.S. Peace Corps, parallel organizations for overseas volunteer service were started in eighteen countries, but none carried the banner "Peace Corps." An

12-1

"International Peace Corps Secretariat" was formed to promote and coordinate all such ventures, but the name was soon changed to the more modest "International Secretariat for Volunteer Service." Only the Americans persisted, without apparent embarrassment, in calling their program the Peace Corps.

That is not quite accurate. A non-governmental movement of community service volunteers, organized in India in the 1950s by the followers of Gandhi, was called the "Shanti Sena"—"Peace Army." And the Soviet government and Communist parties had for years tried to claim a monopoly on the word "Peace," including various international youth "Peace Brigades." Indeed, the Congress of the United States was using the favorite Russian slogan—"Peace and Friendship"—when it declared in 1961, "The purpose of this Act is to promote world peace and friendship through a Peace Corps. . . ."

Although competition with the Russians for the "minds and hearts" of other peoples was no doubt one of the motives of the U.S. Congress, the Peace Corps reflected an older American sense of special mission in the world. "Where liberty is, there is my country," said Benjamin Franklin. The younger Tom Paine replied, "Where is *not* liberty, there is mine." From the founding fathers through Lincoln and Wilson, American leaders have repeatedly declared that the American Revolution was intended for all mankind. In his first year as President, Thomas Jefferson expressed "the hope and belief that the inquiry which has been excited among the mass of mankind by our revolution and its consequences will ameliorate the condition of man over a great portion of the globe."

The sober President John Adams traced the source of America's special mission back a century and a half before the Revolution. He looked on the original "settlement of America with reverence and wonder" because he saw it "as the opening of a grand scene and design in Providence for the emancipation of the slavish part of mankind all over the earth." The new colony, the Puritans had declared, would be a "city set upon a hill" for all the world to watch.

In his first testimony to Congress on behalf of the proposed Peace Corps, Sargent Shriver placed the new plan squarely in this old tradition. He told of the question put to him in India by the Gandhian leader, Ashadevi Aryanayakam. She had traveled three days and nights to say to him: "Yours was the first revolution. Do you think young Americans possess the spiritual values they must have to bring the spirit of that revolution to our country?" Ashadevi added: "There is a great valuelessness spreading around the world and in India, too. Your Peace Corps Volunteers must bring more than science and technology. They must touch the idealism of America and bring that to us, too. Can they do it?" Shriver told the Senate Foreign Relations Committee: "Our answer, based on faith, was Yes."

In the response to the idea—250,000 applicants during the first seven years—it was clear that the idealism of many Americans had been tapped. In the performance of the Volunteers overseas during their two-year terms of service—a total of 25,000 Volunteers from 1961 to 1966, over 80,000 by 1980—it has been shown that American idealism could be applied on a substantial scale.

This applied idealism of the Peace Corps reflected another important aspect of America—the practical Yankee spirit of volunteer service which was also part of America's reputation in the world. In the early 19th century Alexis de Tocqueville described how a direct, neighborly "can do" approach to any community problem and the practice of voluntary association characterized Americans everywhere he went in the new country. In accepting the Republican nomination for President in 1980, Ronald Reagan pledged "to restore in our time, the American spirit of volunteer service . . . a spirit that flows like a deep and mighty river through the history of our nation." The Peace Corps was launched on this river in 1961 as a way to restore that spirit. At the heart of the Peace Corps, Shriver told the Senate Committee in 1961, is the spirit of volunteer service—"that quality in American life which de Tocqueville . . . saw as the central source of American strength."

America was settled, the American Revolution was fought, and the Peace Corps was formed with mixed motives, not all of them so high-flown or above suspicion. If a Yankee is born, as Mark Twain put it, "with the dream of a republic in his head," he has also been known for his shrewd concern for his own self-interest. If a Yankee's instinct is to "invent, contrive, create, reorganize things, set brain and hand to work, and keep them busy," he usually has taken his cut of the gains. (Mark Twain's Connecticut Yankee in King Arthur's Court insisted upon one percent of the increase in revenue his reforms brought Camelot).

The gains that President Kennedy, Congress, and the American public hoped for from the Peace Corps went beyond the promotion of peace and friendship, and the world's response was mixed and not merely applause. The favorable reaction of most leaders of non-Communist developing nations sprang in part from the world's old romance with a young America, and perhaps also from a desire to please John Kennedy, who embodied that America. There was also the natural skepticism of other nation-states in a competitive world. "American P.R.," "Cold War propaganda," "an anti-Russian ploy," "a C.I.A. front" were some of the cynical charges from abroad.

Concern for public relations—for "a better American image"—was certainly one of the factors that persuaded Congress to establish the Peace Corps and appropriate $30 million for its first full year. In proposing the Peace Corps in San Francisco's Cow Palace toward the end of the 1960 campaign, John Kennedy had recalled *The Ugly American*, the 1958 best-selling book by Eugene Burdick and William Lederer which had given shocking examples of how Americans should *not* act overseas. Kennedy wanted Americans to prove they could do better.

Congress and the new President also saw the Peace Corps as a way to counter Communism. "I want to demonstrate to Mr. Khrushchev and others that a new generation of Americans has taken over this country," said Kennedy—young Americans [who will] serve the cause of freedom as the Communists work for their system."

However, in advocating and organizing the Peace Corps, Sargent Shriver sought to downplay any competitive or negative purposes. "It is important that the Peace Corps be advanced not as an arm of the Cold War, but as a . . . genuine experiment in international partnership," Shriver wrote in his report to Kennedy that became the basis for the program. "If presented in this spirit," the report emphasized, "the response and the results will be immeasurably better."

When columnist George Sokolsky warned that Volunteers should present "an ideal that will . . . make it possible for a person to look toward Washington as a Moslem does toward Mecca," Shriver replied:

> Our purpose is peace—not salesmanship. If Peace Corps Volunteers ever did seek to persuade people to 'look toward Washington as a Moslem does toward Mecca,' they would be laughed out of any country I have ever visited. If they even secretly harbored this hope, it would corrupt their approach to their mission. Their mission is not to convert, but to communicate.

Shriver found support for this approach from an unexpected quarter. Secretary of State Dean Rusk advised Kennedy that "the Peace Corps is *not* an instrument of foreign policy, because to make it so would rob it of its contribution to foreign policy." Rusk hoped that Volunteers would help non-Communist nations succeed in their development and in the process promote goodwill toward the United States, but he thought avowed competition with the Russians would be counterproductive.

The presumptuousness of the Peace Corps would cause some irritation anyway, and the sending of mostly young Americans (average age twenty-four) to help less-developed countries must inevitably hurt the pride of some of those being helped. Nevertheless the new program was an opportunity to show other peoples that Americans were interested in them for their own sakes, and Shriver and Rusk insisted that it be presented in that light. Congress finally accepted this formulation, although Cold War rhetoric recurred in committee hearings and the press.

In the Peace Corps Act of 1961, Congress formally specified three purposes which became the charter for the Volunteers' work:

(1) to help other peoples meet their needs for trained manpower;

(2) To help promote a better understanding of the American people on the part of the peoples served; and

(3) to help promote a better understanding of other peoples on the part of the American people.

For the next twenty years, Volunteers and staff of the Peace Corps argued over which of these three purposes was most important. Shriver himself, who directed the program during its formative first five years, thought the perpetual tension between purposes was creative.

For the program to succeed and continue to be welcomed in host countries, it was crucial that Volunteers make a real contribution to the development of those countries. For this they needed to be well-trained and to go in large enough numbers to make an impact. Shriver aimed for 5,000, then 15,000, then 100,000 Volunteers. Large numbers of Volunteers were also necessary if the promised reciprocal learning was to be on a substantial scale. "What the world most needs from this country is better understanding of the world," Shriver's founding report stated. "The Peace Corps is in fact a great venture in the education of Americans and of people in the newly developing nations," the report emphasized. Shriver wanted it to be a big fact, a bold and large venture, and that, too, was very American.

The venture never reached the size Shriver sought, but it succeeded and has survived. It reached its peak with 15,556 Volunteers (and an appropriation of $114 million) in 1966. During the Vietnam War it fell back to about 7,000. Under President Nixon it lost its autonomy and became a division of the ACTION agency, into which most of the former War on Poverty domestic programs, such as VISTA, were folded. Under President Carter and Peace Corps Director Richard Celeste, the program recovered its effective autonomy, which was formally reestablished by Congress in 1981 under President Reagan and Peace Corps Director Loret Miller Ruppe.

The deterioration of America's standing in the world, as a result of the Vietnam War and of other events such as the assassination of John and Robert Kennedy and Martin Luther King and Watergate, led to a cooler reception for the Peace Corps overseas, and to its rejection by a number of countries. Although from President Kennedy to the present, the Peace Corps was declared off-limits to the C.I.A. and there is no evidence that the C.I.A. or any U.S. intelligence agency disobeyed that injunction, there were widespread charges that Volunteers were sent as spies. Revolutions caused the Peace Corps to be withdrawn from countries such as Ethiopia, Iran, and Nicaragua. Budget-cutting under President Reagan caused the Peace Corps to reduce its programs in many countries, and operate in 1982 with just over 5,000 Volunteers.

Nevertheless, at the time of the program's 20th anniversary, Volunteers were serving in 60 countries, and there were standing invitations for them to come to a number of others. The goal of 100,000 Volunteers serving overseas in one year was far out of reach but all told by 1982 more than 100,000 Americans had been enrolled as trainees (although not all of them were selected to go overseas).

At the 20th Anniversary Conference, speaking to more than a thousand former Volunteers in June, 1981, Prime Minister Edward Seaga of Jamaica said: "The Peace Corps . . . is wanted, needed and loved by so many countries of the world."

Similar testimony has come from many sources, high and low, in the countries served. Nigerian journalist and educator, Tai Solarin, wrote that "the lubrication of our teaching force with the Peace Corps is a greater service to this country than Britain did in a hundred years with all of the epauletted and sword-carrying governors who ever ruled this country." Former President of Niger, Diori Hamani, said, "In my travels in Niger, I have always been impressed to note how, even in the remotest villages, Peace Corps Volunteers have shared very closely in the lives of our people, worked side by side with them, spoken their language, adopted their customs and, in sum, done their best to become one of them." In Bangkok, when an American rider spoke in Thai, the taxi driver responded, "You must be Peace Corps."

After observing some of the first Volunteers overseas, Arnold Toynbee concluded that "in the Peace Corps, the non-Western majority of mankind is going to meet a sample of Western man at his best." He predicted that with "even a partial success," the Peace Corps would "help us break down the psychological barrier that now insulates us from the great majority of the human race." Measuring the Peace Corps' accomplishments after its first five years, Secretary of Defense Robert McNamara told an assembly of a thousand returned Volunteers: "I doubt very much that we (3.75 million people in the Defense Department) have influenced the peace of the world as much as the small handful of you have."

These encomiums embarrass former Volunteers who know they were not always at their best, and who tend to emphasize the very partial nature of the program's success. "We know only too well," wrote former Jamaica Volunteer Joan Ambre in 1981, "that the Peace Corps at heart . . . is made up of two decades' worth of thousands of stories of success, failure, striving, disillusion, insight, and unending commitment."

Volunteers were usually their own worst critics, and some of the first Volunteers have been doubly critical of those who came after them. The pioneers found it hard to believe that latecomers could live up to the original standards or have the same kind of experience. But teaching mathematics in the seventh grade in Dire Dawa was about the same experience in 1971 as in 1961, to the new teacher and the new students. In the 1980s, Volunteers leave the United States and return without the fanfare that would have accompanied them in the

1960s, and two decades later it is not as easy representing America abroad as it was in the years of John Kennedy. The main experience of the Peace Corps, however, is the daily work a Volunteer does, and many observers report that the actual work assignments of Volunteers have been better organized in recent years.

After a first-hand review of Peace Corps programs in Africa in 1981, an early Nigeria Volunteer, Roger Landrum, was surprised to find the following:

> The quality of Volunteers is as high as ever it was. Programs are better focused. Africans with whom I spoke—government officials, secondary school students, and villages—view the Peace Corps as a reliable resource when other forms of foreign assistance wax and wane. They don't mince words in saying that a procession of volunteers has made basic contributions in education, agriculture, health and other areas.

Volunteers continue to be observed, studied, and analyzed. The first *Peace Corps Handbook,* in an overly somber section entitled "Living in a Goldfish Bowl," warned them:

> Like the proverbial goldfish, the Peace Corps Volunteers will be 'in view" constantly. You never will have real privacy. . . . Your every action will be watched, weighed and considered representative of the entire Peace Corps.

Such a city-set-upon-a-hill view is never quite as true as in serious moments it may seem. On the first Peace Corps Advisory Council, David Riesman warned against expecting Volunteers to be saints, since if there was one around, he or she would not need a Peace Corps, and would not fit readily within its structure. "You want healthy, representative Americans," Riesman said, "whose motives will be mixed, like most people's."

That is what the Peace Corps got in its first decade and appears to be the kind of Volunteers the Peace Corps is getting in its third decade.

What the world has gained from the Peace Corps is as hard to measure as the gains of the individual Volunteers. Approximately half of all Peace Corps assignments have been teaching in classrooms or in some form of adult education. The other half of overseas assignments, whether in agriculture, health, or community action, have involved teaching by example, learning by doing. How does a teacher ever determine what has been taught or how much the teacher has learned from the teaching?

Senator Paul Tsongas of Mssachusetts, the first former Volunteer to be elected to that body (followed by a second Volunteer, Senator Chris Dodd of Connecticut), has given this account:

My two years as a Peace Corps Volunteer in a small Ethiopian town were a learning experience that surpassed any formal study before or after it. There I lived and learned with students whose lives had been vastly different from my own. I was a Peace Corps teacher, but I hope my Ethiopian friends know how much they taught me. We had a very personal sense of depending on each other, so it was natural for us to know that nations also must depend on each other. Nothing before or after that time has shaped my view of the world so deeply.

*   *   *

If the Peace Corps is very American in its idealism, optimism, and pragmatism, in its spirit of volunteer service, and in its sense of democratic mission, its partial success took it beyond American values to universal values. This is one of the funny things that happened to the Peace Corps on the way to counteracting *The Ugly American.*

"The Great Society requires first of all Great Citizens," President Johnson remarked in convening the first Returned Volunteers Conference in 1965, "and the Peace Corps is a worldwide training school for Great Citizens." It has also been a training school for world-wide citizenship. A Volunteer colleague of Paul Tsongas in Ethiopia, John Schafer, wrote that the Peace Corps was resulting in "a new kind of world-wide patriotism, a patriotism which involves feelings of universal rather than merely national brotherhood."

Concluded Atomic Energy Commissioner Mary Bunting of Radcliffe, after many hours with a group of Returned Volunteers: "You went out ambassadors, and came back world citizens." Or as a 1965 Volunteer in Malawi, future author, Paul Theroux, wrote in a poem: "We are pure until faced with fruit but the seen shape takes away our history so we open our fat hands to a new world."

The encounter between America and the world has long been a source of comedy. *Call Me Madame, South Pacific,* and *The King and I* are modern musical comedies on themes Mark Twain pursued in the nineteenth century. They harken back to the song the British band played at their surrender in Yorktown, at the end of the American Revolution: "The World Turned Upside Down."

It is in the nature of comedy that characters in it do not consider themselves comic. "Your sense of humor doesn't ignite until quite a lot later," wrote Paul Theroux later. (He was sent home from Malawi and "terminated" as a Volunteer for involving himself in anti-regime politics in that country.) John Kennedy sent forth the first Volunteers saying, "Come back and educate us." A lot of them have come back, and more will be coming. It is in the nature of education to have unintended consequences.

The Volunteers went forth representing American values. They came back having learned many lessons. One such lesson is expressed in an Ibo proverb, brought home by Nigerian Volunteer David Schickele: "When the right hand washes the left, the right hand becomes clean also.

The Future

What lessons has our country—or other countries—learned from the Peace Corps? After twenty-one years the program has come of age. What should be expected of it in its third decade?

One study in 1981, by the Youth Policy Institute of the Robert F. Kennedy Memorial Foundation, has urged Congress to authorize the Peace Corps' three-fold growth, from just over 5,000 Volunteers to 15,000 by 1985. That report, *The Peace Corps: More Today Than Twenty Years Ago,* concluded: "The time could not be more propitious for the American people, the President, and the Congress to reaffirm our commitment to the peaceful development of the world through the strengthening and expansion of the Peace Corps."

If President Reagan wishes "to restore, in our time, the American spirit of voluntary service," it would make sense at least to bring the Peace Corps back to that level of its top previous operation in 1966. If the President's vision of this spirit of voluntary service flowing "like a deep and mighty river through the history of our nation" is to become a modern reality, it may be time to move toward the larger goal of 100,000 Volunteers.

To achieve that kind of escalation, the idea of spending two years in full-time volunteer service would need to win much larger public acceptance than it now has. This might most likely come as part of a general program of National Service under which all young people would be encouraged—or perhaps required—to serve for one or more years in some form of military or non-military program, at home or abroad. Robert McNamara proposed such a program in the early 1960s, and in 1965 President Johnson called on the nation to draw on the experience of the Peace Corps and "search for new ways" through which "every young American will have the opportunity—and feel the obligation—to give at least a few years of his or her life to the service of others in the nation and in the world."

In the 1980s, as the difficulties and limitations of the All-Volunteer Armed Forces become more apparent, universal national service may be an idea whose time has come. If a standby military service is deemed necessary in peacetime in order to assure an adequate non-nuclear defense capacity, it is probable that nonmilitary options such as the Peace Corps or domestic volunteer programs would be provided. Even outside the context of a military draft, the idea of large-scale voluntary National Service has been gaining ground. In 1979, a foundation-backed private study committee recommended such a program in its report, *Youth and the Needs of the Nation* (Potomac

Institute, Washington, D.C.). That committee, co-chaired by Jacqueline Wexler and the author of this chapter, and including former Secretary of Labor Willard Wirtz and Father Theodore Hesburgh, called on the country "to move *toward* universal service by stages and by incentives in either civilian or military National Service will be as generally accepted as going to high school."

In 1980, a bill for a presidential commission to develop a plan of National Service, sponsored by Senators Alan Cranston and Paul Tsongas, and by a number of their colleagues in Congress, passed the Senate but was blocked in the House. In the summer of 1982, House hearings were held on a renewed bill for such a commission on National Service.

Large-scale domestic National Service may become one unintended consequence of the Peace Corps' partial success overseas. Another consequence, proposed originally by Sargent Shriver but never intended by Congress, is the spread of volunteer service programs by other countries and by the United Nations.

Shriver had said: "The philosophy of the Peace Corps really is the philosophy of America. And when you cut down deep with honest politicians in the Congress, they understand that. And therefore they support it because it is a genuine American enterprise." But Shriver's original report had also emphasized another point. "Although this is an American Peace Corps, the problem of world development is not just an American problem. Let us hope that other nations will mobilize the spirit and energies and skill of their people in some form of Peace Corps." To underscore this point, the Shriver report had proposed that one of the channels for assignments of American Volunteers be the United Nations and its overseas development projects of United Nations agencies. It further recommended that in presenting the Peace Corps, the United States should "propose that every nation consider the formation of its own peace corps and that the United Nations sponsor the idea."

Congress did not respond favorably to this United Nations approach. In the mid-1960s, when the U.S. Peace Corps initiated a reciprocal program of Volunteers to America, Congress refused to appropriate any funds for its support. Foreign leaders had reacted positively to the idea of making volunteer service an international and reciprocal venture. The first head of state to whom Shriver presented the Peace Corps, Kwame Nkruman of Ghana, had agreed to welcome American Volunteers but asked: Why the one-way traffic? Didn't the United States want some young Ghanaians to volunteer for service to America? Shriver had said yes, he would welcome them and find them assignments. Several years later the "reverse Peace Corps" was formally inaugurated, with temporary funds from the State Department's Bureau of Education and Cultural Affairs. By 1970, more than 100 foreign volunteers from twelve countries of Africa, Asia and Latin America had taught in American schools or worked alongside VISTA volunteers in community action programs. But Congress brought the program to an end by voting down a Peace Corps request for $100,000 (one tenth of one percent of the Peace Corps' 1970 budget), and Volunteers To America was disbanded.

The United Nations in the late 1960s did initiate its own program for international volunteers serving in U.S. technical assistance projects. This program has continued at a level of several hundred volunteers a year, but has not expanded to realize the potential imagined by its proponents. U.N. Secretary-General U. Thant had declared in 1965 that he was "looking forward to the time when the average youngster—and parent or employer—will consider one or two years of work for the cause of development, either in a faraway country or in a depressed area of his own community, as a normal part of one's education."

If the U.S. Peace Corps is to realize its own full potential, the concept of universal volunteer service, advanced by Lyndon Johnson and U. Thant in that same year of promise, 1965, will need to be revived and widely accepted, and the United States may need to open itself again to a reverse Peace Corps to America. Within such a general international and reciprocal framework, China, Russia and Eastern Europe, as well as many other countries, might open their doors to volunteers from abroad. During the Carter administration overtures toward a program with China were made, but Chinese pride made the acceptance of one-way traffic unacceptable. American Volunteers going to teach English in China while Chinese went to teach their language in America was a proposition that aroused friendly interest among Chinese.

The Peace Corps was not originally intended to be limited to poor countries or non-Communist countries; the Peace Corps Act specified only "interested countries and areas." If world peace remains the primary purpose of the Peace Corps, the time may be at hand to find new ways to include those countries whose doors have so far been closed to American Volunteers.

The U.S. Congress to the contrary notwithstanding, the founders of the Peace Corps would not consider such an extension and inter-nationalization of the idea to be an unintended consequence. Nor would the founding fathers of the American Republic be surprised to find that the "deep and mighty river" of voluntary service flowed not only through the history of our nation but ran into a world-wide sea.

IV. AMERICA
AND THE WELL-BEING
OF MANKIND

Secular and sacred America have tended to view the world from the standpoint of the unity of mankind. For secular thinkers, reason is common to men everywhere. It is the quality which distinguishes man from beast. Religious thinkers point to the brotherhood of man as the source of world unity. All men are children of God and thus brothers (and sisters) of one another. To the extent American values rest on the western tradition, the idea that Americans are linked with people in the rest of the world has solid foundations.

The early American foundations who reached out to give aid and technical assistance to peoples in other countries justified their international programs in both rational and religious terms. Science and reason, it was said, transcended national boundaries. Progress was possible wherever the free play of reason was safeguarded and preserved. The most far-reaching scientific discoveries were never monopolies of the peoples of a single nation state. Rationalism could justify concern with humanity because of man's reason. From a religious standpoint, human need was everywhere; the call "to come over and help us in Macedonia" was quoted when the Rockefeller Foundation Trustees sought a basis for extending programs in health beyond the boundaries of the United States. It was the well-being of mankind, not of some narrower and politically definable group, that the international foundation undertook to serve. The grounds for the foundation's approach can be found in philosophy and religion and the distinctive American values resulting therefrom.

Another historic American institution whose efforts at home and abroad have had their source in fundamental American values is the church. American and religious values interacted from earliest colonial times. It is the purpose of the chapter by Professor Julian N. Hartt to trace some of the changes which have occurred regarding these values. The issue for the church often unresolved is how it can accommodate the clash among conflicting values. In Professor Hartt's words the church confronts a persistent problem of defining its mission when the values on which it must rest are antinomies or opposites. A large part of the debate within the religious community, and therefore in the polity, results from an ongoing clash between those who choose one or the other operative principle or opposite in the doctrine and symbols they invoke to justify themselves. They fail to accept the need for the church, as for society at large, to learn to live with antinomies.

Whatever the United States may do in cooperating with others to serve the well-being of mankind, its largest and most sustainable international effort is likely to come through bilateral policies and programs. Officials and legislators accountable to the American people provide and administer the large-scale funds for development assistance. Clifton Wharton, the president of the State University of New York and chairman of the board of trustees of the Rockefeller Foundation argues in the final chapter of this volume that Americans have neglected their responsibilities in this important sector of public policy. We have tended to view urgent international problems primarily in military terms. Dr. Wharton puts forward three challenging new observations to inspire and guide development assistance in the future.

CHAPTER THIRTEEN
AMERICAN VALUES AND THE FOUNDATION
Kenneth W. Thompson

General purpose foundations in the United States are predominantly a phenomenon of American life. There are approximately 26,500 such organizations with assets of more than $30 billion. They are non-profit and are created under state or federal law to serve the common good. Their activities are made possible through privileges and immunities accorded by established tax laws. They enjoy freedom to innovate and a flexibility that public bodies subject to continuous scrutiny and committee hearings seldom enjoy. The staff and chief executive officers of foundations are responsible to boards of trustees in whom there resides a public trust. Since 1969, however, foundations have operated under a revised tax law which imposes more constraints than had previously existed.

Private foundations in the United States are non-political, staffed by professionals, problem-centered, and responsive to urgent community needs; some of them see their mission as worldwide without reference to national boundaries. Their sphere of interest is social and economic and includes health and sanitation, agriculture and nutrition, and environment and culture. They foster international cooperation by bringing professionals together to attack a common problem and by mobilizing their skills and talents without asking what nationalities they represent. The goal of foundations, at least those whose activities go on outside their own countries, is to build networks of cooperative relations that bind peoples together. The work of general purpose foundations with international concerns is transnational in character, not confined to a given locality and nation. In mode of operation, the foundations have tried to teach by building in this way habits and attitudes of cooperation without discussing such cooperation in the abstract or erecting theories about transnational cooperation.

Over the years, I was impressed by the limited appeal of broad theories of international relations to most of the practitioners of foundations. The functionalists talk about the importance of attacking the problem of sovereignty indirectly and reducing its controlling influence by erosion rather than by substituting a powerful international authority for the sovereign State. I do not recall any foundation leaders with whom I worked in the field ever addressing themselves in any way to such an issue. Such men are for the most part highly practical workers in disciplines such as agriculture or medicine who are seldom concerned with broader issues.

Notwithstanding, it cannot be denied that consequences flow from scientists working side by side on an urgent problem whatever their national origins. Common efforts across national boundaries bind men together. The large foundations have provided a meeting ground for educators and scientists from around the world.

The History of Foundations

The American foundation with broad purposes functioning within and outside the nation's borders had its origins in the first and second decades of the twentieth century. The cynics have charged that foundations were the result of robber barons turning their efforts and some of their profits to charity. Strong individuals who had welded together mighty industrial empires through means which were at best morally ambiguous sought to reconstitute the family name and image and to perpetuate their influence. At the same time, first generation foundation leaders were not driven to seek fame through their philanthropy. They were men of immense self-confidence who were prepared to give independence and responsibility to professional staffs charged with the day by day operation of the new organizations. There was less outright interference in the work of highly skilled scientists and qualified educators by the donor or his family than was to be true in any subsequent era.

The first foundations were born in an atmosphere of extreme public skepticism. Their founders' intentions were questioned and there was debate by law-makers over their enfranchisement. For some, it proved more feasible to establish the new organizations under state rather than federal charters. The earliest charters, much like the early state constitutions, established broad general mandates and left the details to responsible trustees and officers. Thus the Rockefeller Foundation was established to serve "the well-being of mankind" everywhere. It was assumed that foundations, to contribute to society's most urgent needs, required flexibility and the capacity to adapt to changing social problems and demands. The founders had the foresight to resist burdening their successors with the dead hand of the past.

Some of the early foundations were international from the start, a characteristic which has been conspicuously missing in some latter day ones. The thinking of certain founders was a blending of Christian and humanistic impulses. At one of the first meetings of the Board of Trustees of the Rockefeller Foundation, a spokesman for the extension of a particular health program into their countries found his justification in the Biblical command, "Come over and help us in Macedonia." It was also a tenet of faith that reason applied to human problems would bring them under control and lead to their solution.

The giants in the foundation world have been established at several important periods in United States history. The Carnegie Corporation and the Rockefeller Foundation were established early in the twentieth century. The Ford Foundation was a product of the years following the Second World War as were the Johnson Foundation, the greatly expanded Lilly Endowment and the Edna McConnell Clark Foundation. The MacArthur and Hewlett Foundations came into prominence in the 1970s.

The Foundations' Mode of Operation

The early foundations in particular recognized from the start that their success depended on their identifying urgent social problems. Their Boards of Trustees drew a clear line between policy determination and the execution of policy. The province of the Boards was to deliberate and choose a problem or series of problems to which the foundation staffs would seek answers or solutions. For some of the first American foundations, response to the problems of public health was basic to the amelioration of every other problem. While private resources were never considered sufficient to solve such problems, the foundation took it upon themselves to make a start. The concept of assisting through providing seed money had its origins at this time. Foundation leaders proceeded on the assumption they could try out an idea or approach through one or more pilot projects. If these proved successful, other funding agencies with greater resources would take over. Foundations from the beginning had links with local, state, and federal agencies who observed the pilot project, sometimes participating and eventually carrying it forward when a solid experimental based had been laid.

A second assumption which was fundamental to the foundation's mode of operation was that not the symptoms but the root cause of a problem provided a point of entry. The question arose as to what were these root causes, and here the task of identification exceeded the competence of any single group of lay trustees. To assist in defining the problem, trustees and senior executives of the foundations recruited top educators and scientists. Close links were maintained with universities, medical schools and schools of public health. The foundations were organized by professional divisions such as medicine, public health and the social sciences; and members of these divisions were granted a large measure of independence and freedom to conduct professional studies, discussions and investigations. The advantage that foundations enjoyed *vis-à-vis* agencies operating under political controls was reflected in the autonomy of their staffs. Strong and respected individuals who gave first priority to their trusteeship and carried over few if any divided loyalties to other organizations and special interest groups to which they belonged stood watch over the independence of their staffs. They showed unparalleled restraint in becoming spokesmen within the foundation for outside groups. Trustees seldom tried to impose their private interests and as a result an *esprit de crops* and a large measure of self-respect grew up among staff members which has not always been matched in the more recent past. Trustees were prepared in a field such as medicine to trust their professional staffs. A mystique of professional competence dominated their efforts. The papers and writings of these early scientists reflect an inner confidence and pride in their work which may have diminished as concern over public relations and popular images have come to replace concentration on results as the paramount criterion for measuring the foundations' work.

It should be noted that while these first efforts did not carry an anti-government viewpoint, the early foundations reserved the right to be independent of government. Part of the sense of pride of the officers stemmed from the fact that staff members could act quickly to meet human needs and were less constrained to call on image makers or high cost public relations technicians to justify themselves to government and a broad and undifferentiated public. There was less obsession with self-justification and the claiming of institutional credit and more concern with showing that other institutions and individuals to whom the foundations had given their funds and their confidence had produced significant work and achieved important scientific breakthroughs that served the well being of mankind.

Foundation representatives operated from "a packed suitcase." They came and went in their work, especially abroad, not from concern for their nation's foreign policy or the demands of international politics but because there was a job to do. Up to the point they judged they had a contribution to make, they continued their labor subject only to the decision of scientific peers and superiors that the work should go on. They were largely free of the need to justify their efforts to non-scientific decision-makers. They were not victims of the quarterly , semi-annual or annual hearings of political bodies; their foreign assistance was seldom plagued by what has been called the problem of one-year appropriations and two-year budgets designed to meet twenty-year human needs.

Finally, in their work these men and women sought for answers both in national and international laboratories. They moved back and forth between American and foreign settings where the problem and the solution took on different forms and expressions. What was learned about infectious diseases in the United States was applied in

Brazil and vice-versa. The world was their laboratory; and they followed where problems took them in their search for medical and public health solutions that would serve not Americans alone but mankind throughout the world.

Shifting Programs and Problems

The foundations have for the most part been free to shift their priorities and main points of focus. The aim has been to identify the single most urgent problem to which foundation resources and professional capacity could be applied with some prospect of success. Health was an early focal point in the work of the Rockefeller Foundation and some of its related bodies such as the International Sanitary Commission and the International Health Division. Poor health was identified as the primary scourge of mankind. A decision was made to proceed by concentrating on a few specific diseases wherever they constituted major health problems: yellow fever, yaws, hookworm, and malaria. The quest for remedies and cures was one aspect of the approach. The other was improved health care and better health delivery systems. The foundations were instrumental in creating schools of public health. They pioneered in new concepts and better and more relevant training. They sponsored studies of medical education, the most famous resulting in the Flexner Report in which the distinguished medical scientist and public health leader, Abraham Flexner, described existing medical schools as made up of "a few doctors and a bag of bones." These efforts taken together led to the transformation of medical training in the United States and the role of medical personnel in the better medical schools. The health researchers found that economic underdevelopment was a prime cause of sickness and as a result they concentrated their attention on regions such as the southern States.

The work which the foundations began in health was eventually taken over by governments. The National Science Foundation, the National Institutes of Health, and other public bodies picked up where the foundations left off. They were able to devote far more resources to the task and to mobilize a wider range of scientific talent and manpower. The intervention of governmental agencies on so massive a scale was confirmation of the principle on which foundation-programming was based. It proved that foundations could use "risk capital" for demonstration projects and experimentation. When these efforts showed what could be done, government was able to move on and build on more solid and lasting structures.

The feeding of mankind has come to be another important focal point for foundations. The successes of international scientists working together to improve the world's health helped pave the way for cooperative agricultural programs. One of the first fully organized coherent international projects was the Mexican Agriculture Program of the Rockefeller Foundation inaugurated in 1943. It illustrated what private foundations can do to meet an urgent problem. Proposed by a politician, Henry A. Wallace, and authorized by a humanist, Raymond Fosdick, the project from the first was integrated into the structure of the Mexican Government. Its home was the Office of Special Studies in the Ministry of Agriculture. Its objective was to help free Mexico from a foreign exchange deficit brought about by the need to import corn and wheat. Its more concrete purpose was to expand corn and wheat production several-fold by such modern agricultural practices as introducing or discovering new varieties of these basic crops. What followed the Mexican success was the creation of country programs in Colombia, Chile, the Philippines, India, Nigeria, and East Africa—all drawing on personnel and agricultural methods which had been tried and tested elsewhere. These country programs led, in turn, to the establishment of international agricultural institutes intended to serve not a single country but a region, if not the world.

With the progression of these efforts from one country to many countries making up a world-wide network of functional international agricultural centers, the foundations were laid for involving large-scale public agencies. The beginnings of public funding are traceable to the so-called Consultative Group on International Agricultural Research, a coalition of some 25-30 agencies representing governments and foundations. Here public and private funding combined to make possible a quantum leap in the numbers and outreach of the international institutes. More recently, a clearinghouse of personnel and ideas has been formed, the International Agricultural Development Service. What began as a tiny private endeavor in Mexico with an annual research budget of $30,000, has now reached the proportions of a world-wide effort the budget of which approaches nine figures.

More recently, foundations have undertaken to generalize their activities in health and agriculture through broad-gauged assistance efforts in university development. One foundation, the Rockefeller, has concentrated in assistance in six to eight selected universities: the University of the Valley in Cali, Colombia; the Univeristy of the Philippines; three universities in Bangkok, Thailand; the University of Ibandan in Nigeria; the three universities in Uganda, Kenya and Tanzania that once made up the University of East Africa; the University of Khartoum in the Sudan; the National University of Zaire; and the National and Catholic Universities of Chile. The procedure used resembles those employed in health and agriculture: provision of visiting professional staff and research and teaching materials, establishment of fellowships for national scientists and educators, creation of seminars for local policy makers and civil servants, and the setting up of interdisciplinary projects and leadership training. The spread of educational activity and the diversity of departments involved have made for greater demands on foundation initiative and imagination. The impact of successful programs have been potentially greater because of the status of overall educational institutions in their particular societies and regions. More recently, the twelve largest donor agencies whose assistance efforts have included higher education joined in a far-reaching review of the contributions these institutions have made to development in their regions. (Some foundations have since terminated their programs including Rockefeller.) The report was published under the title *Higher Education and Social Change* issued by Praeger in 1976-77 under the authorship of Kenneth W. Thompson and Barbara Fogel. Once again, modest efforts at institution-building by private foundations have attracted support from public agencies and their work will, it is hoped, continue into the future. The decline of interest in higher education in some of the largest foundations in the mid-1970s would seem to reflect the personal preferences of a few individual leaders rather than a careful assessment of the urgency of the problem.

Foundations have also led the way in new assistance areas such as rural development, basic education, environmental studies, and the training of government planners. In some of these fields, it is true that public programs have preceded private efforts. The foundations' participation has nonetheless been of utmost importance and while it would be premature to claim results such as those in other fields, the continued use of well-tested foundation practice cannot help but have significance for the future.

Whereas foundations have conducted programs in the developing world which have, for the most part, been non-political, they have also displayed a variety of patterns in their work. While the aim has been to remain apart from local political forces, they are never wholly free. If they had insisted on total independence of government, they would have sacrificed the influence they have exerted to a considerable degree. It must also be remembered that the sharp distinction which is often drawn between the public and private sectors in the West, is absent or less clear in the developing world. Leaving this aside, professionals and technicians from abroad more often than not work with technicians in such government ministries as health, agriculture, and education. Successful assistance programs, moreover, normally require matching contributions by the host governments. Foreign technicians who succeed must make it their business to know and work with key officials in the host government. The first Director of the Mexican Agriculture Program of the Rockefeller Foundation, Dr. J. George Harrar, has stated that he made it his first responsibility and concern to study the personal ambitions and cultural and political viewpoints of the incumbent Mexican Minister of Agriculture.

All this notwithstanding, the success of cooperative educational programs has depended upon their having both the appearance and the reality of being non-political. Cooperation has been achieved when educators speak to educators. In most educational assistance programs abroad, official contacts with local or national politicians have been best left to the "resident representative" of the foreign group. Outsiders of American-based representatives visiting these programs have generally prefered to concentrate their visits or meetings with local educators rather than the political representatives of their own or the host country. I made it a practice in advance of any visit to contact the educators or scientists with whom I sought discussions and frequently they, rather than embassy personnel, met me at the airport and scheduled my educational appointments. In their minds, I was a nonpolitical officer of an international foundation not tarnished by strong nationalistic or colonial ambition nor caught up in my nation's struggle for power.

Private assistance agencies working abroad have taken pains, however, to assure they not act in contravention of the policies of their own government. Cultural exchange programs with the Soviet Union and several East European countries were not initiated until the public policies of the Government of the United States made it acceptable. The representatives of private agencies working abroad have as a rule been somewhat reserved about establishing formal contacts with their own embassy. The courting process has often gone the other way. Some who make an absolute out of the separation of private American and official governmental efforts will have nothing to do with United States representatives abroad. They argue that the price in their relations with host educators or scientists of appearing to be on governmental leading strings is too great.

The other side of the question has to do with keeping governmental representatives informed. It is said that the progress of the Mexican Agriculture Program would have been accelerated if governmental agencies such as the International Cooperation Agnecy (ICA) had joined with the Rockefeller Foundation earlier to give the program a push. Instead ICA and the Rockefeller Foundation representatives kept a polite distance and the closest they came to communicating was when the ICA representative in Mexico asked Dr. Harrar to fill out a fifty page application—which he promptly consigned to the wastebasket. As the priorities of private and public agencies have come to correspond with one another more and more, the distance between their representatives in the field has diminished. At home in the United States, foundation executives have become more inclined to play the political game, some having acknowledged political aspirations. Despite such strategems, congressional investigations and the Tax Reform Act of 1969 have increased controls on foundations and held them to their nongovernmental role. Thus, foundations seek independence while respecting public policy.

Foundations that work in the non-governmental sector are by

definition likely to be concerned with social problems such as health and education. At the same time, most such problems have both a social and political dimension. Beyond this, foundations have created institutes for the study of public policy and of war and peace, problems that cannot be restricted to the social sphere.

The foundations from their birth have made it clear that their main focus would be on urgent problems. It was on this basis that health was chosen as the first foundation interest. The urgency of a problem has not led foundations to believe that their first mission was to respond to each successive crisis or merely to put out fires. Instead the accent has been on ferreting out the root causes of problems. Leaders have talked about initial efforts in basic sciences, culture, the humanities, and the arts. They have lectured their non-science colleagues on what they have called the usefulness of useless science. They have helped usher in new sciences such as biophysics and biochemistry. Their motto has been, "It is better to teach a man to fish than to give him a fish to eat." They have put great stress on leadership training and faculty development, rather than on the attacking of every problem directly.

The work of the foundations, then, started not with a theory but a problem. It was not health in general but certain specific diseases that set in motion the first program in health. It was not the desire to feed everyone everywhere but to help individual countries turn around foreign exchange deficits brought about by imports of certain basic food crops that spurred the Rockefeller Foundation to inaugurate its country program in agriculture. It was not the desire for worldwide education but the hope that a few pace-setting universities could train the doctors and agronomists, physicists and economists, and engineers and managers needed in a given region. Foundation leaders from their earliest history learned one essential lesson. In philathropy as in baseball, you score runs only by bunching hits. Foundations cannot do everything; if they are to contribute, it must be in certain well-defined areas and according to methods that are known to have worked.

The importance of professionals working together is a self-evident strength throughout foundation history. Functional cooperation is not a matter for dilettantes; when programs have had a lasting impact, it has resulted from men of great experience and knowledge bringing their talents to bear on an urgent problem. The larger foundations have drawn their staffs from professionals in the fields to which paramount attention was being given. Thus Rockefeller until recently has been a foundation of medical doctors, agriculturalists, and social scientists. Ford has been one of lawyers and former governmental officials. Carnegie, with a broad spectrum of concern in education and related areas, has been a foundation of generalists. Among newer philanthropies, Johnson has been one of doctors, Edna McConnell Clark of lawyers and psychologists, and Lilly of university, government and business leaders. The smaller foundations have sometimes been no more than a banker or lawyer at the other end of a phone or occasionally a donor who answers his own phone.

The need for professionals who work together is obviously greatest when staff moves into the field. Where foundations produce results in one or the other action fields, it is generally because of clusters of professionals who make up an operating field staff. Having observed the value of such groups in the private sector, John Gardner, formerly President of the Carnegie Corporation and Secretary of Health, Education and Welfare in the Johnson administration, called on the government to set up a similar career service for educational assistance in other countries. When governmental and foundation programs fail, it frequently happens because personnel have not been recruited on a full-time basis, as in the ill-fated environmental program of the Rockefeller Foundation in the Hudson Basin from 1973-75. The failure is frequently due to new and inexperienced leaders ignoring the importance of professional cooperation.

In addition to professional cooperation, there is also a cultural dimension to working abroad. Living side by side with nationals of other countries for a substantial time period can engender empathy and respect that transcends professional relations. There are few experiences as likely to change attitudes. Learning another language, sensing what is unique in other societies and coming to understand the native lore—all these are means of throwing new light on prevailing similarities and differences among cultures. The story is told of a Mexican legend according to which corn should be planted only during a certain phase of the moon. The Rockefeller team disputed this lore only to find that at every other phase of the moon, ants destroyed the seed corn. Cooperation is assured between people of different cultures only when they agree to seek mutual understanding and build new habits and attitudes towards one another based on both rational and traditional perceptions.

The foundations assume that regional or international cooperation in one field helps pave the way for cooperation in another. This seems to be confirmed in the experience of private foundations. Once an outside agency has been successful in giving help abroad, it in effect establishes an identity and a presence. Trust and respect carry over from one set of relations to another. Those who come later are the inheritors of a legacy of respect which they themselves have not earned. When the Rockefeller Foundation returned to Thailand in the early 1960s, its way was eased because a Rockefeller group helped put Thailand in touch with modern medical practices and had built a teaching hospital in the 1930s. Nothing serves international cooperation better than to be known as a member of a respected international body with named leaders and a tradition of continuity and responsibility. In India during the 1950s and 1960s, it was said that American "ambassadors come and go but the country leaders of Ford and Rockefeller remain." These two leaders, Douglas Ensminger and

Ralph Cummings, were symbols to the Indians of the best in American life. They had demonstrated their competence and had proven that they and their colleagues had something to offer. They were also good listeners and generally knew what the Indians wanted. Because these men and their professional colleagues were part of the culture, employed local personnel, and administered functional programs in health, education, and agriculture, they were looked on as trusted friends. They did not speak for fly-by-night agencies but for organizations with long-term commitments to India.

Only four or five of the largest foundations have operating programs that span national boundaries. These include Ford, Rockefeller, Carnegie (though restricted to members of the old British Commonwealth), Kellogg, and perhaps one or two others. A few more have given support to international studies. This group includes Exxon, Compton, Danforth, Hewlett, Lilly, Rockefeller Brothers Fund, Bydale, and Edna McConnell Clark. The fact that primary and fundamental problems know no boundaries has tended to lead to a transnational outlook. However, it is a mark of the provincialism which still exists that so few foundations have selected central problems as their focus and followed where they lead.

A body of political science thought maintains that if national sovereignty is ever to be overcome, it will be by erosion, not constitutional change. There are few present signs of sovereignty being limited by political means. Insofar as the foundations are concerned, they try to avoid being a threat to national governments. Professionals and technicians have not shown much interest in discussions of political questions or national sovereignty, and it is important to remember that relations between governments and education or governments and science in most of the developing countries are far closer than in the West. This means that functional advances are more likely to augment prestige and power than to take any of it away.

It is apparent that national governments almost imperceptibly take a broader view as a result of functional cooperation. However, they remain sovereign states. Political leaders change and even where the heads of functional programs have had some influence and contact, they lose it with political turnovers. Still it is true that participants in functional programs exercise some degree of influence over government officials. Successive Mexican governments turned for advice on agriculture to George Harrar, Norman Borlaug, and Edwin Wellhausen of the original Rockefeller team. Their nationality as Americans rarely limited the role they could play. In another context, cooperation developed through second generation efforts. Mexico has given funds and agricultural materials and tools to certain Central American states, returning perhaps the debt they feel to the Rockefeller Foundation which first helped them. The influence of the functionalists on political leaders has occurred through the former introducing an international, and even a global outlook into governmental circles. In another way, spillover has taken place. Country agricultural programs have evolved into international agricultural institutes, and government ministers who administered the one have been elected to the Board of Trustees of the other. Some functional specialists who began in one country go on to staff specialized agencies such as the World Health Organization (WHO) and the Food and Agriculture Organization (FAO).

What has occurred is what might be called a half spillover, as what is accomplished in one functional area does carry over into another. Whether or not it persists and how lasting its influence will be depends on personal factors that cannot be measured in advance. Yet functional specialists as such do have influence on nationally oriented leaders, and to this extent what is done in a social or economic field influences the political arena. The foundation has unique resources and capacities. It is properly recognized for its persistent efforts to ameliorate enduring social problems.

CHAPTER FOURTEEN
THE CHURCH AND CHANGING
AMERICAN VALUES
Julian N. Hartt

I

The intent of this essay is to deal with manifestations of Christian beliefs, attitudes, and dispositions in present-day America. More particularly, the focus is on Christian engagements with social forces generating and reinforcing rapid and inclusive change in the life of the national and the international community.

This is a theological venture. Of course there are risks in so identifying it: "theology" has recently risen so high in the ranks of pejoratives that it now threatens "metaphysics." So it is important to say what sort of theology is undertaken here. I do not mean a social-scientific sort of enquiry into pronouncements of denominational, ecumenical, and *ad hoc* special interest organizations on the great problems confronting America at home and abroad. The aim, rather, is to improve understanding of the proclamations and performances of self-acknowledged Christian interpreters of social change. For this purpose normative questions are unavoidable. So a theological-philosophical concern is to be identified: What warrants are being educed for certifying religious-ethical critiques and policy reformations as Christian?

Conceptual clarifications are part of the philosophical purpose of this essay. Accordingly, the prime concepts are: (1) Values, (2) Valuations and (3) Revaluations.

Values

In common discourse this term signifies ideals, principles, criteria. The phrase "American values" also denotes institutions in which idealities are embodied: the State, the judicial system, the market-place, the home, school, church. Anxieties about American values are just as likely to swirl around the institutions as around the ideals as such. It is a theological assumption, all but universal in human history, that the good life is, or would be, an enduring and humane synthesis of what the gods require and man can achieve, a coadaptation of ideal aims, categorical obligations, and human resources.

Valuation

In common discourse this term signifies an appraisal or assessment, as in real estate transactions or used car deals. Valuation also denotes the process in which the behavior of an institution is assessed relative to the ideal or ideals presumptively embodied in it and thus supplying its reason for being. So today we hear such questions as: Are the courts *really* just? Are the schools teaching the truth? Are the churches preaching and practicing the *real* Gospel? Indeed nothing is more common today than our concern to determine whether a given institution, or even society as an inclusive system, is living within the terms of its charter; and if not, why not.

Valuation so understood, it is a persistent feature of any enduring society. Large theological questions lurk just beneath the surface. These assumptions are synthesized with large and inescapable facts of human existence. Of these none is larger and none more formidable than the fact of change. All the enduring religions acknowledge and variously construe this fact of facts. They all teach that the ultimately real is in some significant sense changeless—everlasting, eternal, timelessly perfect, etc.—relative to the mutable and transitory world here below. Thus the essential religious task is to discover and pursue that pattern of life, social or personal or both, which best imitates the life of the gods.

Revaluation

The meaning and something of the weight of this social-personal process is suggested in the common phrase, "I'm having to re-think the whole thing." "The whole thing" can mean one's profession, fundamental beliefs, aim in life, marriage—the full range from the sublime to the ridiculous. In any case, what is suggested is something revolutionary, as in sharp reversals, dramatic discontinuities, conversions and counter-conversions. No facet of existence or institution is immune to revaluation, so understood. At any time it can reach out to grasp institutions, personal life-styles, and hitherto regnant ideals. In the process of revaluation the commanding question is not, Are the courts just? The revaluational question is, What is *real* justice and why are we ignoring it? Consider the Marxian attack on bourgeois justice and freedom, or Nietzsche's attack on Christian love. Marx and Neitzsche are powerful critics of "false consciousness" that is, in their interpretations, the entire fabric of moral-political-religious values. As critics they mean to be *radical:* they claim ability to get to the roots of the systematic and deadly corruption of authentic human possibility.

Valuation assumes that certain ideals are valid and are appropriately embodied in institution and character. Such institutions and characters can be evaluated and if necessary corrected by reference to traditional idealities. Revaluation assumes that those idealities themselves are at least questionable, if not illusory and actually mischievous.

I take it to be a fact that the mainline churches in America are sympathetic to *valuation* and have profound reservations about *re-valuation.* Conservative and liberal seem to agree that it is a Christian duty, incumbent upon church and individual, to ask whether institutions and our commitments to them conform to the will of God. "Will of God" is the conservative formula for the ultimate criterion of value. "The ethical structure of Reality" is the liberal criterion of value. The conservative is sure there is something normatively good to get back to. The liberal is just as sure that the normative ethical-religious fulfillment lies ahead in the future and we must resume our march towards it. Accordingly both parties believe that reformation is called for, however profoundly they may disagree on the model society and model citizen. Both parties are made uneasy by the protagonists of revaluation, though the discomfiture is not the same for both.

Despite their respective diseases, liberal and conservative have both been instructed by the protagonists of revaluation on at least one weighty matter. That is the charge that American society, and notably its religious institutions, is a tissue of value-antinomies. Discrepancy between ideals and actual existence is part of the human condition, long noted and variously addressed in all enduring religions. Diagnosis and treatment of hypocrisy are as much religious specialties as they are stalking-horses mounted by unbelievers. But value antinomy goes farther, cuts deeper, than hypocrisy. A value antinomy is a contradiction between ideals, both of which are held to be good and necessary.

What are the value antinomies of capital importance for a theological interpretation of the proclamations and performances of the churches? I list them here; they are developed in the next section of this paper.

(1) Justice vs Privilege
(2) Peace vs Conflict
(3) Consensus vs Dissent
(4) Rights vs Obligations

The third section is an appraisal of the distinctions between Priest and Prophet applied to the churches as they interpret the forces of change in American life.

In the fourth section I explore an argumentative theological proposition that is also a question: *Given the fraudulence of modern philosophical individualism, what do the churches proclaim and embody as the Christian alternative?*

In the fifth section a profoundly vexatious and inescapable issue is developed. That is the way in which the churches project their role in America on the screen of the international community.

"Churches" signifies mainline Protestant denominations. Departures from this usage are indicated where they occur, such as Roman Catholic and Mennonite.

II

Justice vs Privilege

Stated in stark abstractness it would be a rare person who would put his/her church on the side of Privilege. How could a *Christian* knowingly and deliberately side with Privilege, especially if Privilege means unearned, unmerited, or illicit advantage? How could a true-blue *American* do that, whatever her/his church affiliation?

In the real world, avowedly Christian indictments of injustice are not predictably the number-one item in the church's preaching. Nor is there a predictable consensus, church or secular, on who is being treated unjustly at any given time. Prior to the Civil War the churches, north and south, did not speak out in one clear winning voice against the rank injustice of slavery. In the churches as well as outside them one of the criticisms of the Emancipation Proclamation was that it worked an economic injustice upon the owners of the slaves.

Indifference or insensitivity to the profound immorality of "the peculiar institution" is partly a function of theological convictions. According to such convictions, cardinal social institutions directly reflect God's wisdom and benevolence. Therefore it is sinful to tamper with them. And it is profoundly wrong, perhaps even blasphemous, to undertake the abolition of any institution so ordained.

Here we are close to the heart of Christian conservatism as a social philosophy. In addition to this belief, conservatism incorporates another principle, this one at the price of considerable tension: by reason of a spiritual corruption so profound and pervasive as to be innate, human beings are incapable of creating institutions morally superior to the traditional ones. The will to do so is a manifestation of that corruption of spirit, in this case Pride—which conservatives find particularly oppressive. It is the root of the injustice of the Welfare State.

Theological dispositions of this order have long created severe dissonance in the soul and visible life of this nation. Puritanism is an important part of that legacy. The Puritan commonwealth in America was predicated on the proposition that Godly, righteous and courageous men could create here an enduring society morally superior to anything the Old World could offer; to do so was a divine and holy calling. This sentiment reverberates in one of the canonical texts of American piety: ". . . and dedicated to the proposition that all men are created free and equal."

The Puritan mind is one source of a persisting dissonance. The frontier mind is another one. The frontier inspires the proclamation that a man is what he makes of himself. With this goes the conviction that what he wrests from the earth, and from his fellows, through audacity and sharpness of vision, he is entitled to keep. Looked at under a theological microscope this is hardly a Puritan doctrine of Providence. American piety has rarely been celebrated for its theological precision.

So experience teaches, and theologians concur, that the putatively divine gifts of freedom and equality are disproportionate, relative to each other and to any known state of affairs. We are not born free nor at any starting-line are we equal. But we ought to be free and we ought to treat one another as equals, in some decisive respect or other. For those are the demands of justice.

The institutions of justice are the law and the judicatory system in the first order of importance. Religious opinions on the way these institutions are functioning are sharply divided. For instance, some churches enthusiastically endorse tightening legal restrictions on aberrational sexual activity. Others are as evangelistic about freeing consenting adults to enjoy all known forms of sexual activity without fear of legal reprisal or of social disapprobation.

There is at least as much disagreement over the bearing of economic factors on the institutions of justice. Are the courts likely to treat the poor as they treat the comparatively affluent? If so, how do we account for the disparity between sentences levied for white-collar crimes such as embezzlement, and those imposed for drug-peddling in the black ghettoes? Is the law really color-blind? Is it deaf to blandishments of big money?

Such questions are related to a more general one: What is meant by "economic justice"? A member of the Reagan administration asserts "there are no entitlements" when he is talking about the welfare system. As a devout, if not predictably candid, subscriber to the free enterprise system, he clearly does *not* mean that as a universal truth. That system embodied part of the frontier idealities: a man is entitled to keep what his enterprise has netted for him. In terms verging strongly on the theological domain, in a free market economy things will tend to even out—increasing corporate profits means increasing wages, thus a general rise in standard of living, etc. Does this mean that if the system were allowed to run on its ordained tracks there would be no built-in losers?

Beyond a point quickly reached, debate about this with free enterprise theologians is fruitless. It is fatally easy to say that the system has never been given a fair chance. Not even under Grant, McKinley, Harding-Coolidge? Well, unfortunately the rationalization of free enterprise got mixed up with Darwinism. The Law of the Market became indistinguishable from the Law of the Jungle: Capitalist Man emerges gory red in tooth and claw; fit to survive, no doubt, but otherwise contemptible.

That last note of course represents the liberal persuasion. There was a time when the conservative found argument with it unprofitable. That was not so long ago, really, but it is over, irrecoverably. The star of the Social Gospel has set. For that matter, it never commanded a majority in or of the churches. Today the prevailing sentiment concerning the economic order is that people by and large in the long run get what they deserve—except when hardship is too widely generalized across the nation. Which is to say depressions are bad things and anybody who enjoys them is sick in head and heart. But too much "regulation" and "government interference" are bad; only bureaucrats and the wrong sort of politicians enjoy them.

The prevalence of such sentiments can be fairly taken to mean that there is no coherent dissonance-free socio-economic theology in the churches today. Church life is thus a fair, though hardly an inspiriting, mirror of secular culture.

Does this mean that "antinomy" is an inappropriate characterization of justice in relation to privilege? A fair test of this can be made by substituting "rights" for "privilege," for the time being. Today people are claiming to have certain rights because they belong to a group historically disadvantaged. These are claims for compensation, generally in the form of preferments over people belonging to groups historically over-advantaged. Thus "affirmative action" policies and programs. They collide with the dogmatic policies and programs. They collide with the dogmatic individualism popularly associated with the American Way as its theological foundation. According to that dogma, my rights do not derive from membership in a group, whether or not the group is a voluntary association or one determined by circumstance of lineage and birth. I have a right to freedom of movement in the divinely-ordained struggle to improve my position in society. But society does not owe me compensation or initial advantage because I belong to a group historically oppressed. If my personal qualifications for a job are inferior to those of someone competing for the same job, I am not entitled to it.

Perhaps the dogmas of individualism are rarely proclaimed or practised with the kind of rigor or calamity I have suggested. But these dogmas, nonetheless, are persistent factors in pervasive sentiments and feelings. In fact, public affirmation of them as eternal trusts is becoming more frequent.

Do the churches sense the dissonance generated by agitation in behalf of rights? I do not think so. Liberal Christians endorse a wide spectrum of rights and contend for a wide and permanent place for them in foreign policy. The spectrum includes a right not be be penalized, in pursuit of a fair share of the goods and services because of one's personal life-style (to which the key seems to be sexual preferences). It also includes a right to preferments in that pursuit because of one's membership in an historically oppressed group or class.

So liberals are engaged in a revaluation of human conduct hitherto regarded as deviant, to the point where *deviance* as a category becomes unacceptable. Conservatives are attacking this revaluation as unchristian, unbiblical, and unholy.

What is largely missing in such controversies is systematic, or even serious, attention to the theological problem underlying and sustaining the value-antinomy, *Justice vs Privilege.* That problem is anthropological: the modern synthesis of philosophical individualism with the Christian faith has broken down. Discussion of this issue is found in Part IV of this essay. I note here that theological issues larger than the anthropological one are involved in the quarrel over the legitimacy and finality of the cardinal institutions of American society—notably the American interpretation of the doctrine of Providence.

Peace vs Conflict

Other things being equal, the Christian church endorses peace. Given the New Testament, how could it not do so: Christ the Prince of Peace, peace the sign and work of the Holy Spirit in the church and in the believer, "Blessed are the peacemakers," "Peace I give unto you." In these recognitions God is certainly in the peace business. So the church had better be there, too.

History has an incurable habit of making things unequal. So the churches have repeatedly felt constrained to endorse, sometimes to sanctify, conflicts of every degree of destructiveness. Nor are we likely to forget another item of history, viz., that churches have initiated a remarkable number of wars on their own.

No doubt history thus reminds us that the church is "an earthen vessel." Yet, we are sometimes perplexed to answer the question, Who is the potter—God, Mammon, or Caesar? Historical reflection and theological vexation together should help to put in place the value antinomy, *Peace vs Conflict.* This antinomy is imbedded in the life of the church as it is imbedded in American culture and in Western culture more generally. This is to say that the apocalyptical conflicts of this century are not inexplicable aberrations in the behavior of the social system. They are natural expressions of the system. They are manifestations of its inner 'logic.'

I do not believe this means that the system is predetermined to raise the stakes in successive conflicts until finally it self-destructs. In the face of Marxist theological assertions of the inevitability of that final apocalypse, we must contend that a revaluation of the value-structures of the system would avert that tragedy. But not only that. So fundamental a transformation might bring the world real peace, peace beyond the antinomy, by which it is now embraced.

Is the church in America proclaiming the urgent need of that revaluation of our values? Or does it have a blinding and sound-deadening commitment to the antinomic value-structure?

A fair symptom of the mind and heart of the church on this issue is found in the prevailing attitudes of Christians towards Communist revolutions.

The Marxist-theological core of Communist revolution holds that the class conflicts inherent in capitalism will become increasingly violent and comprehensive until the last vestige of exploitation has been expunged from the human community, and a peace thereafter forever inviolable ensues. Thus run the "iron laws" of history, an indispensable part of an iron-clad faith in an utopian outcome of the world-process.

These dogmas liberally employ passion-charged concepts and images, e.g. *exploitation.* What in Marxism is demonic exploitation of the workers of the world is in capitalism's creed a divinely ordained *entrepreneurship,* i.e., making the most of an economic opportunity and creating such openings. The victims of such enterprise (so runs the creed) are, or ought to be, the objects of private benevolence, so far, that is, as the victims are morally deserving; that is so far as they honor in word and comportment and character of the values of the system, such as frugality, patience, and gratitude for favors large and small.

This is not to say that American Christianity consciously and systematically endorse the classical creed of capitalism. I do propose, however, that the mainline churches in America overall endorse economic freedom, as this is understood in the creed of free enterprise, and hold it to be the necessary foundation of democracy. The churches do not exhibit a matching enthusiasm for the second law of capitalism, inevitable conflict, generally spelled and celebrated as competition; the first law being the natural right to maximize individual profit.

So we come to the church-authorized translation of Peace as the providential combination of social harmony and private happiness derived from acceptance of the realities.

Such dedication to social harmony makes one to wonder how the people of the churches understand the saying of Jesus, "I have not come to bring peace, but a sword" (Matt. 10:34. RSV). Would they be likely to understand it to mean that the value of social harmony can be bought for a price much too high, namely the perpetuation of unjust social-economic structures? Or that the spirit of Christ might engender the sturdiest resistance to such a social system?

As noted above, the church-authorized translation of Peace includes private happiness derived from acceptance of the economic and social realities. So the first citizens of the City of Privilege, the people at the top, do not need to feel guilty about their advantages. The people in the middle do not need to feel guilty about striving—or at least dreaming—to rise in the world; so long as their striving and dreaming are not tainted with low-level covetousness, i.e., *envy.* (Here nice theological footwork is called for to define a course between *cupiditas*—ambition, greed, avarice, lust—and *invidia*—envy, hatred. You can't be a Commandment Christian and embrace covetousness.) The people on the bottom in the City of Privilege ought to feel guilty only for rebellious thoughts, bitter resentment, and revolutionary sympathies.

Each level in this City has virtues appropriate to it: *noblesse oblige* at the top; ambition in the middle; patience at the bottom. At the risk of seeming sacrilege, one might feel that this discriminative value system is a triumphantly secular translation of the Pauline trinity of values, Faith-Hope-Love: at the top, benevolent love bestowed on the system's innocent victims, in the middle, faith in the system; at the bottom, hope for redress in a Great Future and gratitude (thankful love) for hand-outs and hand-me-downs in the meantime.

It is reasonable, though not overwhelmingly charitable, to surmise that a disposition in the church to endorse such a social system, and thus to preserve the value antinomy *Peace vs Conflict,* is a product of a persistent effort to serve two masters, God and Caesar. If that surmise is plausible one might again be given to wonder how the church hears the commandment of Jesus concerning the absolute priority of the Kingdom of God.

It would be naive to expect from the church an unequivocal confession of a shortcoming so grievous. It would be quite as naive *not* to expect prompt and passionate justifications for the church's record in serving Caesar. For instance, we must acknowledge that there are scriptural warrants giving Caesar what is owing him (Mark 12:17), in this case your tax assessment. Then there is Romans 13:1—"Let every person be subject to the governing authorities." (Revised Standard Version) Morever, theological sensitivies are especially acute in discerning the complexities in the service of the Kingdom of God. To be *simplistic* in so great a cause must surely be itself a serious sin. The fact is, we hear that the Kingdom of God can be served only through the service of finite historical institutions, such as the state, the economic system as it was before secularistic humanists started to tinker with it, and the traditional Christian family.

The cogency of such techological demonstrations is very largely dependent on what "service" is supposed to mean. Over the Christian centuries a considerable body of doctrine on that matter has evolved. Inevitably difficult questions arise, such as: Can the church and the Christian support a civil institution given either to the pursuit of unholy ends or committed to using unholy means in pursuit of honorable ends? Is civil authority *ever* entitled to absolute devotion? How could Jesus or St. Paul be cited in support of an affirmative answer to that second question?

Asked in abstraction from heart-chilling and mind-numbing crises in the social order, such questions tend to produce automatic answers. The threat of a world-destructive nuclear apocalypse should serve as a fair specimen of such a crisis—hearts are chilled by it the world over and many a mind in high places is certainly numbed. The automatic answers of coventional pieties, church and secular, are placeboes so bland they are nauseating.

Consensus vs Dissent

The churches in America are the beneficiaries, as their colonial forebearers were the creators, of a remarkable freedom, viz., freedom from overt state-political regulation. This history, too, has its harsh dissonances. The Puritans in Massachusetts were cruelly inhospitable to the Quakers, indeed to everything non-Puritan in the religious line. An overwhelming majority of Americans were relentlessly hostile to the Mormons, and gave them many opportunities to prove they were willing to fight and die for their faith. The persecution of Hutterites and Mennonites, in times of peace as well as war, is yet another evidence of a profound antimony in the American spirit in relating to marked differences from what is held to be mainstream Christianity.

We must undertake to make this phenomenon more particular. Beneath the celebration, now so common, of the great providential benefits of religious pluralism there is a theological conviction that America is a church-like institution grounded unalterably on a Judeo-Christian divine dispensation. To dissent from that creed by precept or example is barely to be tolerated. It is certainly not be be encouraged. But this has not meant that alien creeds and bizarre religious practices have been systematically opposed by Christian majorities. Nevertheless it is largely true that minority religious groups, Christian and other, have been tolerated subject to two conditions. One, alien groups and bizarre practices can fairly be seen to be personal and/or ethnic eccentricities, perhaps intriguing ones, in any case harmless ones. Two, the differences are not such as to deny to the majority the right or power to maintain the proper public pieties of creed and ceremony.

Recent developments in this country illustrate how these conditions function. Here is the issue of Christian observances in public schools, such as readings from the Bible, common prayer, and Christian celebration of Christmas. The effort to make such observances the functional equivalent of a religious-political establishment clearly count on a consensus comprising Protestant white constituencies. They are not seeking a constitutional warrant for intoning the Hymn to Osiris at the beginning of the school day. No doubt a few Hail Marys would be preferred to anything clearly pagan. But there is a presumption that Roman Catholic prayer is not the real article; at least for display in *public* schools it is probably closer to pagan rites than you might think.

On this matter, then, "Judeo-Christian" does not mean a conflation of the best of Judaism with the best of Christianity. "Judeo-Christian" is cashed out as a Jesus-centered version of Protestant piety. It is held to be normative because it reinforces a value system presumptively derived from the Bible.

The phenomenon we are reviewing has manifestations beyond the specifically religious area. American majoritarianism has long been ambivalent about persistent and principled dissent. Dissonance accompanies this ambivalence. Individualistic conceptions of freedom, applied to conscience, private property, livelihood and religion, are extraordinarily difficult to square with the belief that the values and interests of the majority have a social reality, virtually metaphysical as well as patently normative. Thus the friendly critics of the system, as well as its avowed adversaries are put at a distinct disadvantage. They are saddled with a burden of proof all but impossible to honor. This situation is symbolized in brutal clarity in the bumpersticker, "Love America Or Leave It!"

Viewed from an appropriate aesthetic distance, this situation is laced with absurdity. So perceived, the "majority" is hardly a nation-wide reality. The actual religious majority is one thing in Holyoke, Massachusetts, and a very different one in Eureka, Ilinois; different still in Canton, S.D., to say nothing of Washington, D.C. Assume that in each of these places a majority had voted for Reagan. What is the make-up of that majority, in each case? In any case, how clearly and persistently are its constituents committed to the preservation or reinstatement of Judeo-Christian values?

The comedic aspect of this situation loses most of its appeal when one ponders how the majoritarian principle is exploited in the interest of political and economic power. People who do not in fact comprise a *demographic* majority are manipulated by appeals to self-regarding interest and become a functional political majority. The correlative is even more formidable: by the same process a demographic majority can be denied the power it deserves, given the validity of the majoritarian principle.

So to a generalization concerning American political life: A majority is something artificially created rather than being a simple given. Indeed the givens may be so unpromising that they must be treated with psychological violence to make them tractable. Churches have always been at hand to produce theological warrants for those mind-bending, spirit-corrupting exercises.

Rights vs Obligations

Among American institutions the church has been the most persistent proponent of natural rights; given, that is, the antecedent conviction that natural means God-given; given also that some duties are divine imperatives.

How is it, then, that an antinomy can be discerned here? To answer that we must ask two questions in return. *One:* What rights are regarded as God-given? *Two:* Upon whom (or what) does the obligation to honor such rights legitimately devolve?

Two such rights are treated here: (i) The right to life; (ii) the right to liberty.

(i) The church has generally regarded human life as God's gift. So if it is ever morally legitimate to take a life it would have to be done or authorized by an institution certifiably divine in its origination. It would not be right for the American Bankers Association to order the execution of bank robbers—it is not recorded in the Bible that God created banks.

It is only the state that is theologically and morally licensed to take human life. Such is the church's view. It would be an odd thing indeed for the church to give such a license to an institution for which merely human origination were postulated, to say nothing of an institution so prodigal in death-dealing that Satan rather than God or man ought to be postulated as its ground.

In this connection it may be appropriate to take note of the impact of nuclear weapons on the theological appraisal of the state. *Prima facie* here is a weapon and instrument of policy nearly diabolical in its power. As a weapon it is violently self-contradictory. It is a frightful symbol of the hegemony of technology over the life of the planet. Is it possible for the church to give even an inferential blessing to a weapon that casts an obscene pall over the right to life of priest, president, and prairie dog without distinction either provincial or metaphysical? What sort of theological sense does it make to say that a state that makes such an instrument the center-piece of foreign policy can rightfully exact obedience in life-or death situations?

(ii) The right to liberty carries a much larger theological inventory than freedom of worship. Accordingly, church protests against the suppression of political liberty in Communist countries must be correlated with theological celebrations of free enterprise or as the social system in which the individual can best exercise his or her economic rights.

Concern for fairness requires a distinction between the endorsements of capitalism as the happiest possible marriage of political and economic liberty, and solo performances on that theme. Here our concern is with the church because in the church the fourth value antinomy is nearly engulfed by ambiguity. Is there salvation in that? That remains to be seen. This leads us to consider the persistence of philosophical individualism in the church's proclamation of the Christian faith.

Whatever its philosophical lineage, the individualistic bent of American society continues to be powerfully reinforced by pietistic religion. Religious liberty is understood to mean the right of the private self not only to worship as she or he pleases. It is also the right to accept as divine revelation, indeed as the veritable presence of the divine, those movements of the heart, those sublime private feelings, that confirm the ego's appraisal of its own value, present or future or both.

Antinomy reasserts itself when the self, so conceived and so dedicated, begins to wonder about its obligations to other selves and to society. Here voluntaristic pietism encounters heavy seas. These are against the church itself.

A church obedient to scriptural faith must confess that to be a real church is above all a calling of God. Only thereafter and therefore is it a choice for us. The New Testament is very clear about this: Because and only because God-in-Christ has chosen us can we as persons and as a people choose to follow him, accepting his life and way and truth as binding upon us now and evermore.

Of course one might still be free to be a Methodist rather than a Unitarian. But one is not free to be a *Christian* if that means being-for and being-with Christ. One cannot choose to be related to something God has not offered. But if God has offered it, and it pertains to the root, trunk, and flower of our existence, to decline it is to decide for a death infinitely bleaker than the grave.

In foregoing I have deliberately waxed homiletical. The intent in that is to suggest what is preached when the church preaches the New Testament faith. I do not profess to know how often that occurs. We can be quite sure about what is generally heard, whatever is preached. What the people of the church hear is an increasingly unstable compound. One part of the compound is a residual conviction that this nation, America, as a people under God, has a divine and holy calling. The other part, just as much a theological principle, is a voluntaristic-anarchical conviction that duty is real and binding only when—if!—I choose to accept it.

The theological wonder is that this compound was ever stable, widely appealing, and efficacious. Today the driving anxiety in the church can be put as a double question: What is taking the place of the value antinomy, *Rights vs Obligations?* What ought to?

III

Beneath the antinomies in the church's relation to American values there is a constitutive anxiety about its fundamental calling under God. Is the church called to be, above all else, Priest or Prophet?

Here Priest is used to signify an institution dispensing forgiveness and in other ways as well disposing its constituency to accept the ordained givens of the everyday world. The church as Priest does not recommend a radical restructuring of that world or of ourselves as individuals. In the priestly view it is not humanly possible to walk blameless through life in this world. Only Jesus was without sin. Since we are bound if not determined to sin, the great religious question is how "to accentuate the positive." The priestly response is to urge acceptance of the guilt-reducing structures of the church (the means of grace). Concretely this means living faithfully and gratefully in the institutions God has provided. The blessed certainty that sin is forgiven lies in readiness to achieve a moral character. In this way the church as priest provides nourishment for the soul unto the end of life in this world and admission into the everlasting glory of the next.

What then of Prophet and prophetic church? The prophetic church is committed to a radical restructuring of individual and society in order to make them conformable to the ethical teaching and example of the Jesus of history. In the prophetic view, Jesus has the value of the Kingdom of God because he is the supreme exponent and representative of the divine ethical imperatives. Dedication to fulfilling those ideal aims brings the Kingdom of God ever closer to realization in history.

So defined, Priest and Prophet are idealizations. As such they are the creations of theological liberalism. There Prophet was the supreme representative of true religion, pure and undefiled. Priest stood for the inexplicable persistence of conterfeit religiousity.

The Priest vs Prophet antinomy was engrained in seminary education during the great days of liberalism. Thus the real revelation of God in the Old Testament is found in the great and true prophets, Amos, Micah, Hosea, Isaiah and Jeremiah. Even these revealers of God's righteous will, we were told, had to be read discriminately because Priestly editors in Judaism had systematically softened and adulterated the severity of divine-prophetical judgment on social injustice and the conterfeit religosity which hallowed it. It was important to note that the implacable and apparently victorious foes of Jesus was seriously distorted by Paul; Paul was the founder of Christianity as a religious system through which the priestly element from early on wove its devious and triumphant way.

The liberal idealizations of Prophet vs Priest made a complex conjunction with pieties already well-entrenched on the American scene before the advent of liberalism. One of these was pietistic voluntarism. The arch conviction of that tradition was, "You can be saved if you really want and will to be saved!" Under liberal revaluation that became, "The ethical transformation of American life can be effected if you will give up your self-centered life and pitch into the divinely mandated tasks of social reconstruction."

Pietism had an inverterate distrust of priestly religion: it was hierarchial, it cultivated superstitious attitudes about religious ceremony and trafficked in idols. The liberal appropriation of this distrust converted it into an attack on the social conservatism of the priestly church. That aberrant form of Christianity promotes passive acceptance of the status quo. Worst still, the priestly church encourages its people to rise in the world by exploiting the economic-social system for private ends. That ego-centered life is acceptable to the priestly church so long as the striver makes a suitable material contribution to the church.

Another component of the religious situation into which liberalism brought its revaluational faith presented more formidable problems.

This was the apocalypticism inherent in some forms of pietism. The problem was not only the expectation of an imminent end of this world and perforce of American society. That was hard enough to assimilate to liberal doctrine aimed at the progressive moral improvement of society. It was harder still to prove that liberal socialism had no connection either with Christian communitarian piety, as seen in Hutterite and Mennonite societies, or with godless Marxist Communism. Christian communitarianism had no bearing on the massive problems of contemporary society. In its own way that was a perfectionism as unrealistic as that of Marxism.

A third component of the religious situation liberalism had to cope with was more promising and less threatening. That was Protestant moralism. The works-righteousness of this tradition was not wholly inimical to liberal doctrine and program. Of course the critical question was the kind of works God through the prophets had mandated. Moralistic piety concentrated on the achievement of virtuous character. It had something to say also about social evils such as the liquor traffic, gambling, and prostitution. The moral energy thus manifested was a challenge for the liberal; it had to be rechanneled and made available for unrelenting attack on more fundamental and more destructive social evils. Poverty and illicit wealth (the deadly twins), war, political oppression, racial bigotry: all were the fruit of injustice. Surely a society prodigal in the production of such fruits offends the God who through Amos had said, "Let justice roll down like waters, and righteousness like an ever-flowing stream." (5:24 RSV) And through Jesus this same God had said: "Woe to you, scribes and Pharisees, hypocrites! For you tithe mint and dill and cummin, and have neglected the weightier matters of the law, justice and mercy and faith." (Matthew 23:23 RSV)

Protestant moralism had another component that was much more problematical for liberal revaluation. That was the conventional Protestant valuation of the nation. There America appears as a particularly valuable People of God, a people under a special covenant. America is an especially favored nation destined for a unique role in world history. Of course with this Election go inescapable conditions: weighty payment for unparalleled satisfactions. The conditions are summed as a virtuous citizen and a morally-spiritually wholesome society. Therefore decadence and licentiousness in the covenanted nation are more abhorrent by far to God and righteous people than the immoralities of lesser folk outside the covenant.

Liberal revaluation of this element of American piety was at best a partial success. It involved an attack on the provincialism and chauvinism of this revival of tribalistic religiosity. America-First Christianity enshrined a morally corrupt and historically unreal nostalgia: it made the Village the paradigm of the good person in a good society. In that view, the Kingdom of God on earth—and one

14-15

could honestly hope in Heaven—was very like a self-affirming homogenous neighborhood, the Town Common in its exact center. The City was the sinister converse of this. In the City alien peoples with priestly church, bizarre manners, and old-world ideologies dominate the scene.

Liberal revaluation found the Village hopelessly archaic as the paradigm of the good man in the good society. Moreover that back-worlds mentality corrupted the Gospel of Jesus at a fundamental point, namely, Who is my neighbor? The liberal answer: The neighbor, who through Jesus we are unconditionally obligated to lovingly serve, is not our racial-religious-economic-class compeer. The real neighbor is *any* human being who needs the best we have and are as moral agents.

So the liberal revaluation of American piety demanded the substitution of a universal ethical covenant for a particularistic American one. In liberal envisagement the real covenant constitutes a universal divine-human community.

The liberal revaluation of American pieties did not survive world wars in any integral form. Orthodox Marxists were bitterly dis-appointed in the summer of 1914 when the Communist party in Germany, generally regarded as the intellectual elite, the theological *Curia* of Communism, voted support for the war credits. So much for international solidarity. Nothing quite that dramatic has afflicted Protestant liberalism in America. Its failures are partly the con-sequences of its successes. Its revaluations were largely absorbed by great political movements such as the New Deal. These movements, in turn, have largely fulfilled their destiny. In the imagination of the general public they survive mostly as targets for reactionary abuse. In fact, their achievements are now part of the American system; they have been brought under the covenant.

IV

The argumentative theological issue mentioned at the outset of this essay has two parts. (1) It ought to have dawned on the church that modern philosophical individualism is fraudulent. (2) What then does the church proclaim as the Christian alternative?

The first (1) part inspires a question: To whom has the fraudulence been revealed? The popularity of resurgent Capitalist doctrine suggests that the aforementioned revelation has not been universally accepted as such. This is not totally devastating, however. When was any revelation given that reception?

The question about the revelation of fraudulence in the theological system requires a more serious response. I make it in three parts.

(a) Niebuhr is a pivotal theological figure for understanding resurgent capitalist dogma. It is well known that the greatest prophet-theologian of our times passed through a Marxist, or semi-Marxist phase (*Moral Man and Immoral Society*). Neither then nor at any other time did he accept a Marxist-materialist anthropology or a Marxist interpretation of history. Just where he stood on the theological-anthropological issue was not sufficiently clear until *The Nature and Destiny of Man* (1941-43). There he rejects the dogmas both of capitalist and Marxist philosophy. The really existing individual, the person, is grievously obscured and distorted by those dogmas. Their evangelists have divided the world; they systematically deface the fragments thus created. Their views of human destiny-in-community are travesties. The tragic mischief wrought by them now runs through the world.

I suppose that if Niebuhr had had then to choose simply between traditional Christian supernaturalism and Marxist materialism he would have sided with the former against the latter. But the fervent efforts to convert him into a neo-conservative fail and fail disastrously. For that strategy the great obstacle in Niebuhr's thought is original sin. He certainly did not accept all of the traditional freight of that doctrine. Nor does he view it as a poetic symbol expressing a certain waywardness in human nature. The waywardness is profound and persistent throughout history:

> The fact of sin introduces an even more stubborn force of corruption into the inertia of nature and finiteness. The man who is limited by time and place does not merely fail to sense the needs of others . . . . He resists the claim of their necessities upon his conscience and makes demands of his own which are incompatible with their interests. (*Nature and Destiny of Man,* Vol I, 296-297)

(b) Niebuhr believed that the biblical view of human nature has the status of divine revelation. As a Christian he believed that the revelation of God in Jesus Christ of the New Testament is unsurpassably true. In Jesus Christ, God's righteous judgment falls with infinite weight upon all human claims to perfection either of self or society in history. And in Christ God also affirms unconditionally a perfection of self-in-community beyond history. That, however, cannot be made to function as a blueprint for the reconstruction of life in this world; nor does it authenticate any existing state of affairs, or condition of the soul, as fulfilling the divine will.

Niebuhr did indeed grant the merits of a free-market economy. But what holds for every social system holds also here: Its value evaluations and revaluations must be tested against the ultimate standard of the Kingdom of God, i.e., Christ's love commandment, the supreme value of values. So judged, no system and no individual can lay valid claim to perfection or to perfectability on the time-line.

(c) The fraudulence of the individualism enshrined in capitalist dogmas concerning the self and society cannot be established by any imitation of scientific proof. The real issue is the criterion for determining when and how practice and policy and theological theory are authentically Christian. I do not propose that Niebuhr's views on this matter are adequate. But I believe he was right in holding that no social order or individual can be called Christian if that were to mean that here and only here is what God in Christ ordains realized. Who will dispute the propriety of using "Christian" in an infinitely more modest sense, viz., to distinguish one religious community from another one but without judging which alone is worthy of all acception?

(2) What does the church proclaim as the alternative to the fraudulent dogmas of the Left and of the Right? No one doctrine or system of doctrines can be accurately and positively identified as that alternative. Nonetheless some persistent themes can be made out; I do not suggest that any of them is consistently advertised as being the great alternative to modern frauds. A body-mind dualism is the most persistent of these themes; antiquity as well as persistence can be claimed for it. According to this doctrine the soul of the individual, being purely immaterial as well as essentially good, is separable from the body. The soul has a native capacity for either a blessed existence in heaven or an exquisitely painful one in hell. The outcome is decided by God on the basis of his just assessment of moral-spiritual merit attained by the individual in this world.

For our purposes the supernaturalistic elements in this doctrine are not the most important ones. A rational person is not likely to linger long over the choice between everlasting happiness or everlasting torment, assuming the reality of the offerings. How are such doctrines translated into the policy choices and their justifications in the everyday here-and-now world? That is the compelling question for this essay. I think that translation worked in the following way.

The Body is the social system in which for the time being the innately or inherently good ego-self, the Soul, perforce lives. The overriding purpose of the soul's assignment to a body is to demonstrate that the individual deserves a proportionate share of the benefits of that social system; correlatively, that a given individual deserves a proportionate share of that system's deprivations. "Proportionate" has to do with justice. Traditional Christianity held that the justice of God is beyond all human calculations and this-world paradigms. Long ago the great American pieties decided that this lofty and uncomfortable doctrine had to be revaluated, as we have seen. This does not mean that any cardinal component of the traditional teaching was simply and thoroughly rejected. Rather, all the components are transmuted, and none more tellingly or dramatically, than the notion of the body-world as a network for demonic temptations. Of course this body can be made responsive, indeed obedient, to spiritual interests and transcendental values. That requires moral effort. Successful expenditure of that effort, a triumphant acceptance of that price, are exactly what God in his pure benevolence and justice rewards both here and in the hereafter.

American piety of this temper achieved, and continues fitfully to celebrate, the providential congruence of ethical merit and this world gain. Blessed is the entrepreneur and his supporters: they are entitled to the loot. This beatitude is not found in the Sermon on the Mount, which perversely says something about the extreme value of the poor. No exercise of theological ingenuity can rationally derive that capitalist beatitude from anything said anywhere in Jesus' teaching. But where is it said that theological man must not try to improve upon sacred history?

Some elements of propheticism are displayed in the transmutation of traditional Christian views of God's justice noted above. One of these is a demand for a return to a traditional rectitude of character and society; the tradition is Victorian, hardly more ancient. A second prophetic element is a dire warning of the imminent and terrible punishment God will visit upon ungodliness and immorality. The third element is correlative with the second. It is a promise of power, prosperity and security for the nation and its loyal people, contingent upon that conversion to traditional morality and its cognate piety. A fourth element in neo-propheticism is more ambiguous: the place of Covenant. Israel's prophets appealed to a covenant in which justice and mercy are divine imperatives. The neo-prophetic church appears to honor two convenants: the Law of the Old Testament, represented in the Ten Commandments, and the Constitution of the United States of America. The neo-prophetic church proclaims a carefully edited version of the Ten Commandments. This church is eager to change the second covenant, the Constitution, where it conflicts with particular pieties concerning abortion, federal fiscal policies, and the place of prayer and other Protestant pieties in the public schools. A more radical reevaluation of the Constitution is also envisaged, viz., revising downward the rights and powers of the Judiciary.

At another point neo-conservatism is hardly ambiguous. That is how compassion is to be related to justice as a political-economic imperative. Recrudescent Republican preaching cultivates resentment against government welfare programs and the philosophy behind them, sometimes described as runaway dogoodism. It is preached that all that is unjust because it takes from the deserving and gives to the undeserving. This stultifies the springs of compassion in the private heart, the true source of benevolence. Again then: *real* justice demands that benefit be proportionate to merit. Returning to faithful adherence to that principle would guarantee freshets, all but miraculous, of benevolence for the comparatively innocent victims of the social system, on a one-to-one basis.

How is it possible to believe that anything like that view of human existence and worth under God is biblical? It was made possible by assimilating biblical history and biblical faith to American history and the American creed. That assimilation required theological work, a religious-theoretical grounding of an inclusive value-structure on an economic principle and paradigm. So freedom came to mean in the first instance the right to aggrandize one's property base in society. Perhaps the other higher freedoms are not strictly derivable from that but they are answerable to it. Thus economic freedom, as defined, emerges as the *sine quo non* of a democratic and Christian society.

Expressed so nakedly the doctrine is materialistic. It is tempting to say it is as materialistic as Marxist dogma but the American version is everyday materialism, not metaphysical. It is passionately proposed and defended as alone compatible with the authentic moral-spiritual life for the individual and society. So to a conclusion.

V

Popular theology—that proclaimed from pulpit and pamphlet—has long been at odds with itself in its condemnation of materialism. The church believes that philosophical materialism is clearly wrong and would not be worth bothering with if Communism were not avowedly a kind of philosophical materialism which its believers persist in calling scientific rather than metaphysical. On the other hand popular theology represents God's promise as having a this-worldly content as well as an other-worldly one. God ordains prosperity in this world for the faithful keepers of the convenant. What is prosperity, then? It means owning sufficient property to satisfy any one or more of the following: (1) the need for economic security; (2) social-status elevation; (3) the pursuit and enjoyment of political power, especially under the commitment to lead the people back—or forward—to rectitude moral, economic, and political.

What thus appears as a contradiction in this gospel is rendered acceptable, for those who do accept it, by placing it in a church ministry—lay and clerical—priestly in its decisive functions; priestly, as we have seen, so far as it provides rites of forgiveness and acceptance. Such a church offers little incentive for or sympathy with a revaluation of the social givens, unless it is a revaluation regressive in aspiration, paradigm and principle. There is then little to wonder at in a steady and strong preference in this country for revolutions and regimes of the Right. This is one of the products of homegrown church-endorsed materialism. It is a remarkable priestly-religious achievement.

There is however a more perplexing development in contemporary religion in America. That is the stirring of a more traditional-biblical prophetic ministry in a church otherwise easily identified as priestly. It involves the insistent use of a doubtful translation of a biblical text. The text is Proverbs 29:18. The familiar and doubtful translation is: "Where there is no vision the people perish." The Revised Standard version has it: "Where there is no prophecy the people cast off restraint." Now to catch something of the sense of that prophetic stirring in the church we should combine the options: "Where there is no genuine prophetic vision the people will lose their way."

For the prophetic vision stirring in churches Catholic and Protestant is a perception of the inviolable interconnections of Justice, Love, and Peace. On this reading of the realities it is self-denying, other-regarding love that is the divinely mandated motive for the pursuit of justice. And on this reading there is no peace without justice. For without justice there are only truces during which people are lulled into thinking that the roots of conflict have finally been extirpated. History gives the lie to that optimism. The lesson is generally bloody. We have all begun to wonder about the last lesson in that book.

But is the prospect of any kind of lasting peace any less illusory? The kind of neo-propheticism exhibited in the Moral Majority involves a return to the naive, brutally naive, strand of optimistic piety. It is mixed with a so far incurably provincial version of Peace and Safety Through Military Strength.

At the moment the people of the church who do not accept this regressive gospel lack voices as well-schooled in the tricks of the mass media trades. They also lack money to pay for a larger and more expert exercise of those tricks. But there may be comfort in biblical wisdom: the false prophets always outnumber, and often outshout, the real and true prophets. There is richer and more legitimate comfort to be found elsewhere—or maybe it, too, is biblical. That is, it is not excessive popularity or numerical strength or decibel output that gives away the false prophets. It is the deadly ease with which they become false priests as well. In Bonhoeffer's telling phrase, they are altogether dispensers of "cheap grace."

VI

The value antinomies manifested in the life and message of the American churches appear to block effectively the expression of a "consensus Gospel" in the international community. For example, liberals decry the oppressive and blatantly racist regime in South Africa. Conservatives praise it for being avowedly Christian and a bulwark of social-political stability in an area where vertiginous and violent change is the rule.

Beneath such striking and apparently irreconcilable conflicts there may be the rudiments of a "consensus Gospel" after all; but an unconscious one. It is conceivable, and I suspect it is the case, that the warring factions in the churches agree that America has a unique salvific mission in the family of nations. America, "the almost chosen people," the Kingdom of God in the new world, the last best hope of glory: these are some of the traditional heiratic terms in which the ordination of America is celebrated. In more prosaic terms, this nation combines enormous power with dedication to ideal aims; human history has never seen its like before; it must be the authentic adumbaration of history's goal, thus of history's God.

We have here a shared conviction that America's ideal values are in principle universally valid. The historic mission is to teach them to the world.

This consensus dissolves around the question of the societal embodiment of these ideals: Ought American institutions—economic, political, religious—to be replicated across the world? The very possibility of consenus is ruined, apparently past any repair, by the question of revaluation: Are not American idealities as provincial and self-serving as those of any other empire?

Granted the all but cosmic sweep of revaluational forces in the present world situation another element in an unconscious "consensus Gospel" may appear. It is more paradoxical than the first one. It is the supposition that Marxist-Communist revolutions are for all practically viable purposes, if not for all legitimate theoretical ones, the authentic paradigms of the revaluational process ordained for our situation. The paradoxical character of this consensus derives from the Marxian principle that economic forces and relations are decisive for the explanation of human behavior. So President Reagan insists that the nations of the Third World should adopt the free enterprise system for their salvation; of our patent, of course. We hear liberals claim that poverty is the root of all social-moral pathologies. According to the one prescription, the underdeveloped countries need more IT&T and Chase Manhattan. According to the other prescription, sweeping redistribution of land and other resources is the first order of the Day of the Lord. According to the one, regimes that are violently oppressive are to be supported so long as they are anti-Communists and provide a ready market for our surplus weapons. According to the other, the liberation of the oppressed masses may very well involve support for leftist insurgents whose respect for human rights is not always meticulous, due, no doubt, to the exigencies of their situation.

This paradoxical spectrum is a persistent feature of the commentary on world affairs provided by American churches. It is evident also in their prescriptions for the productive management, if indeed not for the solution, of the formidable problems confronting the entire world. What is missing in this display is the will to push the revaluation of the Marxian paradigm all the way home. *That would require a revaluation of the manichean outlook that is part of the unconscious "consensus Gospel."*

Here is a spiritual condition more fundamental and more ruinously fruitful than a theological shortcoming. Lamentable indeed is the stark failure of the churches to present an authentically Christian alternative both to capitalist individualism and Communist collectivism. This deficiency the American churches share with their sisters elsewhere. More disastrous by far is the innate disposition to construe historical existence as the ordained conflict between the children of darkness and the children of light, between the Good Guys—all our kinsmen—and the Bad—all aliens. Whoever is not a declared ally is an enemy, unwitting or otherwise. This is the predictable underside of the messianism and apocalyptical triumphalism which have attended the celebration of America's unique historic mission. In the main the churches have not been persistent or passionate critics of this spiritual condition.

VII

I have not attempted to portray the role of the churches in the exercise of the remarkable virtues of America, the genial generous giant. We think of the great overseas programs to feed the hungry and heal the sick and educate the masses. We think of the hundreds of thousands of refugees admitted here just in the last ten years. It is wronghearted as well as wrongheaded to view these performances as manifestations of corporate guilt.

We can properly be grateful for the sterling achievements of American Christianity. I do not believe that they are diminished by the things discussed in this essay; not even by the persistent conviction that America must somehow be able to save the world from the world's own sin and folly. That is an effect of the primitive image of this nation as sort of a church. So to perceive, so to esteem and cherish it, does less than justice both to the nation and to the Christian church.

CHAPTER FIFTEEN
U.S. BILATERAL DEVELOPMENT ASSISTANCE: THREE OBSERVATIONS FOR THE FUTURE
Clifton R. Wharton, Jr.

It was some thirty-four years ago that I sat in the seat that one of you graduates occupies today.* Like most of you, I had a sense that I stood on the threshold of my future. I was exhilarated: the challenging course of study was finished. I was proud: I felt that I had added to my intellectual skills and expanded my critical view of the world. As I neared the end of my program, attending classes in that marvelous old building at 1906 Florida Avenue, I considered two possible directions. First, I could follow my father's footsteps into the United States Foreign Service. He had already completed half of his diplomatic career that would span forty years. Diplomacy was the time-honored field for anyone who sought a professional life in international affairs, and it was the career for which a great many of my most talented fellow students had been preparing themselves. The other possibility was the field of technical assistance for international development. It was an almost entirely new concept—not just a road less traveled, but a trail that had yet to be blazed. Yet I was persuaded that foreign development assistance would become an important part, even a critical part of U.S. foreign policy. That conviction remained unchanged throughout my career. I still believe it today.

I went to work for the late Nelson Rockefeller, in a nonprofit organization he had established as a result of his experience as Coordinator of Inter-American Affairs. Foreign development became my full-time occupation for some twenty-two years. While today I seem to have strayed into academic administration, I have never ceased to devote a major portion of my time and energy to the development field.

---

*This paper is on Dr. Wharton's commencement address at the School for Advanced International Studies in the spring of 1982.

Development Assistance at a Crossroads

The three-and-a-half decades since my graduation from the School of Advanced International Studies are virtually coterminous with the emergence of development assistance as an integral part of foreign policies. Dating from President Harry Truman's famous Point Four Speech, in which he announced his program of bilateral assistance to the world's Less Developed Countries (or LDCs), the evolution of development assistance has continued through the postwar years, the Cold War, and detente into our own increasingly uncertain and anxious era. The U.S. now has had some thirty-five years' experience in development, attempting to help Third World societies modernize and improve their people's lives. Our activities have included not only government bilateral porgrams such as those conducted by AID and its predecessor agencies, but also multilateral programs and those mounted by corporations, private philanthropy, and voluntary agencies.

Despite this very substantial fund of experience at our disposal, I believe that international development assistance has reached a crossroad as we enter the penultimate decade of the twentieth century. The familiar roads diverge into unknown directions, and the road signs of the past give little indication as to how we are to reach the destinations of the future. If we are to make the right choices about which way to turn, I believe three broad observations must be taken into account.

Three Observations

1. *International Development: The Limits of Assistance.* My first observation is that while the drive toward development is clearly one of the most overwhelming global forces of our time, there are limitations to the part of that formal development assistance programs *can* and *should* play at the present time. In the first place, we have a limit of knowledge. We still do not know nearly enough about what "causes" development. Trying to explain why growth does or does not occur in socio-economies has been a central preoccupation of economists and other social scientists since Adam Smith, whose famous essay was suitably titled *An Inquiry into the Nature and Causes of the Wealth of Nations.* Thousands of books later, we development types are still not fully in accord. Oh, we have our theories: investment theories, human capital theories, innovation theories, technology theories, psychological theories, cultural theories, political and historical theories (dare I add "supply-side" theories?)—it would be pointless to mention them all. If we could spend the time analyzing all the development theories and empirical studies of the last thirty years, I believe the important conclusion we might draw would be that there is no single key, no "fundamental" factor that

15-2

catalyzes growth and maintains its impetus. We know that growth takes place because of many factors in combination; but the factors and the combinations are not the same in every case. We have yet to draw up a universally valid chart of theory of how socio-economic conditions combine to cause growth and what combinations are most successful in any given situation.

Although we have yet to assess and fully understand the successes and failure of our bilateral development assistance ventures, compared with the late forties we know a good deal more about the process. Consider for example, the very important development area of food. In the years between 1951 and 1980, food production in the developing nations rose faster than population—at a compound annual rate of 2.9%, compared to 2.4% for population. This was in fact faster than food output growth in the developed nations themselves (Barr, 1981, 1088). Now, it is true that there were wide variations among countries and regions in the LDC bloc, as regards food production, population, and other aspects of development. But overall, the LDCs' food output grew faster during these years than that in the developed countries—in part because of international agricultural development projects carried out by the U.S. and other assisting nations. What else have we learned? Well, in recent years, U.S. bilateral programs have tended to over-emphasize massive commodity and credit transfers without sufficiently looking at ways to help target countries build indigenous capacities for meeting their own needs on a long-run, self-sustained basis. For example, in agriculture we have learned that direct supply of, say, large supplies of fertilizer may not be the best way to improve food production and farm family income on a permanent or lasting basis. Unless we work to strengthen the indigenous institutions and human capital, an external "quick fix" cannot by itself have a lasting impact on food production and can only accentuate dependency. (Wharton, 1982, 6&7).

Similarly, the congressional mandate that assistance programs focus directly on the "poorest of the poor" population in host nations was no doubt motivated by the best of intentions. Nevertheless, if narrowly construed it may not be the best use of scarce development resources. For example,

Using a U.S. agricultural research scientist as a county extension agent working with 200 (small farmers) in an underdeveloped nation may be balm to one's conscience because the scientist is responding directly to human needs. But is it the best use of that scientist if alternatively his time were spent on an experiment station where he might discover a new higher yielding variety or technique of cultivation that might double the productivity of millions of such farmers? (Wharton, 1978, 6).

15-3

We know that macroeconomic or national planning is a necessary but not a sufficient condition for growth. We know that the social and cultural context in which the planning takes place—the public response—is equally important. We know that science and technology in and of themselves are hardly panaceas, if they are unsuitable or at odds with deeply-felt human values or basic social institutions in the nations where assistance is taking place. Failure to look more attentively at these larger questions of "context," if you will, seem to me to have a good deal to say abut why development has been notably more successful in some areas—say, India—than in others such as subSaharan Africa.

Against the backdrop of both our progress in and our continuing need to know more about development must be projected another important limit on what development can achieve: the emergence and maturation of the independent nation states of the Third World. The outcome has been the predictable and understandable dominance of nationalistic political forces. The self-determination of the early post-colonial period has blossomed into the full-blown peer dialogue of North vs. South. Hence, in bilateral development assistance it is no longer a case of our paternalistically choosing or even influencing the developmental goals of the LDCs, much less their implementation. Just as in the United States, domestic political considerations of international political factors in the LDCs often submerge or defeat the realization of developmental goals and programs. (Wharton, 1977). The political limitations on developmental assistance are real and will continue to grow.

But perhaps the most fundamental limitation is that formal technical assistance efforts are, in the last analysis, only a small part of the development process. Quantitatively speaking, at least, Western tariff policies, OPEC oil prices, or even fluctuations in the U.S. prime interest rate have a greater impact on the economies and societies of the developing nations than the relatively small amounts that have been devoted to development. Growth and modernization throughout the LDCs are world-historical processes, involving structural patterns of trade and resource flow, clashes of techniques and ideologies, and realignments of political and cultural forces. These are all matters that one does not manipulate or shape unilaterally, either behind the scenes or in the field.

In other words, the most important limitation affecting bilateral developmental assistance is that it has severely constrained financial and human resources at its disposal, and it operates on a world-historical stage where it is but one of a whole constellation of forces— many of which carry quantitatively much more weight. Hence it becomes a matter of paramount necessity that developers take steps to make sure that their relatively small available investments bring the greatest possible returns—to ensure that development programs provide what my corporate friends would call the "biggest bang for the buck." This goal requires that assistance—whether the most direct kinds of resource of fund transfers, or the most complex, long-range kinds of institution-building—take place on the strategic margin of effectiveness.

2. *Changing Conditions in the Third World.* My second observation is that the Third World is no longer what it was in 1949 or even 1957—not least because there *has* been development.

Three decades ago, for example, well-trained scientists and professionals were mainly imported Westerners. Today, thanks to both U.S. exchange programs and the development of indigenous educational institutions, many LDCs have a large and growing pool of scientific, technical and managerial power. (The major exception is subSaharan Africa.) Over the years 1961 to 1980, U.S. colleges and universities alone have produced something in the neighborhood of 74,000 foreigners with Ph.Ds. (Syverson, 1981, 8, 19). We do not know exactly how many past and recent graduates are working in development in their own lands, but the point is that the numbers are vast orders of magnitudes larger than was true during the early years of technical assistance.

What are some other differences? Well, the U.S. once held almost a monopoly on development assistance, but that is no longer the case. In addition to aid provided by the seventeen member governments of the Development Assistance Committee, in which the U.S. is a participant, there are also the sizable assistance efforts of the OPEC bloc (2.34% of GNP) and the much smaller commitments by centrally planned nations of Eastern Europe (.12% GNP). In these, as in our own program, there is considerable intermingling of true development aid and military assistance. Even so, it is clear that the field we once occupied virtually alone has now become quite crowded.

Another change over the years has been the increasing differentiation among the Third World nations. We have "graduate nations" no longer eligible for bilateral assistance, "middle income nations," "resource rich" nations, and "resource poor" nations. This increasing differentiation among developing countries raises a number of questions. Should our aid be focused exclusively on the poorer nations? If not, what policies and instrumentalities should be adopted on our work with "graduate nations?"[2]

Finally there is the fact which I mentioned earlier, that bilateral assistance is no longer the dominant or sole actor on the development stage.

All these changes are particularly relevant for the conduct of our bilateral development assistance. Unfortunately, the program and project methods employed by today's bilateral development assistance programs operate as if the Third World were essentially identical to what it was in the late 1940s and early 1950s.

From 1953 to 1956 I had the privilege of being a part of a group studying U.S. technical assistance in Latin America. In thinking about the need to re-examine the administrative mechanisms for the conduct of U.S bilateral assistance, I took from my library one of the books produced by the project—Philip Glick's *The Administration of Technical Assistance* (1957). At the time, Gick's book and its two companion policy pamphlets were the state-of-the-art for the conduct of U.S. technical assistance. When I skimmed through the table of contents under the section headed "The Choice of Instruments for Effective Cooperation," I found such topics as: "The broad economic survey," "The technical mission," "the university contract," "the training grant for training abroad."

The striking thing about the list is that although there have been significant, even radical changes throughout the LDCs during the last 25 years, most of the same mechanisms still shape our development efforts today!

A World Commission on U.S. Bilateral Development Effectiveness

The pressing needs to update our assistance methods and enhance the strategic effectiveness of our scarce development resources lead me to propose that there be established an international commission to examine the conduct and mechanisms best suited for U.S. bilateral technical assistance in the 1980s, 1990s, and beyond.[3]

The commission would be sponsored either by a private U.S. foundation or by a neutral agency such as the National Academy of Sciences. The commission should have a duration of no more than two years.

The composition of such a commission should be broad, including not only personnel from the agency for International Development and the U.S. Congress but also leaders and scientists from the LDCs and other donor nations. Educators from the LDCs and the United States would take part, as would foundations personnel and perhaps representatives of other voluntary agencies with substantial development experience and commitments.[4]

Even though the commission's focus would be upon U.S. bilateral assistance programs, an international membership on the commission is vital. Despite the superficial appearance of a "conflict of interest" in having non-U.S. members or even persons from aid recipient nations and other donor nations on such a commission, the net gains in securing helpful insights far exceed any such dangers.[5] (Moreover this view is validated in other experiences as the Canadian organization IDRC.)

It would be the responsibility of the commission to collect data on past, present, and alternative methods or mechanisms for the conduct and execution of U.S. bilateral assistance projects and programs. We need to know what has worked and what has not—and why.[6]

The commission would need to look at established practices in light of changing circumstances. For example, bilateral assistance has traditionally involved stationing U.S. administrators and professionals overseas. Yet long-term overseas personnel are extremely expensive to maintain, absorbing a disproportionate part of total assistance funding. With the growing reservoir of foreign talent available, the commission would need to ask itself whether past practices for in-country administration and oversight can and ought to be revised.

Because bilateral assistance is now a more scarce development resource, every effort must be made to assure that it is used with maximum effectiveness. U.S. bilateral assistance must concentrate on those areas and activities where it has the greatest comparative advantage. For example, U.S. scientific and technological skills may have much to contribute to the long-run research efforts of LDC's; on the other hand we may have little that is unique to provide in improved methods for relief efforts or the delivery of food aid, important as they may be in the short run. (Wharton, 1978).

Determining the effectiveness of our current mechanisms and practices cannot be done in isolation from the problems or subject matter area of development. The linkage must be made. But the commission would differ from other study groups in that the problem areas will not be the primary focus. We have more than enough recent analyses delineating the problems of development (CEQ 1977; Linowitz 1980; Brandt 1980; FAO 1981). But such efforts rarely go beyond defining the problem with a few overbroad recommended solutions. The detailed solutions and the methods for their implementation and execution are rarely touched. What we need now is to concentrate attention upon the administrative mechanisms, program techniques, and project instrumentalities used in our development assistance.

Innovations in the execution of U.S. bilateral development assistance have taken place over the years and are taking place now. Two recent examples are individual U.S. university linkages to specific AID overseas missions for technical support, and the development of a "joint career corps" whereby U.S. faculty members will alternate their work assignments between their universities and service to AID in Washington or overseas[7] (Wharton, 1982, 6). But what is needed is a far more systematic and objective look at all areas of U.S. bilateral assistance to determine the possibilities for new approaches and mechanisms more appropriate to today. With a broad mandate, I believe that the proposed international commission could conduct valuable investigations to achieve a streamlined, modernized, and more effective U.S. bilateral development assistance.

3. *Development: The Centerpiece of U.S. Relations with the Third World.* Once under way, the commission would, of course, be at liberty to explore a whole range of issues and questions pertaining to the conduct and mechanisms of U.S. bilateral assistance. Its goals,

however, should be visionary. It should seek to make concrete the ideal explicit in my third observation for today: The United States must forge a foreign policy in which technical assistance and overseas development are recognized as the core of long-run world stability, and in which development is the centerpiece of U.S. relations with the Third World.

The U.S. still provides the largest amount of overseas development aid in absolute terms—but this figure can be misleading. In comparative or relative terms, the U.S. once gave the largest share of Gross National Product as well. Now we give a smaller share of GNP than twelve other nations—including such currently beleaguered economies as France, Belgium, the United Kingdom, and New Zealand. In 1949, official U.S. development assistance amounted to 2.7 percent of GNP. In 1980 it was .27 percent—shrunken by a factor of 10! Note that at $7.1 billion, the 1980 net "overseas development assistance" total was *lower* in real terms than what we provided in *1961* (Hansen *et al.,* 1982, 226).

At the same time, the U.S. is spending twenty times more on defense than on development assistance (Linowitz *et al.,* 1980, 13), and 1981 expenditures for military assistance are estimated at 28.3 percent of total U.S. foreign assistance (Hansen *et al.,* 1982, 226). What rankles even more is that much of what hides under the cover of "development aid" today is really nothing of the kind, but rather military, political, and economic assistance to nations which U.S. policymakers have designated as strategic allies. In fiscal year 1980, over half of all commitments of economic assistance by AID were in the Economic Support Fund category, formerly called Security Support Assistance. Of that amount, some $1.65 billion—over forty percent of AID's total disbursement—went to Egypt and Israel alone! (Hansen *et al.,* 1982, 242). For FY 1983, the administration's foreign aid appropriation request essentially straightlines development assistance, which is up five percent, somewhat below anticipated inflation. But the security assistance request seeks an increase of thirty-five percent above 1982.

More people have died from hunger in this millennium than from all its wars, but I am not downplaying the importance of defense. I am questioning the persistent entanglement of military and development assistance, which has so far been much to the disadvantage of development. Moreover, I find it necessary to point out that precisely those conditions that development seeks to remedy—grinding poverty, failures of land reform, and a thousand other manifestations of human disenfranchisement—often play a major role in precipitating internal strife in the LDCs and rendering them so vulnerable to both domestic upheavals and the adventurist meddling by foreign superpowers.

At a time when weapons proliferation of all sorts verges on being out of control, and when a spuriously fashionable "tough-mindedness" makes it possible for supposedly rational leadership to discuss the winability of nuclear war, it is certainly clear that an overriding concern of foreign policy should be arms limitations. We must indeed pull back from the abyss of final holocaust: hence the urgency of arms control and de-escalation of hostile rhetoric and actions alike. Nevertheless, I believe that the threat of nuclear war, appalling as it is, is basically a symptom rather than a root of international discord—a symptom with vast potential for catastrophe, but a symptom for all of that. Arms reduction is desirable for many reasons, economic as well as political; yet arms reduction alone will not address the foundations of international instability. Rather, what is needed is a development-centered policy that recognizes and seeks to reduce the social, political, and economic inequities that undercut order, progress, and prosperity worldwide—inequities between and among individuals, and inequities between and among nations. Only when these deeply rooted, structural ills have been acknowledged and addressed will the more symptomatic problems of international conflict become amenable to lasting resolution.

Development goals are almost inevitably long-term ones, which day-to-day political and security crises have a tendency to crowd aside as secondary priorities or idealistic visions. Yet I am compelled to point out that we live in an increasingly interdependent and yet increasingly pluralistic world—a world in which the material capacity to end human want coexists in pathological tension with nuclear brinkmanship. Under these circumstances I would argue that the only workable foreign policy is one in which long-term and short-term interests converge, in which ideal visions are recognized as the sole ones that are ultimately practical.

Conclusion: The True Goals of Development

You, the graduates of SAIS 1982, are tomorrow's leaders. Regardless of the career path you may have chosen—government, business, private agencies—the issue of U.S. development assistance will touch and affect your lives. For you—for us all—the challenge of development is greater today than ever before. Let us not forget the concrete, human dimensions of the problem:

—One human being out of every eight now alive is hungry most of the time.
—Sixteen percent of the world's children are malnourished.
—More than 600 million people live on the equivalent of less than $50 per year.
—The developing nations have one soldier for every 250 people, but one doctor for every 3,700 people.
—More than 100 million agricultural workers own little or no land of their own.

—While development assistance has brought LDC food production today to a level equal to 87 percent of consumption, by the end of the century the figure could fall to seventy-four percent. (Linowitz, *et al.,* 1980, 3)

When I underscore the importance of development assistance programs, I do not mean to imply that they can—or should—gather up the entire LDC world into its arms, sweeping it forward and depositing it with appropriate fanfare on the doorstep of a Westernized twenty-first century. In the first place, nothing of the sort is possible. In the second place, many thoughtful leaders and citizens of the LDCs are by no means certain that they want their own societies to emulate our industrialized, compulsively consumptive example. Development assistance as a profession needs to acknowledge candid reservations about both the *possibility* and *desirability* of development conceived as the globalization of contemporary Western values.

As I have set forth these three observations for the future, it may have seemed to you that I have been painting a contradictory picture of U.S. development assistance.

On the one hand, I have suggested that U.S. bilateral development programs must deal realistically with a range of theoretical and practical limitations. On the other, I have recommended that development become the centerpiece for U.S. relations with the Third World and an integral part of U.S. foreign policy generally.

Here, I have talked of what is practically achievable. There, I have called for idealistic—some might say utopian—commitments to a visionary future.

Well, I am tempted to play the role of the patronizing elder, admonishing you that all great truths are paradoxical and that the answer to most of the multiple choice questions posed by real life is "all of the above."

What exactly does this "all" entail, as regards bilateral development assistance for tomorrow as well as today? Well, development assistance programs aim to improve food production, education, housing, health,and other aspects of material life. But material well-being is not the ultimate goal of development. Income, and indeed all other indices or components of material prosperity, are at best a means to an end. The end itself is the right and capacity for human beings to live to the fullest, as social beings at peace with their world and their fellows.

At its core, the challenge of development abroad is the challenge of human community. Employment, income, and all the goods and services that spill from the cornucopia of knowledge and technology are, at best, tools—tools we use falteringly in our continuing attempt to ease, once and for all, the strains and tensions that ever threaten to tear apart the fabric of the human race.

From the dawn of humanity to the present, our greatest preoccupation has been with the quantitative aspects of life: enough food, clothing, shelter, and fuel for ourselves and our families. Only recently have a few nations, the U.S. in the forefront, been capable of devoting serious attention to the qualitative aspects of life—not only for an elite, but for *all*. Still at the margin of survival, the remaining three-fourths of the world are determined to develop . . . and they will succeed. But while they are still overwhelmingly concerned with the quantitative aspects of life, they look to us for more than just material aid. They are also watching to see how we face the qualitative issues that have arisen in the wake of our prosperity: the issues of freedom, of equality, and of self-fulfillment. In these areas no less than in others, the developing nations are watching us closely, and they are watching with agonizing hope. The challenge of development demands our deepest commitment to these intensely human hopes. Only from their realization will there come a viable future for all of us, or for any of us.

V. SUMMING UP

CONCLUSION
Kenneth W. Thompson

We have traced some of the routes by which American values have been projected abroad through institutions and organizations. Our journey has helped us discover the broad diversity of organized efforts through which American goals and practices are shared with others. We have observed, in part at least, the variety of purposes and goals on which institutional efforts are and have been founded.

In order to study institutions involved in the transmitting of values, we have distinguished among human survival values, economic and social well-being, international cooperation and the well-being of mankind. In so doing, it is obvious that the institutions operating within the four sectors cross boundaries and overlap with other institutions and values. Human survival values and economic well-being overlap; institutions serving one set of values contribute significantly to another. For example, American determination to help the plight of refugees is both a human survival effort and a contribution to economic and social well-being. New approaches to development assistance or to preserving priceless resources of the global environment represent human endeavors that touch all four areas.

Any discussion of human needs and problems that is broken down into separate and discrete spheres for commentary and analysis serves an intellectual and historical purpose. It constitutes a form of abstraction useful perhaps for highlighting aspects of reality without exhausting the limits of reality itself. For those who would point out that abstracting one aspect of reality to illuminate it more fully verges on distortion, we concur. The purpose of abstracting a portion of reality from the whole is to throw the spotlight on that portion of the whole, not to illuminate or explain the whole. The organization of the book proceeds on this assumption.

What remains important and deserving of attention is the breadth and depth of institutional endeavor in the projection of American values abroad. Some institutions have a long and respected history.

They have their roots in early religious and missionary undertakings launched before the turn of the century. In the twentieth century, programs in health and agriculture followed the missionaries addressing themselves to basic human survival needs. Observers describe these early endeavors as secularized versions of the American missionary movement. They were sustained by values which presupposed that human needs spanned national boundaries and that from him "to whom much has been given will much be expected." The privileged had obligations to help others in greater need.

If a survey of the institutions and organized efforts within American society engaged in service to mankind everywhere helps to record the variety of worldwide enterprises in which Americans have been engaged, its objective will have been achieved. Patterns have changed and been adapted to a variety of human needs. Nuances and motives shift in response to the times but underlying all such efforts are certain core values. Each author has sought to identify these values as well as to point out the particular problems and emergent requirements of every organized effort. The essays seek to make explicit what otherwise might be taken for granted or only partially understood. It should be obvious that the challenges are as great in the 1980s as they were for the early pioneers in public health or food production in the first decades of the century.

In raising issues of America's responsibility in the world, we recognize that a survey of this kind conflicts with powerful trends of thought that are pushing Americans to look inward. Problems of inflation, unemployment and human suffering at home are forcing society to throw up drawbridges separating Americans from the rest of the world. In the long run, however, the tendency to manifest concern only for ourselves is likely to be short-lived for two important reasons. One is the set of values to which this little volume calls attention. Given the kind of people we are, Americans are unlikely to rest content with a narrowly parochial view of human problems. The other force which continues to push Americans outward is the kind of world in which we live. It is true that what happens anywhere in the world affects Americans. We cannot escape John Dunne's proclamation: "Ask not for whom the bell tolls, it tolls for thee." As I write these concluding sentences, three highly publicized wars in the Falklands, in Lebanon and in Iran and Iraq are raging, to say nothing of eight so-called lesser wars. If human deprivation, disease and suffering is not the primary cause of these wars, it is an important contributing factor exploited by those engaged in the conflicts. The scene of the vast majority of the bloody conflicts since World War II has been the developing world. Not by accident, that world is the locus of the most dire human need.

Therefore, the words of this volume must close on a note of urgency. The problems with which American values projected abroad are concerned are urgent human needs likely to influence America's survival as well as the survival of all mankind. What may have seemed at first glance a mere intellectual exercise becomes a matter of life and death. It is to such an issue and its amelioration to which we dedicate this survey.

CHAPTER THREE

[1] John W. Gardner, *AID and the Universities,* New York: Education and World Affairs, 1964.

[2] It is obvious that departments within the same university may be in different phases of development at the same point in time.

[3] Dr. Wortman's paper, entitled "The Technological Basis for Intensified Agriculture," was prepared for a conference sponsored by the Rockefeller Foundation at Villa Serbelloni, Bellagio, Italy, April 23-25, 1969. The paper appears in a report of that conference, "Agricultural Development: Proceedings of a Conference."

[4] Institute for Development Studies, University of Nairobi, Research and Publications, January 1972, Foreword, p. 1.

CHAPTER FIVE

[1] Robert Pear, "U.S. Panel Says Indochina Refugees May Increase," *New York Times,* August 14, 1981.

[2] Richard C. Holbrooke, Assistant Secretary of East Asian and Pacific Affairs. Statement before the Subcommittee on Immigration, Citizenship and International Law of the House Committee on the Judiciary. The Department of State, August 4, 1977.

[3] J. Bryan Hehir, U.S. Catholic Conference, Washington, D.C. Fr. Hehir was helpful in providing guidance and support for this research. See also, Kenneth W. Thompson, *Ethics, Functionalism and Power in International Politics* (Baton Rouge, La: Louisiana State U. Press, 1979), chapter 1.

[4] Kenneth W. Thompson, *Christian Ethics and the Dilemmas of Foreign Policy* (London: Duke U. Press and Cambridge University Press, 1959), p. 4.

[5] Kenneth W. Thompson, *Ethics and National Purpose* (New York: Council on Religion and International Affairs, 1957/1967).

[6] Raymond McDermott, anthropologist, in a lecture to students in Asian Education class, EDFD 777, March 6, 1982.

[7] Kenneth W. Thompson, *Ethics, Functionalism and Power in International Politics.*

[8] Ibid., p. 48.

[9] Barry Wain, "Malaysian Fears Social Upheaval from Refugees," *Asian Wall Street Journal,* June 23, 1979.

[10] Guenter Lewy, *America in Vietnam* (New York: Oxford U. Press, 1978), p. 112.

[11] Larry A. Niksch, Robert G. Sutter, and Pham Chi Thanh, *Vietnam's Future Policies and Role in Southeast Asia,* prepared for the Committee on Foreign Relations, United States Senate, by the Foreign Affairs and National Defense Division, Congressional Research Service, Library of Congress, April 1982 (Washington, D.C.: U.S. Government Printing Office, 1982), p. 68.

[12] Bruce Grant, *The Boat People. An "Age" Investigation* (New York and Middlesex, Eng.: Penguin Bks., 1979), p. 211.

[13] Ibid.

[14] Niksch, Sutter and Thanh, *Vietnam's Future Policies,* pp. 1 and 2.

[15] Ibid., p. 3.

[16] Ibid.

[17] Grant, *Boat People,* pp. 80-81.

[18] Ibid., p. 29.

[19] Ibid., pp. 26-28.

[20] Barry Wain, "How One Vietnamese Became a Refugee," *Asian Wall Street Journal,* April 5, 1982.

[21] Denis D. Gray, "In Burma, Buddhism Still Finds a Home, *Asian Wall Street Journal,* December 28, 1978.

[22] Barry Wain, "How One Vietnamese Became a Refugee."

[23] Interview with Marjorie Niehaus, Congressional Research Service.

[24] Niksch, Sutter, and Thanh, *Vietnam's Future Policies,* p. 79.

[25] Grant, *Boat People,* pp. 84-87.

[26] Ibid., p. 217.

[27] Niksch, Sutter, and Thanh, *Vietnam's Future Policies,* p. 120.

[28] Ibid., p. 121.

[29] Ibid., pp. 122-123.

[30] Ibid., p. 124.

[31] Grant, *Boat People,* p. 138.

[32] Niksch, Sutter, and Thanh, *Vietnam's Future Policies,* p. 125.

[33] Dick Clark, *Department of State Bulletin,* October 1979.

[34] Don Oberdorfer, "Hill Warm Toward Plan to Help Boat People," *Washington Post,* July 26 1979.

[35] Bernard Weintraub, "The Problem of Finding U.S. Policy to Deal with the Need for Haven for the Boat People," *New York Times,* July 2, 1979.

[36] William Branigan, "Hill Delegation Backs Curbs on Asian Refugees," *Washington Post,* August 14, 1981.

[37] Eduardo Lachicha, "Agencies in U.S. Dispute Indochinese Refugee Policies." *Asian Wall Street Journal,* August 1, 1981. Also, Robert Pear, "U.S. Panel Says Indochina Refugees May Increase," *New York Times,* August 14, 1981.

[38] Don Oberdorfer, "Flow of Boat People May Rise, State Department Panel Advises," *Washington Post,* August 14, 1981.

[39] Robert Pear, "U.S. Panel Says Indochina Refugees May Increase."

[40] Oberdorfer, "Flow of Boat People May Rise."

[41] Ibid.

[42] William Branigan, "U.S. Changes Refugee Policy to Curb Intake from Indochina," *Washington Post,* April 28, 1982.

CHAPTER SEVEN

1 These figures are from U.S., Department of Commerce, *U.S. Direct Investment Abroad, 1977* (Washington: Department of Commerce, April 1981): pp. 6-7.

2 For general discussions of the relationship between national power and the way in which the international economy is organized, see Stephen D. Krasner, "State Power and the Structure of International Trade," *World Politics* 29 (April 1976): pp. 317-343; Robert O. Keohane, "The Theory of Hegemonic Stability and Changes in International Regimes," in Ole Holsti, et. al., (eds), *Change in the International System* (Boulder: Westview Press, 1980): pp.131-162; and Charles P. Kindleberger, *The World in Depression, 1929-1939* (Berkeley: University of California Press, 1973). For a discussion which makes important general arguments about the relationship between power and economic activity on the basis of an anlaysis of the particular issue-area of foreign direct investment, see Robert Gilpin, *U.S. Power and the Multinational Corporation: The Political Economy of Foreign Direct Investment* (New York: Basic Books, 1975).

3 Analyses of U.S. foreign direct investment after World War II which focuses heavily on technology and managerial expertise were centered most importantly in the "Product-Life-Cycle" approach; see Louis T. Wells (ed.), *The Product Life Cycle and International Trade* (Boston: Graduate School of Business Administration, Harvard University, 1972); and Raymond Vernon, *Sovereignty at Bay: The Multinational Spread of U.S. Enterprise* (New York: Basic Books, 1971).

4 For a discussion of this U.S. analysis, see David P. Calleo and Benjamin M. Rowland, *America and the World Political Economy* (Bloomington: Indiana University Press, 1973): pp. 33-37. Calleo and Rowland associated this view especially with Secretary of State Cordell Hull.

5 For a discussion of the relationship between U.S. domestic political-economic experiences (especially during the Depression) and U.S. approach to post-World War II international economic policy, see Charles S. Meier, "The Politics of Productivity: Foundations of American International Economic Policy After World War II," in Peter J. Katzenstein, *Between Power and Plenty: Foreign Economic Policies of Advanced Industrial States* (Madison: University of Wisconsin Press, 1978): pp. 23-50.

6 For a useful discussion of how the U.S. and other advanced capitalist societies have sought to resolve the public-private actor dilemma in international economic matters, see John Gerard Ruggie, "International Regimes, Transactions, and Change: Embedded Liberalism in the Postwar Economic Order," in Stephen D. Krasner (ed.), *International Regimes*, a special issue of *International Organization* 36 (Spring 1982): 379:416. For an important discussion of the resolution of the question in domestic economies in advanced capitalist countries, see Andrew Shonfield, *Modern Capitalism: The Changing Balance of Public and Private Power* (London: Oxford University Press, 1965).

7 For a more complete discussion see Hedley Bull, *The Anarchical Society: A Study of Order in World Politics* (New York: Columbia University Press 1977).

8 U.S., Department of Commerce, *Survey of Current Business* 61 (August 1981): p. 32.

[9] For a useful review of the relevant literature, see Duane Kujawa, "The Labour Relations of American Multinationals Abroad," *Labour and Society* 4 (January 1979): pp. 3-25.

[10] See Vernon, *Sovereignty at Bay,* op. cit., pp. 231-247; and Jack Behrman, *National Interests and the Multinational Enterprise: Tensions Among the North Atlantic Countries* (Englewood Cliffs, NJ: Prentice Hall, 1970).

[11] See John Zysman, "The French in the International Economy," in Katzenstein (ed.), op. cit., p. 286.

[12] Ibid.

[13] U.S. *Survey,* op. cit.

[14] For a good review of the issues see Thomas J. Biersteker, *Distortion or Development: Contending Perspectives on the Multinational Corporation* (Cambridge: MIT Press, 1978): pp. 1-68.

[15] See Andre Gunder Frank, "The Development of Underdevelopment," in Charles K. Wilbur (ed.), *The Political Economy of Development and Underdevelopment* (New York: Random House, 1973): pp. 94-104. Also see in Wilbur the essays by Celso Furtado and by Thestonia Dos Santos.

[16] See Johan Galtung, "A Structural Theory of Imperialism," *Journal of Peace Research* 8 (1971): pp. 81-117.

[17] Fernando Henrique Cardoso and Enzo Faletto, *Dependency and Development in Latin America,* 2nd Edition (Berkeley: University of California Press, 1979); and Peter Evans, *Dependent Development: The Alliance of Multinational, State, and Local Capital* (Princeton: Princeton University Press, 1979. Other writers in this category would include Gary Gereffi, and Douglas Bennett and Kenneth Sharpe.

[18] For discussions of the strategy of "delinkage" and "national self-reliance," see Carlos F. Diaz-Alejandro, "Delinking North and South: Unshackled or Unhinged?," in Albert Fishlow, et. al., *Rich and Poor Nations in the World Economy* (New York: McGraw-Hill for the Council on-Foreign Relations 1980s Project, 1977): pp. 87-160; and Thomas J. Biersteker, "Self Reliance in Theory and Practice in Tanzanian Trade Relations," *International Organization* 34 (Spring 1980): pp. 229-264.

[19] The key figures in the bargaining school are Raymond Vernon, Theodore Moran, and C. Fred Bergsten. See Raymond Vernon, "Foreign-Owned Enterprises in the Developing Countries," *Public Policy* 15 (Barton: Graduate School of Business Administration, Harvard University, 1966): pp. 361-380; "Long-Run Trends in Concession Agreements," *Proceedings of the American Society of International Law* (April 1967): pp. 85-89; "The Power of Multinational Enterprises in Developing Countries," in Carl Madden (ed.), *The Case for the Multinational Corporation* (New York: Praeger, 1975): pp. 151-183; *Sovereignty at Bay,* op. cit., pp. 49-59, 105-106, 256-257; *Storm Over the Multinationals: The Real Issues* (Cambridge: Harvard University Press, 1977): pp. 139-174, 194-199. Important discussions by Theodore Moran include: *Multinational Corporations and the Politics of Dependence: Copper in Chile* (Princeton: Princeton University Press, 1974); and "Multinational Corporations and Dependency: A Dialogue for *Dependentistas and Non-Dependentistas,*" in James A. Caparaso (ed.), *Dependence and Dependency in the Global System,* Special Issue of *International Organization* 32 (Winter 1978): pp. 170-200; and Moran, C. Fred Bergsten, and Thomas Horst, *American Multinationals* and *American Interests* (Washington: Brookings Institution,

1978): pp. 369-381. Finally, see C. Fred Bergsten, "Coming Investment Wars?" *Foreign Affairs* 53 (October 1974): pp. 135-152.

[20] In addition to the citations in footnote 13, see Raymond F. Mikesell (ed.), *Foreign Investments in the Petroleum and Mining Industries* (Baltimore: Johns Hopkins Press for Resources for the Future, Inc., 1971); Edith Penrose, *The Large International Firm in Developing Countries:* (London: George Allen and Unwin, 1968); David N. Smith and Louis T. Wells, *Negotiating Third World Mineral Agreements: Promises as Prologue* (Cambridge: Ballinger Press, 1975); and Francis Tugwell, *The Politics of Oil in Venezuela* (Stanford: Stanford University Press, 1975).

[21] See Joseh M. Grieco, *Between Dependency and Autonomy: India's Experience with the International Computer Industry* (Berkeley: University of California Press, 1983).

[22] U.S. Department of Commerce, *The Use of Investment Incentives and Peformance Requirements by Foreign Governments* (Washington: Department of Commerce, October 1981); and Bergsten, op. cit.

[23] See Bergsten, op. cit., and "Prepared Statement of C. Fred Bergsten," in U.S., Congress, Senate, Committee on Foreign Relations, *U.S. Policy Toward International Investment* (Washington: General Printing Office, 1982): pp. 13-18.

CHAPTER FIFTEEN
Sources and bibliographical references in text

Terry Barr, "The World Food Situation and Global Grain Prospects" (*Science* Vol. 214, December 4, 1981, pp. 1087-1095).

Wily Brandt, et al., *North-South: A Program for Survival,* Report of the Independent Commission on International Development Issues (Cambridge, Mass: MIT Press, 1980).

Council on Environmental Quality and Department of State, *The Global 2000 Report to the Presidency: Twenty-First Century,* (Washington, D.C.: U.S. Government Printing Office, May 23, 1977).

Food and Agriculture Organization, *Agriculture: Toward 2000,* Rome, 1981.

Philip M. Glick, *The Administration of Technical Assistance: Growth in the Americas* (Chicago: The University of Chicago Press, 1957).

Roger D. Hansen et al., *U.S. Foreign Policy and the Third World: Agenda 1982* (New York: Praeger Publishers for the Overseas Development Council, 1982).

Sol M. Linowitz et al., *Overcoming World Hunger: The Challenge Ahead*—Report of the Presidential Commission on World Hunger, abridged version (Washington, D.C.: U.S. Government Printing Office, 1980).

David Rockefeller, "U.S.-Third World Relations: Time for a New Assessment," remarks to the Council on Foreign Relations, New York (September 14, 1981).

G. Edward Schuh, "Economics and International Relations: A Conceptual Framework," Presidential Address, American Agricultural Economics Association, July 27-29, 1981.

Peter Syverson, *Doctorate Recipients from U.S. Universities* (Washington, D.C.: National Academy Press for the National Research Council of the National Science Foundation, 1981).

Clifton R. Wharton, Jr., "Old Mother Hubbard's Cupboard: Issues of Productivity Versus Equity in the Third World" (Joseph E. Wilson Award Lecture at the University of Rochester, April 18, 1978).

_____ , "Statement before the House Foreign Affairs Committee" (Washington, D.C., March 31, 1982).

_____ , "Feeding the World—Are Politicians the Missing Link?" *RF Illustrated,* Vol. 3, No. 4 (September, 1977).

CHAPTER FIFTEEN (Continued)
Explanatory notes

[1] For a recent insightful review see Schuh (1981).

[2] Both Dave Bell and Ralph Smuckler reminded me of previous efforts to recognize the need to develop policies and mechanisms to encourage U.S. collaborative, scientific, technical and educational activities with "middle income" developing countries. The proposed ISTC, Institute for Scientific and Technical Cooperation, would have been one response to this issue. When an LDC nation "graduates" is precisely the time "when there should be a major effort to solidify and strengthen the educational and cultural ties that have been built under AID and convert them to long-term collaborative relationships for the benefit of *both* the U.S. and the country concerned.": (David E. Bell, private communication April 23, 1982).

[3] Mr. David Rockefeller in a talk to the Council of Foreign Relations (1981) has also proposed the need for a review of U.S. development assistance, but with a somewhat different emphasis and approach. His proposal and mine, however, are quite complementary.

[4] Hopefully the majority of the funding might be from private and foundation sources to assure maximum independence. In particular, I doubt that the commission should be of the Presidential genus—since one president's commission report is often another president's wastepaper. But some federal funding might be provided to assure access to information and an interest in the implementation of any commission recommendations.

[5] Fowler Hamilton, a former AID administrator, in commenting on an earlier draft of the speech made the following trenchant observation in support of the commission's proposed international composition: ". . . No society can solve any of its political or economic problems today by its own unaided efforts. Since every significant problem from nuclear warfare to public health now requires international cooperation and, if the Platonic idea of Western civilization is to achieve change by persuasion rather than by force is to be realized, the fora for discussion must be international." (Private communication April 26, 1982).

[6] Nobel laureate Theodore Schultz made some extremely perceptive comments on this point in his lectures to AID in Washington in February of 1982.

[7] These are just two of several innovations that have recer ly been put into place by the U.S. Board for International Food anc Agricultural Development. Charged by the Congress with overseeing and promoting relationships between AID and U.S. universities, BIFAD has worked since 1975 to promote the greater involvement of U.S. land-grant and agricultural universities in foreign development assistance in the war on hunger. BIFAD has undertaken this via several new administrative and program methods. Two other innovations besides those mentioned above are:

(1) The "CRSP" or Collaborative Research Support Program is designed to provide long-term collaborative funding of research programs involving multiple U.S. universities working cooperatively with those in developing countries. The participating U.S. universities share the cost (a minimum of twenty-five percent) using non-federal funds and the research has a dual goal of benefitting U.S. agriculture and the agriculture of the LDCs. Seven programs are underway involving forty-four U.S. institutions working in fifty developing countries and with six international research centers.

(2) The "Collaborative Assistance Method" of university contracting allows university participation in shaping project design and work plans in advance; heightens flexibility in working out the timing and mix of inputs with institutions in the developing countries; and serves a long-term commitment of professional resources.

My purpose in citing these examples is not to indulge in self-congratulation but merely to illustrate how in just one area of developmental assistance it has been possible to develop new approaches and mechanisms which are more appropriate to today.